Religion in Australia

Studies in Society

Titles include:

Studies in Society

Religion in Australia
Sociological Perspectives

Edited by
Alan W. Black

Sydney
ALLEN & UNWIN

© Alan W. Black 1991
This book is copyright under the Berne Convention.
No reproduction without permission. All rights reserved.

First published 1991

Allen & Unwin Australia Pty Ltd
8 Napier Street, North Sydney, NSW 2059 Australia

National Library of Australia
Cataloguing-in-publication entry:

Religion in Australia: sociological perspectives.

  Bibliography.
  Includes index.
  ISBN 0 04 442342 X.

  1. Religion and sociology – Australia.   2. Australia – Religion.
  3. Australia – Religious life and customs.
  I. Black, Alan W. (Alan William), 1937- . (Series: Studies in society
  (Sydney, N.S.W.)).

  306'.6'0994

Set in 10 on 11pt Times by Jennifer D. Black and Lyndall S. Tucker,
Armidale, NSW Australia

Printed by Kin Keong Printing Co. Pte Ltd, Singapore.

Contents

Figures and tables

Contributors

Alan W. Black	Senior Lecturer in Sociology, University of New England
'Tricia Blombery	Researcher, Christian Research Association
Gary D. Bouma	Associate Professor of Sociology, Monash University
Ken Dempsey	Reader in Sociology, La Trobe University
Barbara L. Field	Tutor, Department of Social, Cultural and Curriculum Studies, University of New England
Phillip J. Hughes	Researcher, Christian Research Association
Michael Humphrey	Lecturer in Sociology, University of Western Sydney, Macarthur
Rowan Ireland	Senior Lecturer in Sociology, La Trobe University
Rachael Kohn	Lecturer in Religious Studies and Semitic Studies, University of Sydney
Frank Lewins	Senior Lecturer in Sociology, The Faculties, Australian National University
Jim McKay	Senior Lecturer in Sociology, University of Queensland
Paul Rule	Senior Lecturer in Religious Studies, La Trobe University
Ruth Sturmey	Project Director, Rural Development Centre, University of New England
Tony Swain	Lecturer in Religious Studies, University of Sydney

Preface

This book is the result of a co-operative effort. After the authors of each of the chapters had provided their material on computer disks, the task of editing this material, converting it into a similar format, integrating the Bibliography and eventually producing camera-ready copy for the book as a whole was carried out at the University of New England. In this process, the editor was ably assisted by Jenny Black and Lyn Tucker, who supplied secretarial services, undertook the typesetting and helped with the compilation of the index. Their assistance is gratefully acknowledged.

1 Introduction: recent studies in the sociology of religion in Australia[1]

Alan W. Black

The first comprehensive sociological study of religion in Australia was written by Mol (1971), who presented a wide-ranging survey of religious beliefs, attitudes and practices in the mid-1960s, together with other relevant Australian data and some comparative material from other English-speaking countries. Since then the number of scholars working in this field has grown significantly, and there has been a growing stream of publications written from a variety of theoretical and methodological perspectives. This chapter will concentrate on work published since 1980. For earlier studies, a very useful bibliography is provided by Mason and Fitzpatrick (1982) and select bibliographies are contained in Harris, Hynd and Millikan (1982), Black and Glasner (1983) and Mol (1985).

Correlates of religiosity

Various recent publications have examined the social correlates of religiosity in Australia. Most of these studies make use of survey data from the 1983 Australian Values Study (Bouma and Dixon, 1986; de Vaus and McAllister, 1987; Kaldor, 1987; McCallum, 1987), the 1984–85 National Social Science Survey (McCallum, 1987; 1988; Graetz and McAllister, 1988: 117–44), the 1986 Joint Church Census (Kaldor and Homel, 1988a; 1988b; 1988c; 1988d; 1989) or the 1987 Combined Churches Survey for Faith and Mission (Blombery and Hughes, 1987; Blombery, 1988; 1989a; 1989b; Hughes, 1988a; 1988b; 1989; Hughes and Blombery, 1990). Kaldor (1987) also uses 1983–84 McNair–Anderson survey data. Several studies use data from older surveys, either as the primary source (de Vaus, 1980; 1981a; 1981b; 1982a; 1982b; 1983; 1985; Black, 1985; Mol, 1985; McAllister, 1988) or for comparative purposes (Kaldor, 1987; McCallum, 1987).

1

These studies show that in some respects the correlates of religiosity in Australia are similar to those found in other Western societies. For example, they indicate that, on a wide range of measures, females tend to be more religious than males. Explanations for this difference vary. Mol (1985: 73) states that there is no evidence that either occupational or marital status can explain the difference. He prefers the explanation that both religion and women have generally been concerned with functions of conflict resolution, emotional healing and integration, whereas men have generally fulfilled more instrumental and aggressive roles. Sometimes Mol speaks of sex roles as being culturally defined and of males and females as being socialised into them; at other times he comes close to a form of essentialism with respect to both religion and gender.

De Vaus and McAllister (1987) systematically test three explanations relating to the structural location of women in society. These explanations attribute the greater religiosity of females to, respectively:

1 their child-rearing role;
2 their lower level of workforce participation; and
3 the relative importance they attach to the family as against paid work.

Their Australian data support explanation (2) but not (1) or (3). These data contrast somewhat with United States findings, in which workforce participation does not appear to be related to degree of religiosity among females (de Vaus, 1984). De Vaus and McAllister (1987: 480) suggest that this difference may be due to a greater integration of religion into mainstream culture in the United States than in Australia. In a workplace that is regarded as non-religious, a religious person will be more readily tolerated, even by those who do not see themselves as religious, if religion is a significant part of the wider mainstream culture, as in the United States, rather than being more marginal, as in Australia. The validity of this explanation clearly needs testing using comparative data from other societies. Other possible explanations for gender differences in religious orientation are discussed but not tested by Bodycomb (1984; 1985), Mol (1985), de Vaus and McAllister (1987), Kaldor (1987), Graetz and McAllister (1988)s and Blombery (1989a).

Kaldor (1987) and McAllister (1988) provide the two most systematic examinations of age variations in religious orientation in Australia, and of the extent to which these are due to life-cycle or to generational factors. This issue is also discussed by Mol (1985), Bouma and Dixon (1986), Graetz and McAllister (1988) and Blombery (1989a; 1989b). The data suggest that, although life-cycle factors explain some of the variance, generational factors have also been important. These results are broadly consistent with findings by Wuthnow (1976) in the United States. Kaldor's (1987) study also breaks important new ground in Australia by examining the influence of contextual factors on rates of church attendance. Included in his analysis are factors such as community size and type, demographic structure, ethnic composition, household and family profiles, housing tenure patterns, levels of mobility and other socio-economic variables. Kaldor's analysis is a good example of the increasing level of methodological sophistication in some of the more recent studies.

The local/cosmopolitan variable is not as significant a factor in shaping religious beliefs and behavior in Australia as Roof (1976; 1978) claimed for the United States. Contrary to Roof's findings for American Episcopalians, Black's (1985) data from mainline Protestants in Australia revealed that theological conservatism/liberalism is a better predictor of frequency of church attendance, degree of involvement in other church activities and views about ecumenism than is the local/cosmopolitan variable. Theological orientation is also a better predictor of attitudes to change in church structures and practices, and of moral conservatism, but it is not such a good predictor of concern for social justice, and of degree of approval for church activism on social, political and economic issues. In the light of these results, it was hypothesised that, at least among Protestant church members, the impact of general breadth of perspective (of which the local/cosmopolitan variable is one measure) decreases, and the salience of theological orientation increases, as the proportion of the total population which regularly participates in church-oriented religion decreases. As that proportion varies both within and across societies, as well as over time, this hypothesis is ripe for cross-national, and perhaps longitudinal, testing.

Writers such as Bruce Wilson (1982; 1983), Kaldor (1987) and McCallum (1987) have pointed to marked declines in church affiliation, church attendance, belief in God, participation in religious rites of passage and so on since Mol conducted his survey in the 1960s. Similar trends have been observed during much of this period in Britain, the United States and other countries. McAllister (1988) sees such changes as evidence of an ongoing process of secularisation. Mol (1985), Kaldor (1987) and McCallum (1987; 1988) see the changes as significant, but not necessarily as part of an ongoing process. Bouma (1983) argues that the fluctuations in church attendance which have occurred for the population as a whole during the past twenty years or so have been relatively minor, and that they should not be regarded as decisive evidence of a process of secularisation. Likewise, Bouma and Dixon (1986) use data from the Australian Values Study to challenge 'the myth of secular Australia'. More will be said about this in a later section.

It should be clear from what has already been said that in some respects religion in Australia is similar to that in many other, especially English-speaking, countries; in other respects it is significantly different. Overall, religion in Australia tends to occupy a position intermediate to that which it occupies in Britain on the one hand and the United States on the other. In terms of denominational variety and especially the relative numerical strength of different denominations, America has the greatest degree of religious pluralism, Australia comes next, then Britain. Likewise, although in each of these countries Christianity claims at least the nominal allegiance of the majority of the population, the rate of church-going in Australia (about 20 per cent of the adult population per week) is about twice the rate in Britain but only about half the rate in the United States (Black and Glasner, 1983). These observations are consistent with Martin's (1978) theory that in Western societies there is generally a direct connection between degree of religious pluralism and rates of religious participation. The main exceptions to this are countries such as Poland, where a monopoly religion has become a vehicle for the expression of cultural identity in the face of external threat.

Religious institutions in their social context

An important series of studies on religion in two small Australian towns has been authored by Dempsey. His first book (1983a) provides an insightful ethnography of a Methodist church in northern New South Wales. This particular local church went through a period of sharp conflict between ministers and laity in the 1950s and 1960s. Paradoxically, the efforts of the clergy to encourage greater lay participation and lay responsibility in church affairs met with both active and passive resistance from the laity. Kinship and friendship networks quickly came into play in opposition to clergy or clergy's wives whose ideas and actions failed to correspond with local expectations. Dempsey does not confine his analysis to the operation of purely local factors. He looks also at forces at work in the wider church and in society at large: for example, trends in theology; the increasing professionalisation of various occupations, including the ministry, yet the declining status and influence of the ministry and of the church itself; the Vietnam war; the challenges, at least in some quarters, to traditional definitions of female roles; and so on. Although some factors might be unique to the particular time and place of this study, many can be found at work elsewhere.

Dempsey's more recent work (1983b; 1985b; 1989) has focused on the main Protestant churches in a small town in north-western Victoria. Here again he has analysed a process of decline, both in the community itself and in its churches, paying particular attention to class, gender, age and kinship as factors influencing church participation and church structures. He has also used material from this study and his earlier one to examine factors affecting the identity of the rural minister (Dempsey, 1986) and pressures to which ministers' wives are likely to be subject in such communities (Dempsey, 1985a). Participant observation and extensive interviewing, together with careful analysis, give these studies a richness of detail which is found in some of the best studies of new religious movements but often lacking in sociological accounts of major denominations. Nevertheless, one must be cautious about overgeneralising from case studies. Not all rural communities and not all rural churches are declining (Black, 1988a).

Bodycomb (1984; 1986) presents a model of 'zones of disposition' towards organised religion, distinguishing four such zones and discussing the likelihood of movement from one zone to another. He then analyses factors affecting church growth or decline, distinguishing between those which are largely outside the churches' direct control (contextual factors) and those which are more amenable to their control (institutional factors). In the contextual category he names demographic factors, location and neighbourhood, availability of functional alternatives, prevailing values, the presence or absence of 'threats and terrors', generalised public images of churches and the placement of the population in the various zones of disposition. The institutional factors he examines are denominational styles and policies, credal confidence, experiential validation, growth orientation, handling of potentially divisive issues, member satisfaction, hard-nosed know-how, internal demography and pastoral leadership. These lists draw upon, refine and extend those developed by writers such as Currie, Gilbert and Horsley (1977) in Britain, and Hoge and Roozen (1979) in the United States.

Institutional and contextual factors are likewise important in understanding the chequered career of the ecumenical movement. Elsewhere (Black, 1988b), I have given a critique of theories of ecumenism put forward by sociologists in Britain and the United States, arguing that they do not deal adequately with all aspects of this phenomenon and that they are unable to account for the outcomes of union negotiations in particular cases. I then proposed an alternative theory based on the analogy of marriage. This theory gives particular attention to the *process* of union, including reasons why some negotiations fail. Other publications have focused more specifically on the phenomena of fission and fusion involved in the formation of the Uniting Church in Australia, which was a 1977 merger between the Methodist Church of Australasia, about two-thirds of the Presbyterian Church of Australia and five-sixths of the churches which belonged to the Congregational Union of Australia (Black, 1983b; 1986). Comparative studies have also been made between this merger and others in Canada and Scotland (Black, 1983a; 1990a; Campbell, 1985), as well as more general assessments of the results of merger movements in various countries (Black, 1988c; forthcoming). Such studies throw light on the irony that the quest for union is itself often a source of division within negotiating denominations.

The interplay between religious institutions and their social contexts in Australia is further analysed by Hogan (1984; 1987). His basic thesis is that:

Many of Australia's most important institutions and traditions have been shaped by forces that have taken religious or anti-religious forms. The

family, the class structure, the school system, the modern political party
system, the pattern of pressure group activity, the terms of Federation, the
very self-concept of nationhood, the rhetoric of political debate, even the
structure of sporting and cultural competition: these are some of the facets of
Australian life which religious groups and their rivals have helped to shape.
(Hogan, 1987: 287–8)

How is this view to be reconciled with historian O'Farrell's (1976: 67)
assertion that in Australia 'what is most significant historically about
religion is its weakness, its efforts to achieve some strength, its tenuous
and intermittent hold on the minds and hearts of the Australian people, its
peripheral or subordinate relation to their main concerns'? Hogan (1987:
288–93) sees the answer in terms of two paradoxes: that democratic
societies are shaped by minorities, not majorities; and that although the
main denominations have not been very successful in their primary
religious mission, religion has gained strength by association with other
important social forces such as ethnicity, class and gender. Hogan gives
little explicit attention to the last of these three forces, but he does explore
some major ramifications of the other two.

The relationship between ethnicity and religion in Australia has also
been highlighted in a publication edited by Jupp (1988) in connection with
the Bicentenary of white settlement, and in two collections of papers edited
by Ata (1988; 1989). Lewins (1983) has examined the tensions between
Australian and migrant (especially Italian) members of the Roman
Catholic Church, concluding that 'culture divides more than religion
unites' (Lewins, 1983: 84). McKay (1985; 1989) has studied religious
diversity among Syrian-Lebanese Christians in Sydney, arguing that
interdenominational factionalism and the assimilative power of Roman
Catholic and non-Catholic churches in Australia have worked against the
development of a strong sense of ethnic solidarity between Catholic and
Orthodox Syrian-Lebanese: for them, religion divides more than ethnicity
unites. In this respect they are different from some other ethnic
populations in Australia, but similar to Syrian-Lebanese Christians in the
United States (Kayal and Kayal, 1975).

An important recent development in many Western societies has been
the growth of various Muslim communities, each composed largely of
immigrants from a particular country, together with their offspring.
Humphrey (1987) has analysed the significance of the mosque in a
Lebanese Muslim community in Sydney, and its relationship to other
Lebanese and Islamic organisations in Australia. The emergence at the
mosque of a popular imam preaching fundamentalist Islamic values led to
concern among some politicians and members of the public that this
would result in the mosque community's becoming culturally and
politically isolated from, and in conflict with, the wider society. Calls
from outside that community for the removal of the imam had a twofold
effect: on the one hand, they helped to unite Lebanese Muslims who had

previously been divided by family, village, regional, sectarian and ethnic differences, making them more determined than ever to maintain the religious values and community autonomy which their critics had sought to curtail; on the other hand, the very effort to assert their autonomy led the Lebanese Muslims to make use of available political and legal processes, and thus to their fuller involvement in mainstream Australian society. Here, as in other instances reviewed above, one encounters elements of paradox or irony. Elsewhere, Humphrey (1982; 1984a; 1984c; 1986; 1989) examines tensions between public law and religious law in the handling of family disputes and community disputes among Lebanese Muslim immigrants, and other aspects of their interaction with the wider society.

Another paradox is encountered in Knight's (1985a) analysis of fundamentalism and education, based on a case study of the Seventh Day Adventist Church. He argues that, despite their otherworldly rationale, Adventists and most other fundamentalists wish to survive and prosper in this present world. They:

> tend to be essentially socially conservative, displaying typical middle class concerns with material prosperity, social respectability and political stability. Hence when (as now) their worldview and style of life is seen to be threatened by national or international instability (e.g. economic crises, exponential technological change, increasingly non-'Christian'and secular life styles, and nuclear annihilation) they are likely to retreat to an imagined more golden past for solutions . . . , pressing for a return to individual and personal moral purity in human behaviour and to 'the basics' in education. (Knight, 1985a: 31–2)

In Knight's view, their rejection of the world is symbolic, a means of providing an 'ethnic boundary' (Barth, 1969) between those who have 'the truth' and those who do not. Despite, or perhaps because of, their emphasis upon particular facets of personal morality, fundamentalists are generally oblivious to deep structural bases of inequality or social injustice. In economics, they generally favour the agenda of the 'new right'. In short, although they vigorously attack some of the lifestyle freedoms found in Western societies, such as those associated with divorce, abortion, homosexuality, pornography, multiculturalism, etc., they strongly defend Western capitalism and 'free enterprise'. Some—here I am going beyond Knight's analysis—also hold to a 'prosperity doctrine', which legitimates success in this world. Elaborations and extensions of Knight's arguments are found in his other papers dealing with controversies over 'creation science' in Queensland, Australia's 'deep north' (Knight, 1985b; 1986; Knight, Smith and Maxwell, 1986).

This section has focused on a number of paradoxes or ironies which may be discerned when one examines conventional religious institutions in the Australian context. From my knowledge of religion in other Western societies, I would suggest that these incongruities are not unique to Australia; similar phenomena occur elsewhere.

Civil religion

Several authors have recently analysed aspects of 'civil religion' in Australia, particularly the beliefs, practices and monuments associated with Anzac. 'Anzac' is an acronym for the Australian and New Zealand Army Corps, which first established its reputation for heroism on 25 April 1915, at Gallipoli in the Dardanelles. Since 1916, 25 April has been observed as Anzac Day, a public holiday on which there are civic rituals to commemorate Australians who have died heroically in war. In this respect it is somewhat similar to Remembrance Day in Britain or Canada, Memorial Day in America and so on. Warner (1959: 248–79) argued that the rituals associated with Memorial Day help to integrate the whole community, and that they give participants a feeling of wellbeing in the face of anxieties associated with death. While some aspects of Warner's ethnography of Memorial Day are applicable also to Anzac Day, there are also significant differences. First, the marches which take place in various towns and cities on Anzac Day do not, as on Memorial Day in Yankee City, make their way to cemeteries. This difference probably springs in part from the fact that Australia has experienced neither a civil war nor an invasion from abroad. Its war dead have usually been buried overseas, in the various theatres of war, rather than returned to Australia for burial. The locales of dawn services on Anzac Day are typically some form of cenotaph or war memorial not associated with a cemetery. Thus, in a sense, the annual ceremonies associated with these memorials give the war dead a funeral they never had (Inglis, 1987).

Second, Warner stresses the important part played by various religious denominations, ethnic associations and other voluntary organisations in the events leading up to, and on, Memorial Day, which thus celebrates the unity in diversity of the community. The events leading up to Anzac Day are neither as extensive nor as intensive as those described by Warner. The part played by the various religious denominations is much more muted, and the recognition—but transcending—of religious and ethnic pluralism is much less apparent (Kapferer, 1988).

Third, in Warner's account there is no equivalent of the heavy drinking and gambling which are significant features of many participants' activities on Anzac Day. Kitley (1979) argues that drinking and gambling on this occasion have several layers of significance: they are assertions of egalitarianism, rituals of rebellion against authority, and means of expressing and assuaging ambivalence about war and its results. Sackett (1985) sees drinking and gambling in the context of the total sequence of events on Anzac Day. This sequence re-enacts some of the experiences of the typical serviceman. He leaves his home, neighbours and regular occupation to become a part of a military unit. Before battle he is fortified with a tot of rum and may also engage in religious rituals, as occurs in the dawn service. Later on he goes on parade in his particular military unit. There are further solemn ceremonies similar to those marking the interment of dead companions. The informal 'booze-ups' and gambling which follow, and which allow the recounting of past experiences, are analogous to the binges troops staged while on leave from the hostilities or when they were being demobilised after the war. Finally, after all this, the former serviceman returns home, with the expectation of resuming his regular activities on the morrow. Although this analysis may be overdrawn and is certainly far from complete, it gives some insight into the events of Anzac Day.

Freeland's (1985) examination of Australian civil religion focuses primarily on the symbolism found in the main war memorials, especially that located in the national capital, Canberra. He concludes that this symbolism derives largely from pagan sources in classical Greece, rather than from Christian sources. This he attributes partly to the somewhat negative attitudes held towards ecclesiastical religion by many Australian troops in World War I in particular; partly to classical Greece's being the supposed source of democracy and of the ideals of freedom for which so many had sacrificed their lives; and partly to general constraints which emerge in religiously pluralistic societies where there is no formally established religion. To avoid alienating sections of the populace, civil religion in such societies tends to be fairly vague in its theology, but it may draw on some primal religious tradition which is part of the cultural heritage of the particular society. Flaherty and Roberts (1989) also trace the roots of Anzac symbolism to ancient Greece, arguing that this symbolism valorises youthful virility and innocence, and the cleansing goodness of fresh air and sunlight.

Though he makes no reference to Freeland's work, Kapferer (1988) would, I think, argue that Freeland has correctly analysed some significant features of Australian civil religion but has not adequately discerned some of the 'deep structures' of the Anzac phenomenon. Kapferer makes a comparative study of what he terms 'the religion of nationalism' in Sri Lanka and Australia. In his view, 'nationalism makes the political religious' (1988: 1), it 'makes culture into an object and thing of worship' (1988: 209); and 'the cult of nationalism has become the dominant religion of modern nation states' (1988: 136). But he goes much further than simply reiterating a purely Durkheimian theme. Building in part, though not uncritically, on the work of Dumont (1986), Kapferer argues that Australian nationalism, which is quintessentially expressed in the Anzac legend and ceremonials, is a variant of the egalitarian and individualist ideology widespread in Western societies; the power of Anzac symbolism and the emphasis on individual autonomy and social

egalitarianism in the Anzac story cannot be properly understood apart from
the ideological structure of Western Judaeo–Christian civilisation. As
Kapferer (1988: 129) puts it, 'this "religion" of the common man is
formed within Judaeo–Christian ideology even as it inverts and rejects it'.
Kapferer discerns in the Anzac legend and rites not only the themes of
heroic endurance and sacrificial death, but also a fundamental tension
between the people and the state. He shows that at various points this
tension can be seen as one between the ideal and the real, between
individual autonomy and social regulation, between the natural and the
artificial. He concludes that 'when Australians mourn at Anzac they may
not only be sorrowing at the death of their comrades in war and since but
also at the experienced reality of their own loss of autonomy and their
inability to determine their own lives in the ordinary social and political
world' (Kapferer, 1988: 165). From this perspective, the drinking on
Anzac Day is not simply an expression of 'mateship' or sociability, nor
just a way of drowning one's sorrows, but also an assertion of individual
autonomy and personal power, putative means by which both the
individual and the nation can be revitalised and regenerated.

   To what extent is Australian civil religion priestly in the sense that it
sanctifies the status quo and to what extent is it prophetic in the sense that
it offers a sharp critique of the status quo? That question is not easy to
answer, partly because of the ambiguities inherent in the Anzac
phenomenon. Though most would say that Anzac is intended to honor war
heroes, not to glorify war, some social critics have suggested that the
former purpose can easily degenerate into the latter. The counter argument
is that Anzac is a reminder both of the dreadful cost of war and of the need
for 'eternal vigilance'. Whether one attributes priestly or prophetic
character to such emphases depends both upon one's particular values and
upon one's perceptions of social reality. The same can be said of other
aspects of the Anzac tradition. Kapferer (1988: 177) sees in that tradition
evidence of a 'powerful distrust of the state'. On the whole, however, the
Anzac tradition currently serves much more to sanctify the status quo than
to challenge it. As Kapferer himself shows, it tends *inter alia* to reinforce
elements of sexism and racism in Australian society.

Explaining distinctive aspects of religion in Australia

Some writers explain aspects of the character and place of religion in
Australia in terms of the circumstances surrounding white settlement.
Thus Mol (1985) draws a contrast between the religious pilgrims who
landed in America in 1620 with many religious observances, and the
officers and convicts who began white settlement in Australia in 1788
with little religious ceremony or motivation. He sees this difference as
symbolic of the fact that religion has always been much more on the

periphery of white society in Australia than in America. While there is some truth in this, it should also be remembered that not all the colonies in America were established by religious pilgrims and that, even in those which were, colonists with primarily secular motivations soon outnumbered the religious pilgrims.

Grocott (1980), Thiering (1982), Turner (1987) and Shaw (1988) argue that in so far as religion had a place in the early Australian colonies, it was regarded by the colonial authorities as a form of social discipline. Various writers have suggested that the convict era left in the Australian psyche a deep-seated aversion to authority, an aversion reflected in the Anzac legend and perhaps still influencing attitudes to organised religion (Bodycomb, 1984: 174ff). Wilson (1983), however, dismisses convict resentment as an explanation for the present state of religion in Australia, arguing that the key factor is a more global phenomenon, namely the process of industrialisation.

Bouma (1988a; 1988b) sees a somewhat different significance in Australia's foundation as a penal colony. He argues that the military middle class, which was dominant for the first 50 years of white settlement, regarded religion as 'something that was done for you by a religious professional'. In Bouma's view, this 'military-chaplaincy' orientation towards religion has persisted, being reinforced by later events such as World War I and perhaps by the work of chaplains in church-related schools. Though there is probably some validity in this argument, it is doubtful whether it, any more than the theory of convict resentment, can adequately account for the prevailing character of religion in Australia today. Historically, the most important influence has been the nature of religion in the various countries from which Australia's population has been drawn. The impact of this has been modified to some extent by generic factors affecting religion in Western societies and by a variety of more specific aspects of Australian society, some of which have already been noted.

Another way of conceptualising the foundation of white society in Australia is to stress the role of the state. The state was important not only in the establishment of penal colonies but also, later on, in promoting and subsidising immigration by non-convicts, in facilitating land settlement, in building roads and railways, and so on. In general, the state played a more active role in social and economic development in Australia than in America. During the first half of the nineteenth century, colonial governments in Australia also provided various forms of financial support for religion (Black and Glasner, 1983; Turner, 1987; Jackson, 1988). By contrast, religion in America at that time was much more self-sustaining, partly because of a stronger revivalist tradition. Jackson (1988) suggests that the absence of government financial support for religion in America may even have encouraged church leaders to cultivate revivals and to employ professional revivalists. Whatever the reason, revivalism has

never been as strong in Australia as in America. Nor has Australia been
the birthplace of new religious movements such as Mormonism, Seventh
Day Adventism, Christian Science and Jehovah's Witnesses, or the host of
other movements which have appeared in recent decades.

Several writers have recently attempted to explore the impact of the
Australian landscape and climate on religion. Jackson (1988) contends that
the landscape which colonists found in Australia was much more foreign
to their eyes than was that found by settlers in North America. Since, in
his view, religious feeling in the British Isles was closely related to the
particular natural landscape there, the colonists found it difficult to evoke a
similar religious feeling in Australia. Arguments akin to this have a long
history, as is illustrated by the lament of the ancient Israelites in captivity
in Babylon: 'How shall we sing the Lord's song in a foreign land?' (Psalm
137:4). Further research is needed to ascertain how central a familiar
landscape was to the maintenance of religious feeling in Britain, and how
significant a radically different landscape was in shaping attitudes to
religion in Australia. Without ruling out this factor entirely, I suggest that
it is inadequate to explain why the current rate of church attendance is
higher in Australia than in Britain.

O'Farrell (1981: 4) sees the contrast between Britain and Australia in
somewhat different terms, arguing that styles of religious architecture,
clerical dress and liturgy were imported to Australia from 'the damp and
gloomy British Isles . . . The whole external image of imported religion in
Australia appeared as sombre, constricting, stifling in a land of colour, fun
and freedom.' As O'Farrell recognises elsewhere in his article, the
Australian physical and cultural environment—and no doubt that of
Britain—is far more complex than these words indicate. Indeed the title of
his article, 'The Cultural Ambivalence of Australian Religion',
summarises his basic argument: that in some respects religious
institutions have occupied a marginal position in Australian culture, yet
'religious matters have also been at the centre of some of the (few) great
debates in Australian history—in education and politics particularly'
(O'Farrell, 1981: 5). Here he foreshadows the argument developed in more
detail by Hogan (1987).

O'Farrell comments, too, on the role of the State, noting the extent to
which it has taken over functions once performed by religious institutions:
in social welfare, hospitals, various forms of counselling, and so on. This
development sprang largely from the belief that the State had both the
power and the money to solve the problems of life, a vision which has
waned somewhat in the 1980s. Though not confident that religion in
Australia is in a fit shape to reassert its cultural relevance, O'Farrell thinks
that such a reassertion might occur, perhaps through the influence of a
relatively small but strongly committed religious minority, especially in a
situation where the 'props of seculardom', such as prosperity and the
welfare state, are dropping away. That remains to be seen.

Some explanations for the distinctive character of 'civil religion' in Australia have already been discussed. There is further material on this in the writings of Ely (1981), Glasner (1983), Turner (1987) and Linder (1988). Taking a lead from Mol's (1976) *Identity and the Sacred*, Ely (1981: 564) has argued that 'the obverse of nearly all processes of secularisation is a parallel sequence of sacralisations. Secularisation in Australian history has been nothing but the displacement of certain sacred objects, beliefs and customs by others.' Ely adopts a broadly Durkheimian definition of the sacred: that which 'as symbol or cause, or both, members see as intimately linked to the group's well-being, and to which, collectively, they accord deep respect' (Ely, 1981: 561). Ely (1981: 563) also speaks of the 'reverent or fearful setting apart of something as sacred', but he regards both Durkheim's and Mol's definitions of religion as too inclusive, preferring instead an exclusive definition such as that of Robertson (1972). In other words, he maintains that not all sacralisations are necessarily religious, but that more insights will emerge from the analysis of what is regarded as sacred than from restricting attention simply to the religious. In his view, talk of secularisation tends to focus on the viewpoints of collective losers, whereas talk about the sacred focuses more on the perspectives of collective winners; it is an examination of the latter which offers the better hope of understanding the dynamic and structural elements of Australian history.

Although Gilbert (1980), a sociologically aware Australian historian, has written an excellent study entitled *The Making of Post-Christian Britain*, he has not published such a comprehensive analysis of Australia. He makes some brief remarks on this in two publications prompted by the Australian Bicentenary (Gilbert, 1988a; 1988b). Rowan Ireland (1988) has provided the fullest attempt so far to deal with the question of secularisation in Australia, relating his analysis both to the work of theorists in other countries and to recent Australian research.

The scope of this book

The present book provides a sample of recent theorising and research on the sociology of religion in Australia. The order of the following chapters has been determined partly by the relative sizes of the religious categories or collectivities studied, and partly by the inter-relatedness of themes or issues pursued from one chapter to the next.

In Chapter 2, Rowan Ireland and Paul Rule turn the spotlight on Roman Catholicism in Australia. At the 1986 Australian Census, Catholics made up 26.1 per cent of the total population, their numbers surpassing for the first time the numbers identifying with the Anglican Church. Because higher percentages of Catholics than of Anglicans attend church regularly, Catholic church attenders have outnumbered Anglican church attenders since well before 1986. Nevertheless the frequency of attendance by Catholics has fallen significantly during the past 25 years. This is one of the many changes within Catholicism since the second Vatican Council. Yet it would be wrong to see such changes, together with the obvious diversity within the Catholic Church, simply as an outcome of Vatican II. As Chapter 2 shows, throughout much of its history in Australia, Catholicism has been characterised by somewhat competing 'projects' or understandings as to what it means to be Catholic. Nevertheless, there seems to be greater diversity within Catholicism since Vatican II than before. And diversity is not confined to Catholicism. Indeed, in recent decades there has been in many religious traditions a discernible trend towards greater individual selectivity in belief. Hence another irony: the above trend is both a form of *convergence* between religious traditions and a source of *divergence* within each tradition. Of course, one of the options which some choose is the traditionalist or fundamentalist one—the attempt to stifle diversity by imposing a rigid definition of the *one* true faith.

Although the term 'project' is not used, the issue of competing projects and also that of social change comes up again in Chapter 3, Ruth Sturmey's historically grounded study of Anglicanism and gender in Australian society. She analyses the ways in which the Church of England in Australia (later renamed the Anglican Church of Australia) has responded over the years to the particular circumstances in which it has found itself, especially as these relate to men's and women's roles in the family, in the church and in society at large. Notable factors which she examines include relationships between church and state, financial pressures on the church and its clergy, the challenges of liberal, democratic and rationalist ideas, processes of secularisation and of embourgeoisement, and changing patterns of education and work. Sturmey's analysis both reinforces and supplements the conclusions of de Vaus and McAllister (1987), to which reference was made earlier in this chapter. She also examines some distinctive features of society and religion in Australia when compared with Britain or America. She notes, for example, that the character of Christianity in Australia has been shaped largely by Anglicanism and Roman Catholicism, neither of which has traditionally stressed individual autonomy or religious dissent. By contrast, religion in America has from the outset been more strongly moulded by traditions of religious dissent and freedom of conscience. Furthermore, religion has never received such strong intellectual input in Australia as it has received in Britain and America through theological faculties in long-established or church-related universities. Sturmey argues that these and other differences have had specific effects on gender roles both in church and in society.

Another perspective on gender-related issues in the Anglican Church is provided in Chapter 4, where Barbara Field applies discourse analysis and semiotics to the conflict over whether women should be ordained to the priesthood. Using insights derived from Foucault (1972; 1979), she argues that people's perceptions of reality are powerfully shaped by various meanings and assumptions embedded in language. Even where people speak what appears to be a common language, there may be different sets of meanings and assumptions, some of which may be at odds with one another. While different discourses, as they are sometimes called, may co-exist within the one society or organisation, some discourses are likely to be dominant over others at a particular time. Patriarchal discourse, which positions women as subordinate or invisible, has long been dominant in most churches. It is often reinforced by essentialist discourse that assumes there are innate differences between men and women in personality and in capacity for leadership, as well as in physiological characteristics. Chapter 4 concludes that many aspects of the theology, liturgical practice and structure of the Anglican Church both reflect and maintain men's dominance and women's powerlessness and marginality. Yet there is also within the Christian tradition an alternative discourse based on notions of full equality, of mutuality and of inclusiveness. It remains to be seen whether this discourse can displace patriarchial discourse from its hegemonic position within not only the Anglican Church but also other churches. The greatest resistance to attempts to displace patriarchy comes from individuals or denominations at either the strongly 'catholic' end of the spectrum (including the Roman Catholic and the Orthodox churches) or at the strongly 'evangelical' end of the spectrum (including Baptists and Pentecostals). Though the proportions vary greatly from one diocese to another, Anglicanism in Australia has both these wings, as well as a more liberal 'broad church' group.

The capacity of churches to achieve equality between men and women is further examined in Chapter 5. This is Ken Dempsey's most recent analysis of church-oriented religion in a small town in Victoria, especially within the Uniting and Anglican churches. In that it has ordained women to full pastoral, preaching and sacramental ministry since the time of its inauguration in 1977, the Uniting Church differs from the Anglican Church, though no woman has yet served in this capacity in the particular town studied by Dempsey. While his data sources are different from those used by Sturmey in Chapter 3, his conclusions about the roles of laymen and laywomen are broadly consistent with hers. He also concludes that the churches tend to mirror, rather than transcend, other hierarchical divisions present in Australian society, such as those of class and age. Such divisions are not unique to Australia, but they raise the question of the capacity of the churches to bridge various social barriers.

Chapters 6 and 7, which interpret aspects of the 1987 Combined Churches Survey for Faith and Mission, provide convincing evidence that high quality sociological research on religion in Australia is going on outside the universities as well as within them. 'Tricia Blombery begins Chapter 6 with a brief review of anthropological and sociological theorising on the ways in which concepts of God or of gods relate to the sociocultural context in which such concepts are held. As social structures vary, so do God-concepts. For example, in societies with clear hierarchical structures, a deity is more likely to be thought of in hierarchical terms than is the case in societies which are more egalitarian in character. Even within the same society, different concepts of God can exist, and these differences can be related to people's different locations in the social structure or different social experiences. Although in religiously pluralistic societies such as Australia, different denominational allegiances may account in part for different conceptions of God, there are also differences within denominations. Chapter 6 gives particular attention to variations associated with age and gender. As was noted earlier, age-related differences may be due either to life-cycle or to generational factors. Blombery discusses both, though her data, gathered at one point in time, do not enable a decisive test of these two explanations. She also finds that differences between men and women in God-concept reflect social expectations that women will be concerned with the expressive, nurturant and affective aspects of life, while men will be more concerned with the wider world. Thus women are more likely than men to favour images of God as a personal friend, an ever-present helper or a comforter, whereas men are more likely than women to favour more distant, cosmic images— for instance, such as of God as the creator and sustainer of the universe.

In Chapter 7, Philip Hughes throws light on the decline of mainline churches during the past 30 years. This decline is manifested both in the falling percentages of the population identifying with Anglican, Congregational, Methodist, Presbyterian or Uniting Churches, and in falling rates of attendance for these churches and for the Catholic Church. In contrast to this decline, some other denominational groups, such as Pentecostals and to a lesser extent Baptists, have expanded during this period and continue to achieve relatively high rates of church attendance. Hughes distinguishes four 'ideal-types' or patterns of faith, which he terms 'conversionist', 'devotionalist', 'conventionalist' and 'principlist' respectively. Only 42 per cent of his sample fit neatly into these categories; many of the rest could be regarded as belonging to hybrid types. Of the four ideal-types, principlists have the lowest rate of church attendance and conversionists have the highest. The four ideal-types are also differentially distributed among the denominations studied by Hughes. In particular, conversionists are over-represented among Baptist and Pentecostal church attenders, whereas principlists are over-represented among attenders of Anglican, Catholic and Uniting churches. This does not mean that most attenders of the latter three denominations are principlists. Rather, principlists make up a significant minority there, whereas they can hardly be found among Baptist and Pentecostal church attenders. It is likely, too, that a significant proportion of people who are only nominally associated with mainline churches are principlists, and that this helps to account for the decline of these denominations.

Further insights into Pentecostalism are provided in Chapter 8. This begins with a brief ethnographic account, noting that Pentecostalism is, in part, an expression of ecstatic tendencies which have been evident from time to time both inside and outside Christianity. It then offers an appraisal of sociological theories that purport to explain the growth of Pentecostalism, especially various forms of deprivation theory, as well as theories which focus on specific characteristics of Pentecostalism, such as its segmented structure, its emphasis on charismatic leadership, its use of face-to-face recruitment by committed lay members, its promise of certitude, empowerment, a strong sense of identity and a way of accounting for both good and evil. Although Pentecostalism is at odds with some aspects of contemporary culture, in other respects it is closely attuned to that culture. Its stress on spontaneity, informality, immediacy, anti-intellectualism, affectivity, involvement of the body, some degree of ecstatic or expressive disorder and popular styles of music are very much in keeping with the 'expressive revolution' which occurred in Western societies in the late 1960s and early 1970s and which left a lasting imprint on popular culture. The chapter concludes that contemporary Pentecostalism mirrors some aspects of present-day society and counterbalances other aspects.

In Chapter 9, Gary Bouma explores the bases of ultimate authority used in ecclesiastical organisations to arbitrate disputes, to legitimate activities and to either prevent or produce change. In a refinement of a typology put forward by Max Weber, Bouma distinguishes three modes of authority, based respectively on appeal to tradition, reason and emotion. Although elements of each type of authority may be present in an ecclesiastical organisation, there is a tendency for any particular denomination to give primacy to one of them. Typically associated with the three different modes of authority are differences in polity, styles of worship, types of lay participation, architectural forms, theological emphases, views of salvation, titles of religious professionals and so forth. Bouma analyses these differences, giving examples from various denominations. Catholic, Orthodox and Anglican Churches, all of which have episcopal polities, tend to stress tradition. Presbyterian and Reformed Churches, all of which have presbyterial polities, tend to stress reason. Pentecostal and Baptist Churches, all of which have congregational polities, tend to stress feelings and emotion. Bouma also argues that national cultures vary, some being more congenial to one type of ecclesiastical authority than another. This relationship is, however, not a simple one, and further work is needed to explore it in more detail.

Whereas Bouma focuses primarily on authority in Christian churches, Rachael Kohn deals with the problem of authority in 'self religions' in Chapter 10. This term was coined by Heelas (1982) to refer to groups or movements which encourage the individual to engage in a quest for self-fulfilment, self-empowerment or self-enlightenment free from established forms of authority. Various such movements have emerged in recent decades, mainly in America, and have spread to other countries, including Australia. The three movements which Kohn examines are those founded by Da Free John (the Johanine Da'ist Communion), L. Ron Hubbard (Scientology) and Werner Erhard (*est*, more recently known as The Forum). She argues that there is an internal contradiction in each of these leaders' teachings. On the one hand they all teach that authentic and final authority resides in the individual and is fundamentally 'self centred'. On the other hand they maintain that it is impossible to recognise one's self-enlightenment or attest to one's self-empowerment, as this very act would negate those desired qualities. One must therefore depend upon the leader or his designates to recognise these qualities as one ascends the scale of enlightenment and empowerment. This analysis leads to the paradoxical conclusion that in movements such as these, which ostensibly encourage radical subjectivism among followers, radical authority is exerted by the leaders. Chapter 10 documents these processes and relates them to other features of these movements.

In Chapter 11, Tony Swain provides a region-by-region overview of Australian Aboriginal religions and of their responses to alien intrusion. At the core of traditional Aboriginal religions is a place-based ontology in which people spiritually linked to land are federated into mutually interdependent socio-religious groups. This is a non-hierarchical and radically pluralistic cosmology. Two features resulting from prolonged contact with aliens have been the modification of the people–land link and the introduction of a belief in beings who transcend socio-geographical boundaries. Such contact occurred before, as well as after, the coming of whites to Australia. For example, trading contacts with Melanesians resulted in the introduction to Cape York of a cult of 'Heroes'—quasi-transcendental beings. Likewise, in Arnhem Land the influence of Indonesian traders is evident in the fertility cult of the All-Mother, a fully transcendent being associated with the Land of the Dead to which souls are believed to depart in an icon of a Macassan prau. Again, in southeastern Australia, where the impact of invasion by whites has been most profound, there is a belief in a sky-dwelling transcendent All-Father, whom Aborigines now generally associate with the Christian God. Such a belief poses something of a challenge to Aboriginal place-based ontology, though the latter still remains important for many Aborigines. Overall, it is clear from Chapter 11 that, contrary to some received opinion, Aboriginal religion is neither uniform throughout Australia nor invariable over time.

The last two chapters of the book deal either implicitly or explicitly with aspects of the relationship between religion and ethnicity. As Jim McKay and Frank Lewins note in Chapter 12, sociological research on this topic can generally be divided into three main categories. First, there are studies which highlight the mutually reinforcing character of ethnicity and religion. This is readily apparent where members of a particular ethnic category (e.g. Greek) profess the same religion (in this case, Orthodox). Second, there are studies which analyse the way in which ethnic differences may divide people who ostensibly profess the same religion. For example, in various countries, including Australia, there have sometimes been significant tensions between Muslims belonging to different ethnic categories, between Catholics of different ethnic backgrounds and so on. Third, there are studies which explore the ways in which religious differences may separate people who would otherwise belong to the same ethnic category. For instance, there are longstanding divisions between Catholic, Orthodox and Muslim Lebanese. Using a theoretical framework derived from Schermerhorn (1970; 1978), Chapter 12 examines cases falling into categories two and three above. McKay and Lewins conclude that different relationships between religion and ethnicity reflect different histories of both religious and ethnic groupings, as well as power relationships within the particular society. Their study provides convincing evidence that the interplay between religion and ethnicity is important in understanding patterns of conflict and integration in polyethnic societies such as Australia.

This issue is further illuminated by Michael Humphrey in Chapter 13. Like many other Western societies, Australia has, in recent decades, experienced an influx of Muslim migrants, especially from Turkey and Lebanon. Although they constitute less than 1 per cent of the Australian population, their concentration in parts of Sydney and Melbourne, together with their distinctive ritual practices and—in the case of women—modes of dress, has given them a visibility out of proportion to their numbers. This visibility has been heightened as a result of media reports on resurgent Islam in the Middle East. Chapter 13 examines aspects of Islamic culture and religious practice in Australia, paying particular attention to the interplay between gender, class, ethnicity and religion. A detailed analysis is made of the significance of Islamic voluntary associations and mosques as sites where gender differences, ethnic background, class interests and religious values are expressed. Clearly, responses to the development of Islamic institutions in Australia will have long-term significance not only in relation to government policy on multiculturalism but also in relation to the exercise of religious freedom.

Note

1 This chapter is an expanded version of a paper originally published in *Sociological Analysis: A Journal in the Sociology of Religion* (official journal of the Association for the Sociology of Religion). It is used here with the kind permission of the Editor of that journal.

2 The social construction of the Catholic Church in Australia

Rowan Ireland and Paul Rule

It is now a quarter of a century since the most important event in the recent history of Australian and world Catholicism: the second Vatican Council. The other modern Councils of the Church—Trent and Vatican I—were notable for creating a renewed centralism and sense of mission, an agenda that shaped the social as well as inner life of the institution and its adherents. Vatican II, while certainly inducing or precipitating great changes, seems to have brought diversity and division rather than a unified purpose to the Catholic Church in Australia. This essay does not claim to evaluate this phenomenon or assign causes, but simply to outline and to a lesser extent document it.

One of the difficulties in such a task is not the lack of survey and other data. In the period since Vatican II, we have, for the first time, a proliferation of quantitative information on the effect of Catholic adherence, belief and salience of religiosity on social, political and moral behaviour and attitudes.[1] Prior to that, there was little besides crude census and public opinion poll material which often, by lumping together nominal or 'tribal' Catholics with committed believers, confuses and conceals the religious factor in social behaviour. The exception is Hans Mol's Religion in Australia survey which, based mainly on data gathered the year after the closing of the Council, serves as a valuable benchmark for change.

Some of the results of recent studies may appear surprising and even contradictory. We will not attempt to reproduce even the major findings here, but will merely point to some of the evidence for the problematic nature of the relationship between belief and practice in contemporary Australian Catholicism. On moral issues, for example, only 48 per cent of Catholics in the Australian Values Study (AVS) survey thought abortion 'never justified'; and the absolute disapproval figures for other issues on which the Catholic Church has a strong public position were: suicide,

53.3 per cent; divorce, 22.8 per cent; extra-marital affairs, 53.3 per cent; homosexuality, 41.8 per cent; prostitution, 34.9 per cent; euthanasia, 31.8 per cent; and tax cheating, 47.9 per cent. On most of these questions, Catholics were close to community norms, with the exception of abortion, where 29.6 per cent was the overall national percentage (Anglicans were at 24.5 per cent). However, as might be expected, Mol (1971) found that it was non-church-attending Catholics who more strongly supported legislation legalising abortion (79 per cent compared with 33 per cent of regular church attenders); and Bouma and Dixon (1986: 129), while they give no figures specifically for Catholics, found that church attendance, belief in a personal God and daily prayer strongly influenced opposition to abortion.

The AVS data on beliefs show similar strong divergences from 'official' teachings, as well as the same variation related to religious practice. For example, 94 per cent of practising Catholics believed in a heaven compared with only 68 per cent of the non-practising. Other surveys show a similar pattern. A 1987 *Age* poll recorded only 59 per cent of Catholics as believing in the Trinity, and 69 per cent in the resurrection of Jesus from the dead (*Age*, 18 April 1987), although this poll did not attempt to measure religiosity.

A comparison of Mol's 1966 survey with the more recent AVS data shows some marked and significant shifts. Mol found in 1966 that Catholics were much more likely than Protestants to agree that 'the most important thing for a child to learn is to obey rather than to think for himself', but by 1983 Catholics (41 per cent) were less likely than other religious adherents to consider obedience an important trait/skill for children to learn at home.

It is clear from the above that the behaviour and attitudes of Australian Catholics—like Catholics elsewhere[2]—can no longer, if they ever could, be predicted by reference to official positions taken by the Catholic hierarchy. Catholics are marching to different drums, only one of which is being beaten by bishops and even Roman authorities.

We have conceptualised these differences by the use of the term 'projects' to distinguish these diverse understandings of the relationship between religious faith and behaviour, specific beliefs and social and moral practice. 'Project' does not necessarily imply an explicit or fully articulated religiophilosophy,[3] but more often must be deduced from statements and public positions and also from the ever-proliferating literature—fiction, quasi-fiction and biography—on being Catholic in Australia. However, it does signify fundamentally different approaches to living in Australia in the late twentieth century and fundamentally different views on the future of Australian Catholicism.

We use the notion of projects to help us conceptualise the Church and discuss change in it. Churches may be conceived of in any number of ways—classically, as distinguished from sects, or in terms of some element like demographic profile or features of formal organisation. In this chapter, adopting perspectives from the sociology of social action, we conceive of the Catholic Church as forever under construction as its members enact their projects for being Catholic. The Australian Catholic Church is the interaction of the rather diverse projects for being a Catholic in Australian society. Any church conceived of in this way must have as many dimensions as the religiosity of its members: the projects of members will focus variously on doctrinal commitments or ethical positions, on ritual and sacramental or devotional life, on the social life of the parish or the 'works' that are performed in and for society at large.

Conceiving of the Church as a set of interacting projects, we leave open, at the start, the questions of boundary and cohesion, though these will be considered in later sections. At this point, though, we note that one of the striking features of contemporary religious consciousness and social expression is a degree of convergence between the religious traditions as well as a loosening of old institutional bonds and loyalties. The tendency towards selective and individualistic religious belief across all religious traditions, documented by Robert Bellah et al. (1985: Chapter 9) for the United States, seems equally verifiable for Australia. And most, if not all, major religious denominations in Australia show at least some signs of the same divergence of projects as the Catholic Church. One little-noted kind of ecumenism is the coming together of liberals and conservatives across denominational lines, whether in defence of a common theological understanding—Biblical scholars are a case in point— or of a common stance on social and moral questions such as abortion, welfare, justice and peace issues. Perhaps the 'project' concept has much wider relevance than to an understanding of Catholic differences.

Projects of the past

At any point in time, we would argue, the Church is the enactment of a variety of projects: it is the give and take, the push and pull between actors who group around the variety of understandings of what it is to be a Catholic in Australian society. In hindsight, at least, it would appear that there have been several moments in Australian history when there has been a sort of ordering of projects around some dominant project. Arguably, the contemporary Church is distinguished by its relative disarticulation of projects as much as for its particular profile of projects. This may well be a distortion—at least of the past—arising because the writing of history imposes coherence, shakes chaos into order and seals the unrecorded as the never-was. It may also distort the present, simply because we cannot yet see theme and coherence in what is a continuous becoming. But a case for relative articulation of projects at various moments of the past can certainly be made.[4]

One early moment has left few traces in the present. It is associated with the names of the English Benedictine monks William Ullathorne and John Bede Polding. Polding arrived as Australia's first bishop in 1835 and became the colony's first archbishop in 1842. His project was to establish a church whose centrepiece and model for the whole was to be a Benedictine abbey, a cultural oasis of European Catholic civilisation. But it was to be a missionary church and the mission was to the Aborigines and to the Irish, most of the latter being folk Catholics of little instruction and, as was the case in rural and often Gaelic Ireland at the time, 'unfamiliar with obligations of regular religious observance and sacramental practice'.[5] The abbey part of the project was dropped by Polding's successor, Roger Bede Vaughan (1877–83), who, although also an English Benedictine, recognised that it had no constituency among bishops and clergy in newly created dioceses, almost all of whom were Irish and not associated with the monastic tradition. A shrewd man, Vaughan also presumably realised that, by the 1870s, a lay Irish project was central to what the Church was. In 1871 the Australasian Catholic Benefit Society was formed. This was parish based, though run by laity, and operated as a benefit society, a fund-raiser for various Irish causes, and in general as the base for increasingly self-conscious defence of Irish Catholic interests and culture.

Vaughan's own central project was, from the beginning, well articulated with the laity's projects. His goal was the development of a separate Catholic education system in the face of the passing of the several *Education Acts* of the colonies between 1872 and 1880. He organised the Joint Pastoral of 1879 which laid the foundations for a Catholic system to be run by European, Irish and Australian teaching orders of nuns and brothers. It should not be forgotten that the educational visions, spirituality and practices of the several orders were extraordinarily varied, with, on the one hand, some orders of French origin attempting to construct a French bourgeois world of intense spirituality and high culture and, on the other, the Australian Sisters of St Joseph, founded in 1866 by Father Julian Tennison Woods and Mary MacKillop, devoted to what they considered to be the basic practical and moral schooling of the Irish-Australian poor. But out of the diverse projects of the orders emerged an educational system whose development and maintenance became the dominant and binding project constituting the Church for the next hundred years.

In the last decades of the nineteenth century, the diverse projects of the teaching orders, the bishops' Catholic schools project and the variety of lay causes overlapped and reinforced one another not only because they were concelebrated in a thousand parish halls on St Patrick's Day and other grand occasions, but because common cause was forged in a sectarian environment. 'Irish need not apply' told you who you were; even if you had better qualifications you had a battle on your hands, and the organised

Catholic community united in symbolic and practical endeavour was the only means for attaining cultural and material survival.

It is easy, though, to exaggerate coherence and articulation and to invest the Catholic Church of this period with something of the solidity of the great monuments of bricks and mortar that were then being erected. An examination of the projects of Cardinal Patrick Moran of Sydney (1884–1911), and of what became of them, reveals elements of conflict. Moran was the nephew of Cardinal Cullen, Archbishop of Dublin (1852–78) who at once symbolised and enormously achieved a transformation of the Irish Church. The nephew became the leader of the attempt to transplant that transformation to Australia.

In neither country was there any simple reworking of Irish traditions. The Cullen–Moran transformation, like those occurring around the globe in the post-Vatican I era, involved a working *on* local Catholicisms with a spirituality made in France and organisational models made in Rome. Undisciplined, relatively unclerical, animistic and local folk Catholicisms were to be transformed into the one Catholicism, organised through a centralised, clergy-dominated hierarchy, its true faith and valid practice codified and minimal standards set for all believers. Lay Catholic religious practice, beyond the minimum of Sunday Mass, yearly Confession and Friday abstinence, was to be developed and supervised through the sodalities of the French Catholic renewal—the Children of Mary, the Confraternity of the Sacred Heart, the St Vincent de Paul Society. But in Moran's plan, a more tightly organised, disciplined and educated Church was not just to work on itself; such a Church would more easily become integral to the formation of a more just and civilised Australia according to the ideals formulated by Pope Leo XIII.

Much of Moran's vision was realised. It was promulgated for the Australian Church through the national plenary councils of 1885, 1895 and 1905. The teaching orders in Catholic schools were enthusiastic missionaries for French spirituality and a simple Roman theology. From Moran's time on, just about all Australian priests destined for the episcopacy were trained in Rome. But though the tide of Europeanisation and clerical bureaucratisation did not result in clashes as bitter as those which occurred in Brazil or the United States, old rival projects remained. The Irish identification and the project of Irish cultural and political defence remained for many Catholics *the* Church project, more important than Moran's Australianism. Against his 'integrationism', the tide moved in favour of defence of a distinct and separate Irish–Australian community. This was perhaps symbolised in the setting up, in the year of his death, of the Australian Catholic Federation, a lay organisation devoted both to pressure group activity for government aid to schools and to action for the protection of Catholic interests. We may infer too, from sermons, 'missions' and pious tracts of the time, that lay Catholics, though contributing with extraordinary generosity to the schools and building projects, needed a lot of working on to bring them around to the faith and morals projects of the clergy. Probably the Church that the bulk of Catholic laity were enacting at this time was a set of public rituals (St Patrick's Day parades), practices (Friday abstinence and sending one's children to be educated by the nuns or brothers) and sacred places, presided over by selected clerical leaders (Moran himself and later Archbishop Mannix), insofar as they provided satisfying religious legitimations for quite secular lay projects. Richard Ely has probably characterised accurately the lay Catholic world of the early twentieth century as focusing around a cluster of sacred 'objects' including 'Irish culture and liberty (variously interpreted), religious-national festivals (such as St Patrick's Day), the right to work, to unionise and to strike, mateship among workmen, ownership of land and home, the special role in the family of motherhood, the rights of "the people", religious vocations and the priesthood' (Ely, 1981: 563–4).

This lay Catholic world held together not only through the disciplines which the laity accepted from the clerical project, but because of constantly renewed symbolic boundaries demarcating it from a British–Australian–Protestant middle-class world. This other world awarded sacredness to such 'objects' as 'the British empire and Britishness, the monarchy, the bible . . . self-improvement and the work ethic, the rights and duties of property, freedom of contract, civil and religious liberty, the "British Sunday", national development, law and order, and perhaps Adam Smith's "invisible hand" ' (Ely, 1981: 563). In this context, Catholic lay and clerical projects could meld in the regular devotional practices and the revered icons that set apart Catholic households, presbytery and lay family homes from their neighbours. On the other hand, the Catholic Church of the early twentieth century was not Moran's project in full swing, as it were, nor the project of maintaining the lay Catholic world; it was the overlap, the give and take between those projects (and perhaps several other less broadly diffused projects as well). The emergent properties of that Church were contained in conflicts and accommodations between these projects.

By the 1930s, new projects involving new constituencies were beginning to have a part in the constitution of a different Church and the pattern of conflict was altering. With the achievement of Home Rule in Ireland in the 1920s, the Irish project became more focused on the maintenance of Irish-Australian culture and less on the politics of Ireland; at the same time, it was gradually becoming less important as a constituting project of the Church *vis-a-vis* other projects. In contrast to the project of defending the material interests of the Catholic community, represented now by the Knights of the Southern Cross, was the project of 'social' Catholicism, itself diverse but international in inspiration, and an outlook that saw the mission of the Church as achieving a more socially just Australia through application of the principles of the social encyclicals of Popes Leo XIII and Pius XI. Insofar as those key principles could be summed up under the headings of decentralisation, distributism, subsidiarity and local ownership, there was little that would have been new to Cardinal Moran. Two things, though, *were* new. One was that 'social' Catholicism came to be championed and developed by new groups of young lay intellectuals. The other was that lay 'Catholic Action' for the achievement of the ideals of 'social' Catholicism had, by the end of the decade, been given a defined position in the hierarchical structure of the Church.[6]

When the Catholic bishops established the National Secretariat of Catholic Action in 1937 they were able to draw on groups of laity and clergy inspired by the visions and apologetics of Chesterton, Belloc and Jaques Maritain and the 'See, Judge, Act' methodology developed by Belgium's Canon Joseph Cardijn in the Young Christian Workers' Movement. The Campion Society, founded in Melbourne in 1931, is often singled out for special mention because from it Mr B. A. Santamaria and some of his later critics emerged. But there were similar groups in other capital cities—for example, the Newman Society and the Aquinas Academy, established in 1928 in Sydney, and the Aquinas Library group in Brisbane. The Sydney Campions were founded in 1934. The Campions, in their Melbourne paper, *The Catholic Worker*, announced a project in every sense of the word. Reacting to what they saw as the disintegration of Christendom under the corruptions of capitalism and the advances of communism, they hoped to awaken society and Church to the need for a radical implementation, in private and public life, of the social teaching of the modern popes. Paul Collins has nicely summarised the concerns and emerging tendencies of the Campions at the end of the 1930s: 'They supported co-operatives of workers, the need for support for the family and emphasised a return to the land . . . The Spanish Civil War changed the direction of these young Catholic idealists. The main enemy became communism rather than capitalism' (Collins, 1986: 198–9).

It would be wrong to consider the Campion project as being in any sense a dominant project of the Catholic Church in its time. Greg Dening (1978), in his history of Xavier College, remarks that Father Hackett, who as founder of the Catholic Central Library was a pivotal figure for the group, never received much of a hearing for Campion concerns among parents and old boys at the school where he was rector from 1935 to 1940. Less privileged Catholics too, however deeply immersed in parish devotional life, were at that time little involved in the projects for a new Catholic Christendom. Moreover, Bruce Duncan (1987) has shown us how naive, confused and at cross purposes were many of those who did consider themselves involved in projects of Catholic Action in the 1930s.

From the early 1940s through to the 1960s, however, Catholic Action as developed by Mr Santamaria did become a dominant project in the Australian Catholic Church. And it was dominant not only because it received strong episcopal support in the form of an official mandate for at least a decade, but also because it was firmly based in Catholic parish life and successfully, if not monolithically, linked its anti-communist crusade to the range of fears, loyalties and religious enthusiasms of ordinary Catholics. The Movement, as it came to be called, retained much of the world view and program of the Campions. But its special project was the harnessing of the organised energies and resources of Australian Catholics for the political defeat of communism. Operating secretly, with a highly centralised command structure not unlike the enemy's and very like the monolith of the Protestant stereotype, it translated Catholic Action into political work to defeat communists and those deemed to be communist sympathisers in the union movement and the Labor Party.

By the early 1950s, such dominance as the Movement had managed to achieve began to falter. Some Catholics involved in Labor politics came to resent the second-class citizenship assigned them in the Church because they were not amongst the Movement cadres. Some New South Wales bishops, with their own channels of influence in the Labor Party, rejected the hegemony of Melbourne that the primacy of Movement strategy seemed to them to involve. A few groups, notably the Young Catholic Workers and the 'university apostolates' in Melbourne and Sydney, questioned and proposed alternatives to the integralism of the movement: they did not see in Church doctrine and structure a sufficient model for a restored Christendom (see Buckley, 1983).

It does not seem to be the case, though, that the decline of the Movement (until it became but one project among many in the Church of the late 1960s to the present) represents a sudden and total disappearance of integralist vision and thought. Catholic 'new left' activists often shared with their opponents an essentially prophetic stance and gained coherence from their self-image as an embattled prophetic minority. They disputed with B. A. Santamaria about his possession of the title *Against the Tide*, which he was to choose for his memoirs. They regarded the National Civic Council's support of the Vietnam War and of the Liberal government's policies on issues such as the United States alliance, trade unions, strikes and recognition of the People's Republic of China as very much going with the tide, and their own positions as oppositional.[7] They appealed to the same Catholic traditions—just war doctrine, spiritual over material values, the centrality of the family, remembered ethnic grievances—at the same time as they challenged the Catholic 'right' over its application of those values. They differed on organisational models, preferring open consensual structures and direct action to hierarchical/cell structures and covert influence. But a very high proportion of them had got their political and social education and impulse to social activism from the Movement. Eventually, many of them were to transfer this activism to exclusively secular spheres and even to abandon religious practice and/or belief, but they could not have been what they were without their Catholic roots.

Contemporary constructions of the Australian Catholic Church

Vincent Buckley, in *Cutting Green Hay*, has reminded us of the variety of ways of being a Catholic in Australia well before Vatican II. His account of the development of the intellectual apostolate and its 'groups' in Melbourne and Sydney in the 1950s shows us young Catholics at the universities intent on the construction of what Latin American Catholics nowadays call 'new ways of being Church' at the very time that, in theological and ecclesiological terms, the Catholic Church was supposed to have been most homogeneous and Catholics most conformist. In the light of Buckley's account, Vatican II does not seem quite the fount of decline and fragmentation or re-animation and diversity in the Australian Catholic Church.

Nevertheless, since the 1960s, the sheer variety of projects and the extent to which they are understood to involve contest over the form and content of the Church itself seem to have increased. Whether this has involved disintegration and a triumph of secularisation will be addressed in the next section. In this our concern is to map the variety, highlighting the sort of Church that is being constructed by the protagonists of each project. The various projects will be seen to involve not only emphasis on one or other of the several dimensions of religion but also contrasting notions of what it is to *be* Catholic on each of those dimensions.

To a greater extent than in the past, important if not sizeable groups of Catholics emphasise what is often called the cognitive dimension of religion, and there is increasing contest between different conceptions of and practices regarding the Church as the repository and communicator of the Truth about faith and morals. In this case there is no problem in the use of the word 'project' to denote the contesting positions. On the one hand, groups like the Pathfinder group of the 1970s or writers in the journal *AD 2000* in more recent years, in their critiques of modern catechetics in general and RE teaching in Australian Catholic schools in particular, express not only a point of view about the teaching functions of the Church but pursue a strategy to restore Church institutions to what they regard as orthodoxy. Theirs is self-consciously a project in which the teaching function of the Church is given pre-eminence; that which is to be taught is doctrine about faith and morals, the content of the Magisterium in the form of propositional theology.

On the other hand, from at least the time of the setting up of the Confraternity of Christian Doctrine in the Melbourne archdiocese in the 1960s, a teaching project, quite different in aim and pedagogy, has slowly developed and gained ground institutionally and in actual teaching practice in the Church's schools. Theologically, the aim of this project is to stimulate reflection on the continuing Christ-event, and thereby to train students to become co-producers of an historical rather than a dogmatic theology. The emphasis is less on the transmission of the formulae of traditional doctrine (though only less than in the *AD 2000* project) and more towards establishing points of intersection between the stories of Scripture, personal biography and contemporary social history. Among Australian Catholic theologians, Father Tony Kelly is probably the best-known exemplar of this new reflective theology-in-the-making. But it is important to note that neither of these projects for the Church as teaching Church is the exclusive domain of clergy or theologians. Both have their protagonists in the letter columns of the Catholic papers (Collins, 1986: 181).

In Australia, the projects for doctrinal development and appropriation are mainly centred in the Catholic Church's formal educational institutions: seminaries and theological colleges, universities and teachers' colleges, Catholic Education Offices and adult education centres. In recent years, perhaps the greatest changes have been in the ever-increasing numbers of laity studying and teaching in such institutions. The theology taught is post-Vatican II theology, biblical and historical, but still often essentially pedagogically propositional and divorced from broader contemporary intellectual currents. The emergence of Catholic universities may change this, but might also facilitate a turn inwards and towards the more conservative doctrinal project. Nevertheless, it is in such institutions that many of the crucial battles for the mind are occurring. Conservatives and liberals alike, to use convenient but misleading labels, see hegemony over the education of clergy and teachers in Catholic schools as vital. Recent Vatican directives on seminaries and the responsibilities of theologians seem designed to create a Roman-oriented conformity. Is Bishop Brennan of Wagga Wagga's recent removal of his student priests from Sydney to place them under his personal tutelage a sign of the times? It would be a great irony if the laicisation of the seminaries were to produce a clerical exodus from them.

Quite traditionally, there has been a division of labour and even tension between those who identify with the teaching Church and those who identify primarily with the Church as the agent for the sanctification of the world. But among those tending towards the latter identification there are at least two contrasting projects in the contemporary Australian Church. On the one hand, among older clergy and laity, being a Catholic is focused on the organised Church and its sacraments. The world is to be sanctified as individual Catholics attain a measure of sanctification, seeking salvation in and through a formal association constructed around the sacramental rites. The priest as celebrant in formal rituals is the central figure in this project of sanctification. Rates of sacramental practice and numbers of priestly vocations are indices of success, or if falling, the signs of decline.

Another project for the sanctification of the world which has engaged many Australian Catholics in recent years is less priest and rite focused and involves building the Church as a people as a priority over the salvation of individual souls. The Renew program, which has been attempted in 650 Australian parishes in fourteen dioceses since 1987, certainly does not eschew individual salvation and it positively seeks renewal of the Church's sacramental practice at the parish level. But it is distinguished from the earlier sanctification project by its focus on the development of lay spirituality and the building of communal rather than associational relations among parish populations. Though the program includes deepening the sense of social responsibility among participants, it is not so essentially concerned with community action for radical social change as the Basic Christian Community movement in some parts of Latin America. Nor is it essentially concerned with a restructuring of the Church itself: it is primarily a project of sanctification, less centred on individual salvation than an earlier project but still centrally concerned with the sanctification of the world through the achievement of a holier Church. However, out of Renew, as its opponents are probably correct in fearing, is constructed a Church that is less priest-centred and probably less amenable to the project of the promulgation of doctrine from above than the earlier sanctification project.

Another set of projects in the contemporary Australian Church explicity contests the structural form of the Church itself. On the one hand there are important individual bishops and groups whose major project is that of 'recentrage'—the restoration of an hierarchical line of command and the centralisation of decision-making in a Church which, according to the apostles of recentrage, has fallen into disarray since Vatican II. On the other hand, there are the experiments in decentring: the transformation of the Church into a flatter and more diffuse structure, a loose network of communities in which a rich variety of ministries is recognised and the boundary between clergy and laity less marked than at present. The recentrage projects, though at times in conflict with one another, have achieved a certain ideological coherence and authority derived from pronouncements of the Cardinal Prefect of the Sacred Congregation for the Doctrine of the Faith, Joseph Ratzinger. Harvey Cox (1988) argues in his *The Silencing of Leonardo Boff* that Ratzinger's world view, even as articulated in the notorious *Ratzinger Report* (Ratzinger and Messori, 1986), is not just reactionary but based on a consistent cultural as well as theological analysis. It involves a rejection not only of 'modern' culture in favour of a classical European Christian culture, but also of any attempt to replace the latter with a cultural pluralism. It calls forth a centralised Church able to maintain a unitary culture and theology.

One expression of the recentrage project in Australia is the Opus Dei Movement. Favoured by the present Pope, Opus Dei has, since 1982, had the status of a personal prelature in the Catholic Church with its own bishop responsible directly to the Pope and secular clergy, drawn from celibate laymen of the organisation, assigned to it rather than, as normally, to a territorial diocese or prelature. Opus Dei was founded in Spain in the

1930s. In Australia, it had about 300 members, including nine priests, by 1987. The number is small but the aim of Opus Dei is to be a model of pure Catholicism rather than a mass organisation. Each Opus Dei group is like a monastery without walls: out in the world, its monks mostly laity ('numeraries' and 'associates' who are celibates and 'supernumeries' who are single or married). All members, striving for excellence in their work, living in their families, try to follow traditional Catholic ascetic disciplines and keep abreast of orthodox Catholic teaching. Some will be engaged in educational and charitable enterprises sponsored by the organisation (in Australia, residences for tertiary students like Warrane College of the University of New South Wales, a number of study centres and the Eremeran Club for girls in Killara). In these 'corporate works', Opus Dei claims merely to provide 'the spiritual care, guaranteeing at the same time that all instruction given there is in line with the teachings of the Catholic Church' (West, 1987: 183–4). In form and function, Opus Dei constructs a Church that harnesses lay energies and professional skills for the promulgation of centrally determined (in Rome) orthodoxy and for ends of justice and charity dispensed from more privileged elites in the Church to the less privileged.

But there are other and more influential groups and individuals urging a tighter, more Roman Church for the achievement of Catholic integralism. Many of the former Movement activists have joined Mr Santamaria, who now edits an integralist theological and Church affairs monthly, *AD 2000,* in campaigning against heresy and disloyalty amongst not only disobedient laity but also clergy and bishops. Others have joined in single-issue campaigns such as Right to Life and CARE (attacking the 'new' religious education in Catholic schools). Significant features of these activities are their appeal to a higher loyalty rather than local loyalties (Mr Santamaria's old closeness to the Australian bishops as a body is a thing of the past) and their links with similar movements overseas (much of the content of *AD 2000* is reprinted from American and European sources).

There are several variations on recentrage. One emphasises a tightening of discipline in the name of anti-modernism and is less wedded to formal command structures than Opus Dei. One of the leading articulators of this centralist Roman 'traditional' vision is George Pell, auxiliary bishop of Melbourne and rising man in the Australian Catholic Church as demonstrated by his recent appointment to two Vatican bodies. In a *Conversazione* at La Trobe University, Pell (1988) urged 'energetically promoting many aspects of the style of Australian Catholicism, which we have been tempted to downplay for reasons of ecumenism or as concessions to modernity', and, in a controversial phrase, that 'the doctrine of the primacy of conscience should be quietly ditched'. An exercise in ecclesial futurology by Pell (1989) envisages a parish-based religious practice involving a return to traditional devotions, a diminution of central bureaucracies and a key leadership role for the parish priest.

A lay exponent of this anti-modernism is Michael Gilchrist, who has produced frequent *AD 2000* articles as well as two books, *Rome or the Bush: the Choice for Australian Catholics* (1986) and *New Church or True Church: Australian Catholicism Today and Tomorrow* (1987). The title of the former is symptomatic. For Gilchrist, any pronouncements of 'Rome', whether newsletters of Roman congregations, interviews or occasional addresses given by popes and cardinals, are authoritative, representing 'the mind of the universal church'. We in the bush, the 'horizontal' element in the church (a term he uses with no suspicion of irony), have no role but to obey. Gilchrist combines a romantic and unhistorical view of the pre-Vatican II Church with an antipathy to all recent developments. His writings are a litany of what he and his major audience obviously regard as horror stories: girl Mass servers, Holy Communion in the hand, Catholic feminists. We are back with the *Ratzinger Report* and its bleak vision of the world and the Catholic Church; and strong, centralised episcopal structure is the condition for a new dawn.

One curious feature of the Gilchrist version of essential Catholicism is its closeness to the parody of mid-century Catholic life to be found in the literature about Australian Catholic upbringings. The present authors, who both came from typical pre-Vatican II Catholic parish and school backgrounds, have concluded that we must have suffered severe deprivation. Our childhoods and adolescences might have been greatly enriched by encounter with the extreme authoritarianism, eccentricity and absurdity that the memorialists deplore and conservatives lament. Our recollections are more of a dull conformity.

Decentrage projects are expressed in some of the experiments in Christian community surveyed by Mary E. Britt (1988). Most of the Australian Catholic experiments in building community to live the faith are probably best considered as projects for the sanctification of the world and involve no self-conscious challenge to the governance of the Church. This seems to be the case with the 'covenant communities' emerging from the Charismatic Renewal movement in the 1970s—communities like the Emmanuel Community and the New Emmaus Family, both found in the Brisbane area. But there are other experiments in which Church structure is at issue. Mary Britt, writing of some small groups in the outer western region of Sydney that seem, in their commitment to action for social justice, to be like the Base Christian Communities of Latin America, notes the sort of decentring of the Church that seems to be integral to their commitment:

> A new model of church is operative here; an open model in which all are called to full participation in the life of the community of believers, to responsible ministry according to one's own gifts and the neighbour's need; where there are relationships deep enough for people to support one another in faith as they grapple with ultimate questions and everyday realities; where

those who are affected by decisions are involved in making them; where actual needs, not maintenance of a status quo, are the criteria for choice of ministries and allocation of resources. It is a model that sees the church not as the kingdom of God, ready made, but as the People of God struggling to build that kingdom and expecting leadership from the church to take a prophetic, not a compliant, stance towards the prevailing culture. (Britt, 1988: 43–4)

The Hesed community, located in rural Victoria, seems to share similar values and goals.

In many of the ethnic communities that comprise the Catholic population there are groups—as of yore among the Irish—whose Catholic identity is very different from both the recentring and decentring Catholics. There are 'tribal Catholics', to use a prejudicial term, for whom Catholicism is alleged (usually, but not exclusively, by Catholics of Irish–Australian background) to be little more than a marker of ethnic identity. Paul Collins (1986: 214) notes that Catholics from the former Eastern bloc countries 'manifest a strong interrelationship between Catholicism, nationalism and anti-Communism', and it may be that when the latter 'isms' have become absorbing projects in an individual life, the former is a sort of prop that is not passed on to succeeding generations. The same might be true of Vietnamese Catholics. The suggestion is that ethnic projects of ethnic Catholics are more important to them than the living of their Catholic identity.

We really don't know, and Cyril Halley (1980) has shown us how little the Catholic Church organisation in Australia has cared to know, about ethnic Catholicisms, despite the fact that 'around 45 per cent of all Catholics in this country are either born overseas themselves or are children with at least one parent born overseas' (Collins, 1986: 213). There is anecdotal evidence that among Italian Catholics there are comparatively few in the second and third generations who retain any Catholic identity. But if this is true, it might in part be a result of the strong and consistent assimilationist policy of the Australian bishops and the insistently Australian style of ritual and devotional life in most Australian parishes (there are some notable exceptions). Adrian Pittarello (1980) and Frank Lewins (1978) have documented the sense of puzzlement and exclusion among first-generation Italian Catholics as they taste 'the soup without salt' of Australian Catholicism. In fact, this may be a rationalisation of the impact of urban industrial society on rural migrants, and similar complaints are expressed by internal migrants from Southern Italian villages to the great cities of the North. But the supposed primacy of ethnic projects among ethnic Catholics is also likely to be, in part, a function of an Australianist project pursued largely subliminally by 'old' Australian Catholics—though it is of interest to note that B. A. Santamaria, in 1939, argued against ethnic diversity in the Australian Church (Santamaria, 1939).

A final set of projects that seems, at least from time to time, to assume priority in the lives of some Australian Catholics, involves identification with the Church as a base for the social transformations that the Gospels and Church teaching enjoin. In 1987 when the Catholic bishops decided to disband the Catholic Commission for Justice and Peace (CCJP), creating instead a new Bishops' Committee for Justice, Development and Peace to be advised by a Catholic Council for Social Justice, many inside and outside the Church concluded that battle lines had been drawn between rival projects for the achievement of social justice. On the one side was the CCJP and supporters who quickly formed a Catholic Coalition for Justice and Peace with branches in all capital cities except Hobart and in some regional centres. Among laity and clergy on this side the announced project was to produce information and critical analysis that would persuade Church, state and civil society to opt for the poor and oppressed on domestic and international issues of justice and peace. From 1969, when it was established by the Bishops' Conference, the CCJP had published reports, approved by the bishops, on such matters as employment, industrial relations, nuclear disarmament, youth and land rights. The research for these reports involved wide consultation with academics, trade unions, government bodies and representatives of groups believed to be suffering injustice. The reports themselves were intended to take a stand: debate and controversy were to be encouraged.

Over the years, the CCJP was attacked as 'communistic', naive', 'anti-American' and 'quasi-Marxist' in *News Weekly,* the journal of Mr Santamaria's National Civic Council; and some bishops dissented from particular reports or expressed reservations about their controversial nature. When the body was disbanded, many assumed that the bishops were backing off from a project for justice that went well beyond simply announcing Church teaching, and that the bishops wished to regain control of the making of the statements so that they would be less controversial. Some years later, it is apparent that this was not the case. The bishops have certainly not gone to the side of the National Civic Council. They have recently adopted the United States bishops' model of major statements produced through a prolonged consultative process. The first such statement, on the distribution of wealth in Australia, is about to appear. A larger number of bishops will have been involved in the making of this statement, but indications are that it will not be blandly consensual, nor will it merely reiterate the principles of Catholic social teaching.

Nonetheless, the very public controversy over the disbanding of the CCJP brought out contrasting projects for societal transformation. Among the various positions could be discerned, at one extreme, a project in which a hierarchically organised Church's leaders would work on and with the elites of the state and civil society for a specifically Catholic version of a

Christian order. At the other extreme, and embodied in some of the experiments in community previously outlined, may be discerned the project in which the Church as a pilgrim and ecumenical people *acts* rather than pronounces, in order to build a new civil society from the grassroots. In this latter project, Catholics engage in the work of the social movements—the women's movement, peace, green, civil rights and Third World solidarity movements—rather than exclusively in within-Church agencies.

A disintegrating church?

Despite the profusion of projects and conflicts we have outlined, we have almost certainly failed to represent the full range of ways of being Catholic in Australian society. Further research will be necessary to show how the various projects distinguished above and more besides (liturgical projects, for example) combine and permutate in actual lives and how salient the various types of Catholicism are in the lives of their carriers. Leavey and Hetherton's cases (1988) help us along on the issue of range and salience, and Hornsby-Smith's (1987) work on English Catholics should help us with types. But if we have under-represented the range of lived projects for being Catholic, what does this imply for the Church which, we are claiming, is sociologically the give and take, the push and pull of those projects? If the range has increased and the integrating mechanisms have declined since Vatican II, is the Church in Australia in a state of disintegration? Have we been surveying not a Church under constant construction but a Church in an advanced stage of self-destruction? In this concluding section we shall advance some considerations against the conventional wisdom that would answer these questions positively.

If the projects outlined above, together with others not listed here, were lived out in little sect-like groups within the Church, then we would have something like Babel and destruction close to hand. In fact, the combinations of projects, and perhaps a certain logic that invites alliances across projects and certainly a privileging of certain clusters of projects over others, preclude the multiplication of sects. We have already noted the difficulty of deciding the heading under which projects should be discussed: some of the community-building projects might have been discussed as recentrage *or* sanctification projects; the *AD 2000* contributors might be considered to be constructing a recentred Church *and* a Church devoted primarily to promulgating pure doctrine in faith and morals.

Indeed, through the diversity there are signs of clustering around two poles, and the Australian Catholic Church is perhaps taking shape as two broad projects for being Catholic emerge ever more clearly in contest with one another.[8] The first broad project, given a certain coherence and awarded privilege by current Vatican policies, includes the following specific projects that we have reviewed:

- the project of communicating doctrine about faith and morals, the content of the Magisterium in the form of propositional theology;
- the project of channelling God-bestowed holiness on a godless world through the organised Church and its sacraments, with a focus on individual salvation in a formal association;
- the project of recentrage, or restoration of a hierarchical line of command;
- the project of working on society for justice and peace from the top down, through the influence of Church elites on the elites of the state and civil society, for a more Christian order.

The specific projects comprising the second emergent broad project might include:

- the teaching project of stimulating reflection on the continuing Christ-event and the building of an historical theology;
- the sanctification project of forming communities of the worshipping faithful engaged in bringing wholeness to a fractured world;
- the ecclesial project of de-centring and the attendant development of lay communities and ministries;
- the project for justice and peace in which a pilgrim and ecumenical people attempt to build a new civil society from communities and networks at the grassroots.

But if there is something like this emergent ordering in diversity, is there not also a destructive polarisation? We would argue no, or at least not yet, in Australia. It is well to remember that there is a long tradition in the Australian Church of disputes, often bitter and prolonged but having the character of family quarrels in which a sense of belonging survives vicious engagement. T. L. Suttor's *Hierarchy and Democracy in Australia, 1788–1870* (1965) and Margaret Pawsey's *The Demon of Discord* (1982) have documented the ferocious intra-church disputes which took place in both Sydney and Melbourne in the middle of last century over the future and government of Australian Catholicism. In these disputes, the several parties accused their opponents of heterodoxy and disloyalty. Yet few were pressed to the point of formal withdrawal. The dynamics of shared ritual as understood by Durkheim may help explain bonding despite deep dispute. But there is also a sort of profile of conflict in the Australian Church which allows for construction of the Church rather than self-destruction.

Though there is not much hard data to go on, inspection of debates between Catholics in journals like the ecumenical *National Outlook* and

Adelaide Voices or the Melbourne diocesan paper *The Advocate* suggest that there is much crossing the line between the two general projects. For example, some of those living a decentring project insist on working within parish structures and are committed to putting new life into old sanctification projects. Some of the rebuilders of civil society carry a very traditional spirituality. Furthermore, the Australian bishops, to the despair of fundamentalists on both sides of the divide, are quite non-fundamentalist when assembled in Conference.

And it is not only the bishops who constitute a sort of buffer: it is the still large mass of parish laity who comprise a sort of uncommitted (though we should not assume bland or disinterested) middle. Apart from the case studies found in Leavey and Hetherton (1988), we know little of this middle except that it is uncommitted to any fundamentalism, and we can guess from a still massive vote of attendance and support that its projects include continuity of the institution of Catholic education and of the existing parish structure.

This is not to suggest that there is no contest between projects and even some tendency to polarisation: it is only to point out that there are other tendencies mediating and moderating polarisation.[9] These same tendencies are read by fundamentalists of the first broad project as symptoms and causes of the Church's self-destruction since Vatican II. Wishy-washy bishops and laity without clarity of project because they have been denied a solid Catholic education cannot maintain the Church against the inroads of secularisation, it is argued. Decline in formal practice among Catholics and a loss of influence in the public sphere are the expected and perceived outcomes, within this viewpoint, of self-destruction.

There is no denying certain signs of institutional decline. The Catholic Church may still be nominated as church of affiliation by 26 per cent of the Australian population. But among Catholic women there has been a decline from 60 per cent attending at least once a week in 1967 to 36 per cent in 1985. Among men, the corresponding decline has been from 42 per cent to 32 per cent (McCallum, 1986: 17). At the same time, clergy per head of Catholic population have been declining. Moreover, taken collectively, priests have been ageing much more rapidly than the population at large. There is every sign that female religious orders will have disappeared by 'early next century' (McCallum, 1986: 24).

On the other hand, the living of some of the projects described above and even the contests between them may be interpreted as signs of vigor. Countering undeniable signs of the inroads of secularisation is evidence of life: increasing numbers of laity undertaking theological education, the cross-fertilisation of religious traditions evident in Australian Catholic scholarship, the experiments in communal living of the faith that we have reviewed, the breadth and depth of concern about issues of justice and peace on an international scale among senior students in many Catholic schools.

None of this is to argue that all is well, that the danger of the Church turning into a bureaucratic shell is not real or that the prevailing privilege of some projects over others is as the Lord intended. It is rather to point to signs that the social construction of a living Church continues.

Notes

1 Hans Mol's two studies, the 1966 survey published as *Religion in Australia* (1971) and the updated *The Faith of Australians* (1985), based on the 1981 census and other data, are indispensable. The Australian Values Systems Study, part of the International Values Study conducted in 1983, is most accessible in Bouma and Dixon (1986). The Christian Research Association's Combined Churches Survey for Faith and Mission includes data for Catholics and has so far resulted in several publications including Blombery (1989a; 1989b), Blombery and Hughes (1987), Hughes (1988a; 1988b; 1989) and Hughes and Blombery (1990). More specifically Catholic in its focus is the National Catholic Research Council's Pastoral Investigations of Contemporary Trends series, of which Leavey and Hetherton (1988) is the most useful volume for our purposes.

2 The European data from the European Values Study Group Foundation survey may be found analysed in the Pro Mundi Vita: Europe North America Dossiers, Nos 27 (1984/4) and 37 (1987/2). Hornsby-Smith and Lee (1979) and especially Hornsby-Smith (1987) survey the English data. The United States data from the National Opinion Research Center are reported in the many publications of Andrew Greeley, most accessibly in Greeley (1985).

3 This useful term is borrowed from the Chinese scholar Tu Wei-ming (1979: 84) who uses it to denote 'the inquiry into human insights by disciplined reflection, for the primary purpose of self-transformation' (i.e. the development of lifestyles informed by a specific religious tradition, but extended and applied through reflection on experience).

4 The following outline of 'moments' is not based on original research but draws heavily on MacGinley (1988) and O'Farrell (1977).

5 J. Bossy, an historian of the English Catholic community 1570–1850, quoted in MacGinley (1988: 25).

6 In a rapid resumé such as this there is necessarily an exaggeration of the consistency and maturity of projects. In fact there was much confusion about what lay Catholic Action entailed and what now appears as extraordinary naivety in attempts to apply diverse European models for Catholic Action in Australia (Duncan, 1987: 4–7).

7 Val Noone is completing doctoral research at La Trobe University on Catholics opposed to Australia's involvement in the Vietnam War.

8 Father P. R. Wilkinson is engaged in doctoral research in Adelaide, in which he is investigating empirically the possible emergence of two movements in the Church, drawing on the theories and 'intervention' methods of Alain Touraine.

9 Father P. Garland (1981) has developed some of these ideas about the profile of conflict.

3 Anglicanism and gender in Australian society
Ruth Sturmey

From the mid-1960s, sociologists of religion have merely confirmed what church leaders had known from at least the late nineteenth century, namely that women tended to be more involved with organised Christianity and do more supportive church work than men (Church of England, 1925: 190–206; Heeney, 1982: 90–1). Some possible reasons for this gender difference in religious orientation were reviewed briefly in Chapter 1, where particular attention was paid to the analysis done by de Vaus and McAllister (1987) on the Australian Values Study. In this chapter I want to make use of historical data to throw light on the way in which the roles of men and women in the church have related to broader trends in Australian society. To do this will require an understanding of the adaption of organised Christianity to Australian conditions, of the influences affecting men's and women's lives in Australia and of the process of secularisation. It is in the complicated matrix of these processes that the differences in men's and women's present religious orientations may best be understood. However, this particular analysis will use only the Church of England in Australia (later known as the Anglican Church) to illustrate the process. It arises out of a much longer study (Sturmey, 1989) which, in exploring the significance of the women's ordination movement in that Church, concluded that the abovementioned processes were crucial to any proper understanding of the present situation.

The place of religion in Australian life

Discussions of the place and character of religion in Australian history have often concluded that Australian life has been characterised by a religious vacuum: that, apart from its 'sectarian strand' (Hogan, 1987), this is a post-Christian society where secular substitutes for Christianity have been created (O'Farrell, 1976; 1981; Bollen et al., 1980). However, it is my contention that the historical debate has *not* yet fully considered the influence of religion on *all* of Australian life, but only on the public sphere of politics, the economy, employment and education. It can be said, therefore, to have primarily mapped the influence of Christianity—or the lack of it—on the lives of Australian men. Likewise, most histories of churches have dealt with the exploits of men, who have dominated its politics and official beliefs. So what has been omitted for the most part is an historical analysis of the role of Christianity in the sphere of family and home life and thus in the lives of Australian women.

Moreover, there have been no significant attempts, apart from that of Jill Roe (1985) on Theosophy to write religious history with a gender analysis, even though there have been specific studies of women's groups within various churches, including a recent history of the women's ordination debate in the Anglican Church (Porter, 1989). Nor has this neglect been righted by feminist historians or sociologists. They seemed little interested in exploring the religious life of Australian women, having apparently assumed like Jan Mercer (1975: 253–73), that there was nothing more to say than that male church leaders had thoroughly socialised women into conservative and heteronomous roles and there was little to be found in this to women's credit. Feminism itself appears to be more highly secularised in Australia than in America or Britain, where a great deal has been written on the religious roots of feminism (e.g. Behnke, 1982, Epstein, 1981). Thus the link between women and organised Christianity, including women's role in maintaining the influence of organised Christianity in Australian life, has not yet been fully explored.

Australian Christianity according to the Church of England

Various expectations and social conditions helped to shape the character of the Church of England in Australia. For much of our history, there have been significant parallels between roles assigned to women on the one hand and functions expected of the Church on the other. In the course of this chapter, some of these parallels will be noted. First, the Church of England in the convict colonies was expected by the authorities to maintain and legitimate law and order by morally reforming and making more obedient, ordered and stable the convict (and free) population, and by sanctioning marriages as it had always done (Grocott, 1980). In nineteenth century England, the Church of England clergyman had been described as the 'mainspring of the police in his parish' and he had been encouraged to co-operate fully with the police and poor law guardians in urban areas (Heeney, 1972–73: 214–15), so his early colonial role as magistrate was an extension of this understanding. For the same reason, and despite increasing opposition to any state support of religion, state aid to the churches was extended into the goldrush period because highly mobile fortune hunters of various races and classes—most of whom were men without families—were viewed by authorities as likely to be socially disruptive and morally corrupt without the steadying influence of women, family life and religion.

Evidence suggests that administrators and professionals also regarded women and marriage as important 'civilisers' and harmonious stabilisers of the raw and immoral society of men. Women were described as God's police by those concerned about corruption and disorder in a frontier society with few of the organisations, rules and established routines they had known in Britain (Dixson, 1984; Summers, 1975). Women, like the churches, were believed to be men's link with culture and refinement, with gentle, co-operative, self-sacrificing virtues, with familial traditions and ties, as well as being the occasion of those responsibilities that steadied and sobered men to the duties of the good citizen.

Moreover, from that beginning, traditional Anglican theology and social ethics have remained largely supportive of law, order and harmony and of the legitimacy of old laws and social arrangements which have best met the needs and ideals of the Church's leaders. These concerns take priority over other motifs such as justice or freedom, which are important in American Protestantism. Australian Anglican leaders have tended to see the ideal social order as being in the past rather than in the future and have therefore been inclined to judge most social changes as eroding God's standards and God's authority. A stratum of intellectually or socially critical clergy for whom philosophical, social and economic change is part of the mission of the Church has not developed as strongly as in some other parts of the world. The great value Anglicans put on harmony and law abiding behaviour is still strongly present in the women's ordination issue.

Second, the Church of England provided a way for many to express their cultural and family identities and traditions and to relieve the psychological stress presented by an alien land and a pluralist society. For many Anglicans in the lower socio-economic categories in particular, the changes to location and lifestyle brought about by an industrialising and urbanising Britain had already broken the habits of church-going. For others, the long journey to Australia, the new challenges of colonial life and the lack of a church presence in many areas broke their allegiance to organised Christianity. Many colonials simply learned to get along without the Church of England, being less familiar than other Protestants with an individualised religion of the heart relatively free of outward trappings, special liturgies, sacraments and a priesthood, and being unused to financially supporting their church. Nevertheless, there were still many colonists who, when it was possible or necessary, sought to re-establish links with the Church of England. Such 'necessary' occasions typically included the birth of children, marriage and death. This suggests that contact was often reinstituted at the request of women because these occasions were more central to their life tasks and status.

The richest and therefore most influential Anglicans in colonial society certainly had the chance to express their family's social and economic status through such Anglican practices as pew rents and donations for church buildings and furnishings that acted as family memorials. Until the late nineteenth century when parish government was reformed along more democratic lines, the system of subscriptions to clerical incomes also strengthened the power of wealthier men to influence church affairs. As in other aspects of colonial society, the Church's severe financial problems allowed those who were prospering in the colonies to proclaim their own success in these ways as decreed by tradition (Hirst, 1988: 58–77). In addition, supporting the Church of England was often part of an overall desire to create a cultured 'English tone' in colonial society, and to express loyalty to the British Empire and monarch (Scarfe, 1974: 120–23; Meaney, 1964–65: 141). Often non-Anglican families became Anglicans as part of their 'gentrification'. The Church of England's emphasis on corporate ritual and more rational or aesthetic worship and doctrine, its greater acceptance of the usual gentlemanly recreational pursuits and its link with the aristocracy suited the growing wealth, status and aspirations of upwardly mobile non-Anglican Protestants. 'Gentrification' was generally overseen by female family members, to whose lot fell the maintenance of social relationships and the arranging of an appropriate lifestyle and material expression of the family's success (Williams, 1980). Family trips back to England and Ireland in the second half of the nineteenth century helped such families stay in touch with and copy the latest English values and lifestyles. To varying degrees, depending on the city, the Church of England therefore reflected the interests and social arrangements of a conservative, relatively wealthy and English-oriented elite. However, this put such Church members at odds with the growing egalitarian, nationalist, labour and later women's movements, and thus further reduced the Church's appeal to those involved.

The influence of liberal, democratic and rationalist thought on educated administrators had already led to a less-than-enthusiastic official promotion of the Christian cause at the time the Australian colonies were founded. Moreover, during the nineteenth century, political leaders in Australia— even more than in Britain—were cutting back the formal authority and privileges of the Church of England, particularly through loosening the church-state nexus. Bourke's *Church Act* of 1836 in New South Wales and similar legislation in other colonies, finally saw the end of Anglican hopes of remaining the established church in Australia. In the second half of the nineteenth century, state aid for church buildings, for clergy salaries and for denominational schools was gradually discontinued, and systems of what was called 'free, compulsory and secular' education were established.

Theological studies were not included in the teaching programs of the universities founded in Australia during this period.

Church of England leaders, both clerical and lay, responded to this secularising of the public sphere in several ways that had important gender ramifications. The first response was to try to prevent their traditional antagonists, Roman Catholics and Protestant 'dissenters', from sharing *in reality* the public positions of influence in politics, education, the economy and culture which were now *in theory* freely open to all. This produced the sectarianism that so riddled Australian public life. Men transfused old religio-cultural arrangements and hostilities into a theoretically 'religionless' public sphere (Hogan, 1987).

The second response was to educate the laity to become more responsible for maintaining the Church. Anglicans could no longer take the services of their church for granted or regard religion as the sole business of clerics. Clergy and lay people alike would have to work especially hard to establish the Church of England as they knew it, given that it depended on very expensive styles of architecture and cultural trappings, and that it supported not only a local cleric and his family but also an episcopal structure. However, the roles that fell respectively to men and women to ensure the establishment and continuing influence of the Church of England tended to to be different. In order to gain the co-operation of its predominantly middle-class colonial laymen with their increasingly liberal, democratic temperament, the Church had to make significant concessions to their demands that they have some political influence in the institution they were being asked to support financially. Out of sheer economic necessity, therefore, the Church of England actually made its most far-reaching adaptation to colonial conditions: clergy and influential laymen were allowed to form a governing church assembly (synod) to be conducted along parliamentary lines. This had first been tried by the Episcopal [Anglican] Church in America. Bishop Perry of Melbourne was the only early bishop attracted to constitutionally limited headship and some form of democracy—those principles which more naturally suited the colonial male population:

> With regard to the Church in these colonies I am convinced in my own mind, that it will never gain a hold of the affections of the people, unless there be something of the popular element introduced into its constitution. Even now there are not a few who talk of what they absurdly call a free Episcopal church! I do not anticipate that this feeling will come to any sort of head here at present, but I feel assured that it would do so. . . if the Bishop should retain the power of appointing ministers at his sole discretion, and exercising an indefinite authority over the clergy. (Bishop Perry, Melbourne, to Bishop Broughton, Sydney, 4 July 1850, quoted in Robin, 1967: 64)

The concessions were at first limited to an elite group with certain property qualifications. Later in the nineteenth century, however, and after it was granted by the state, both parish and synodical government were broadened to allow for a popular male franchise and wider participation by laymen. The same rights to participate in church government were not given to laywomen for almost another century in some dioceses.

On the other hand, women were encouraged and requested to raise the extra money that was needed to feed the rather expensive tastes of this poor church. As few had the personal wealth of a Baroness Coutts (who endowed the Diocese of Adelaide) to be philanthropists in their own right, they gave of their time and labour to make and sell what they produced or to arrange and cater for social and cultural events to raise money, or themselves to carry out the housekeeping tasks that maintained and upgraded the facilities for worship (such as looking after linen, flowers, church cleaning, kneelers, etc.), and made or paid for many of the facilities in theological colleges, church hospitals, hostels, schools and missionary societies (Willis, 1977). Thus women were organised to work co-operatively in auxiliaries and guilds, at fêtes and on rosters to carry out the maintenance work and extra money-raising which was needed to make sure the clergy were materially provided for and that the Church in Australia could reproduce a standard of Anglicanism similar to that of the Church in England (Cambridge, 1903: 43–4, 89, 122–3).

Third, when Australia's intelligentsia, which included many practising Anglicans, decided to keep religious dogmatism out of the universities, the clergy (who, if they were trained in Australia, rarely had a university education) came to regard these institutions as places where anti-Christian systems of knowledge were promoted. Rather than give positive thought to the relationship between theology and ethics and the far-reaching revolutions in knowledge and society which took place from the second half of the nineteenth century, the clergy tended to separate religious knowledge from other knowledge. There were few comparable equivalents to the Oxford and Cambridge academic churchmen or to the American transcendentalists, who might be able to reformulate Christianity in terms which took account of new thought and new social realities. The debates in Melbourne from the 1860s to the 1880s had only Bishop Moorhouse and Judge Higinbotham amongst the Anglicans to answer for and adapt Christianity in a way that was not simply a (frequently quite spirited but characteristically defensive) traditional reiterating of religious authority (Roe, 1968–69: 149–66). The more usual response of separation and defence which the Church used to deal with controversy and 'secular' challenges tended to become a well-worn pattern in the following years (Lawton, 1983), as Anglican clerics became more narrowly specialist in their knowledge and spent more time involved in specifically church matters. If new ideas and social arrangements threatened to change the spheres of life in which the Church was most successful in holding on to its influence—namely the family, personal morality and religious belief—such ideas and arrangements came to be seen as threats to the authority of the Bible and the clergy.

Lastly, it is important for an understanding of the pattern of the Church of England's adaptation to Australian conditions to remember that within 50 years of the establishment of the major dioceses, and as all state aid to the churches ceased, the major towns began to expand rapidly and our modern pattern of suburban living, where men tended to travel away from the suburbs to work and women worked within the home and networked within the suburbs, began in earnest its rise to cultural hegemony. The Church of England, whose parish system was a relic of pre-industrial life and had not suited the vast distances or highly mobile, scattered populations of the earlier pattern of settlement, found a better footing in suburban life, one to which it could more easily adapt its traditionally-organised, parish-based Christianity. The era of rapid surburban expansion between the 1870s and 1914 was also one of the high points of the Church of England's growth and rates of adherence in Australia. The largest church buildings and the biggest congregations were established in the middle-class suburbs of the major towns (Judd and Cable, 1987: 111–14). Church programs were increasingly oriented to the needs of family life, and especially of women and children, as their needs were developing in the middle-class suburbs under this dual-spheres ideology (Sturmey, 1989: Chapter 3). Even among persons who had little other contact with the Church, the traditional life-passage rituals of baptisms, marriages and funerals continued to be used. Suburban family life, and the socio-economic and gender arrangements that undergirded it, became the new base to which the church contracted most of its efforts and over which it claimed its authority. From there it sought to spread its beliefs and values throughout Australian society and maintain its own economic viability. Thus the Church of England gradually accepted that the public sphere operated on secular criteria. This belief suited its laymen in particular, because it left them free to operate on these principles. There developed the modern Christian habit of aligning the increasingly separate sphere of 'work' and public life (of men) with the 'secular', while the private and family world (of women) is regarded as the legitimate haunt of the sacred. This habit, though worldwide, has been particularly strong in Australia.

Women in society and the Church of England

Generally speaking, women in Australian history seem to have been more completely circumscribed by their domestic and family activities than in Britain or America. For most of Australia's history they have been regarded as a scarce resource, necessary to men's, and indeed the whole family's, material comfort and upward mobility, or as the answer to

Australia's serious problem of under-population (Anderson, 1983; Grimshaw, 1979; Grimshaw et al., 1985). Much has been written on the Western ideals about and roles for women that this arrangement entailed and some on their particular Australian emphases (Sturmey, 1989: 115–69). Suffice it to say here that it would seem that proportionately more women in Australia than in Britain or America were able (if only just) and keen to live out the middle-class ideal of devoting their attention to the home, social relationships, the raising of children and some voluntary work, all of which had their own rewards. This has been recognised as part of the process of embourgeoisement of those from lower socio-economic backgrounds under industrialised and liberal democratic conditions. However, whereas in American and English society this process was widely justified and idealised in religious terms, as fitted the greater acceptability of Christianity in the public sphere, it was not so in Australia. Here there were few references outside church circles to John Ruskin's ideal of the gentle, spiritual high priestess of the home; the prevailing arrangement could be more acceptably justified in 'secular' utilitarian and scientific terms.

The lifestyle of the home and family became a universal measure of quality of life or social respectability (Davison, 1978), within the reach of a great many more people once the 'family wage' was established as the ideal by the Harvester Judgment. However, it was no longer middle-class life as it used to be, for Australian women became not so much the managers of households directing servants to do the manual work and care for the children, but managers of households where they themselves did the manual work and raised the children. The short supply and the expense of servants in this working person's 'paradise' were further affected by the establishment of compulsory schooling, which limited the availability of girls who had traditionally helped with housework and child raising either in their own homes or as employees in other homes. Middle-class ideals of womanly skills had to change more quickly and extensively in Australia than in Britain to include skills usually associated with servants—such as how to maintain floors and stoves, cook and preserve, and sew and launder. Australian middle-class women were less likely to complain about the uselessness of inactive or frivolous lives than the likes of those Englishwomen (and Anglicans) Florence Nightingale and Annie Besant.

But not only was useful work required of women in the family, it was also required of women in the struggling Church of England which, like many Australian families, was trying to establish itself according to traditional standards of propriety and success. The poverty of the Church and of its clergy, together with the increasing expectations that the clergy would measure up to job standards similar to those which laymen applied in their occupations (Nicholls, 1987), meant that a colonial clergyman's ability to increase the congregation, the property and the financial resources of the parish and to fulfil the rising expectations of his parishoners would ensure his access to the more desirable parishes—which were usually in the wealthier suburbs of the main towns. This meant that the survival of the parish and the eventual career advancement of the clergyman depended on his use of a great deal of voluntary labour. This was provided primarily by female family members who assisted him as 'unpaid curates' to successfully develop the parish. As in small businesses and on family farms, labour which could not be directly paid for had to be substituted for capital and influence in order to achieve prosperity or advancement. Ada Cambridge reported that the Anglican ministry imposed a 'killing strain', particularly in rural areas, on clergy wives. Relating her own experience, she said:

> I trained the choir, visited every parishoner within reach, did all that hard work unfairly demanded of the parson's wife under these democratic systems of church government; besides the multifarious work at home . . . Certainly my long and intimate acquaintance with the subject leaves me in no doubt as to which of the clerical pair is in the shafts and which in the lead. It is not the parson who . . . bears the heat and burden of the day, but the uncomplaining drudge who backs him at all points, and too often makes him selfish and idle by her readiness to do his work as well as her own. Under colonial and disestablished conditions, he is not largely representative of the class from which our home clergy are drawn; as a general rule he comes from that which . . . is not bred to the chivalrous view of women and wives—regards them, that is to say, as intended for no other purpose than to wait upon men and husbands. The customs of the profession accord so well with this idea that it is not surprising to find a pious man killing his wife by inches without having the slightest notion that he is doing so. (Cambridge, 1903: 87–9)

Moreover, churches were increasingly accepting the role (which Australian politicians, administrators and businessmen have been only too willing to allow them, and indeed have *expected* them to fulfil) of organising and carrying out charity and social rescue work. Clergymen who could not meet these greater expectations eased the pressure on themselves and on female relatives by calling upon other women to do that part of the increased church work which most accorded with women's traditional roles and skills. So laywomen voluntarily taught children, formed support committees, organised groups for women and children within the church community and helped with the charity and social uplift work to society's poor, dependent, sick and exploited (Judd and Cable, 1987: 115–16; Sturmey, 1989: 151–9).

The revival of the women's religious orders and the deaconess order in the nineteenth century enabled some women in the Church of England to earn their living and fulfil a spiritual vocation other than (and not combined with) marriage and motherhood. A deaconess training institution was set up by churchmen in Sydney with the specific objective of training women to take some of the increasing burden of pastoral and educational work from the clergyman and his female relatives. He could then specialise in public spiritual teaching, admonishment and presiding over the liturgy and sacraments, which were regarded as his 'primary' work. Meanwhile, his female relatives could concentrate on their homes and families and the more personally rewarding church work amongst their peers. The formal, public ministry of the deaconess was justified by the cleric who set up the training institution in the following terms: 'deaconesses demonstrated to the wider community the proper supportive role of women' and 'by example . . . sought to develop the home and family instincts of women and thereby regenerate the Christian family' (Mervyn Archdall, quoted in Judd and Cable, 1989: 153–5). It is perhaps significant that such accredited public roles of service within the Church's ministry, set up by men for women last century (and which didn't change substantially until the 1980s) did not become popular in Australia. Between the 1880s and 1966 only 171 women joined the deaconess order (Sturmey, 1989: 158). Missionary work, which allowed a good deal more freedom, power and excitement than parish work, and jobs in church agencies as 'secular' professionals with their higher wages and status seemed, for women themselves, far more attractive ways of expressing a religious commitment through a public vocation.

The social and economic arrangements described above were generally legitimated and given religious meaning in the Church's teaching. *The Divine Master in Home Life*, a devotional book written in the early twentieth century by the Archbishop of Melbourne, Harrington Lees, told men that they were called fathers because they were like God and were to imitate God's fatherly work of providing for, protecting and ruling his special family and the world in general, whilst women, on the other hand, were to imitate the devoted motherly service of Mary to her son and Lord: 'Oh busy needlewoman have you ever thought you would have liked to sew for Jesus as Mary sewed. May I remind you that you can? There is not one single garment sewn at a Work Party or Dorcas meeting, not a stitch put into the preparations for a missionary Sale of Work that may not be done for Jesus Christ, Who says of such work "Ye did it for me" '. (Lees, undated) The middle-class family became for the Church of England the key to the health and harmony of society and the symbol par excellence of the relationship of God to the Church and to the individual soul—that is, the relationship of Husband/Father to wife/child. However, churchmen did not address the issue of men's relative absence from family life in Australia. Both clergy and laymen benefited too much from concentrating both their work and leisure energies outside the home and relying on women to take the greater burden of family functioning. Instead, emphasis was placed by both 'secular' and church authorities on teaching women to focus their energies on fulfilling an upgraded agenda for 'housewife and mother' with all the skill and knowledge that science, education and later psychology could muster. The most important of all Anglican women's organisations, the Mothers' Union (Willis, 1980: 173–89), aimed to defend the family against divorce law reform and liberal, democratic, egalitarian career ideals for women as well as to promote a more skilful, scientific and middle-class commitment to motherhood, home management and wifely conduct amongst the 'lower classes'. For many Anglicans, this was also seen as the ideal way for women to stem the waxing tide of unbelief and immorality without having to step outside the home; husbands and sons could be influenced by quiet, Godly example and by teaching children Christian beliefs and behaviour.

But the most important observation for this essay is that there is evidence from personal records that women located in the domestic sphere did not generally secularise in their world view and behaviour as early or as thoroughly as men. The letters of colonial women before World War I show that a belief in and emotional dependence on God was more likely to be an important source of strength and consolation for them than for colonial men (Frost, 1984: 68–9, 151, 176, 184, 188, 241–2, 254, 268, 279). An all-knowing Providence was often invoked in the context of yet another pregnancy, the sickness or death of a family member or their own loneliness and inner difficulties. It would seem that here, as in other situations of relative powerlessness, Christianity held out the possibility that their sufferings and service might in fact have some value in the long term, if they were good and obedient to Divine commands. Well into the twentieth century such women's lives were still dominated by childbirth, the care of the dependent young and old, the nursing of sickness, presiding over the death of family members and teaching values and social skills to the next generation. These aspects of human life are more likely than the technological, economic and instrumental to rely upon tradition and to raise religious questions. Two of these, birth and death, are the last aspects of human life to be fully secularised in modern culture.

Moreover, even up to World War II, the burden of housework without modern labour-saving devices and of making the items they could not afford to buy for their family and home absorbed a great deal of women's energy, which was then not available for personal education or public involvement (Cowie, 1906; Cambridge, 1903; Hyslop, 1976–77). In addition, fewer women in Australia had the opportunities presented to British and American women by the earlier growth of progressive schools and colleges, their family's established wealth and culture and their own freedom from marriage to appreciate the intellectual changes taking place, to learn to think for themselves and to pursue their own professional training, even though there were notable exceptions like the well connected Rose Scott and the progressively educated Vida Goldstein. So women remained more intimately connected with the less secularised reality of life and death, less connected with an education system that encouraged independent and modern thought, less connected with the work and values of public life, more connected with traditional family identities and culture and strongly socialised to value service to all and acceptance of authorities greater than themselves.

Ideals for Australian men

Yet the more the Church became linked with the home sphere the more it was liable to be seen as 'women's business' by Australian men. By the 1920s, bishops were complaining that the natural leaders amongst men were not offering for the ministry; only the most feeble and conformist men (i.e. those that least fitted the Australian masculine ideal) were offering. Even loyal Anglican laymen were admitting that they never approached their clergy for help or guidance on issues and problems in their own 'secular' sphere (Church of England, 1925: 201-8).

Let us look briefly at the cultural ideals which emerged for Australian men. They are well documented in White's (1981) book, *Inventing Australia,* and Hirst's (1988) article on egalitarianism. Men, it was said, did not need 'frills, formalism or fable' (Zaunbrecher, 1980: 308, 315-19); rather, they should think for themselves, concentrate on solving practical problems, disregard religious differences and forge a new, independent, egalitarian identity unshackled by the status-reinforcing and authoritarian constraints of a degenerating European social order and culture based upon authority and submission:

> They tramp in mateship side by side—
> The Protestant and Roman,
> They call no biped lord or sir,
> And touch their hat to no man. (Henry Lawson, quoted in Hirst, 1988: 75)

Also highly valued was skill and power in facing physical (or, for other groups of men, intellectual or commercial) challenges. These were the character ideals of the Enlightenment, of frontier life, empire building and populism—what White (1981) called 'the ideal of the coming man'. To these Enlightenment ideals was added a romantic idealisation of an earlier tradition of frontier bush life, Australia's own version of the noble life close to nature. These ideals formed Australia's mateship tradition. Women and the middle-class domestic arrangements they preferred were generally kept separate from the ideals and primary activities of men. In the eyes of such men, both women and organised Christianity seemed to uphold a world full of artifice and convention, and to be uncritically accepting of outmoded hierarchical authorities and tales disproven by science and reason. Moreover, women's character and the character of clergy (despite determined efforts to establish a 'manly Christianity') remained linked with cultural ideals for subordinates and saints that had preceded the Enlightenment and been carried through the Evangelical Revival (McCann and Strain, 1985: 85–92). It was therefore not surprising that when the

Church aligned itself with that part of Australian life least resistant to its influence—suburban domestic life—men should be more inclined than women to drop out of all but the most perfunctory or status-reinforcing identifications with organised Christianity.

It is therefore possible to see in the 1968 Lambeth statement of Sydney's Anglican Archbishop Marcus Loane—that the ordination of women 'would mean the death knell of the appeal of the Church for men' (quoted in Sturmey, 1989: 169)—a fear that in the rebellious and rapidly secularising period of the 1960s the Australian Anglican Church was in danger of becoming too woman-identified to attract men at all, particularly if the women were allowed to occupy Church positions presently reserved for men. What Archbishop Loane's comment failed to address, however, was that the numbers of women joining the formal work force and improving their education since the 1960s had been so great that women's ideals had significantly shifted. The Australian Values Survey in 1983 showed that when women are in full-time, paid employment, their rate of church attendance is no higher than men's (de Vaus and McAllister, 1987).

It would seem from the historical account just sketched that de Vaus and McAllister have good reason to prefer the structural location explanation in accounting for gender differences in religious orientation in Australia. Yet the link in Australia between women's entering full-time employment and their decreasing participation in churches is not inherent *simply* in women's structural location. One also needs to take into account the characteristics of the Church in which they are becoming less involved. The nature of Christianity in Australia has largely been set by Anglicanism and Roman Catholicism, neither of which has emphasised the authority and freedom of the individual or valued a founding myth of minority dissent and independence as have American Puritanism and Protestantism. Instead, these two churches have emphasised—for women in particular—socially adaptive and conserving/caring behaviour and allegiance to external, hierarchical authorities. In addition, religion has been more separated from, and has less acceptance in, the public sphere of life in Australia than in America.

Australian women, when they have moved out of their domestic roles, have had few adequate models to help them express a Christianity that addresses their newer experiences and learning. Therefore it can be surmised that they are more likely than American women to move out of the churches altogether when they mix in the public world of men (Franklin and Sturmey-Jones, 1987). Thus the concern should be not only with whether the death knell has sounded for men in the Anglican Church but also with whether the Church can change the socio-cultural basis of its influence fast enough to retain the interest and involvement of its present majority of women. As women's structural location, education, sources of fulfilment and everyday experiences come closer to those of men, Australian women may yet prove to be just as secular as Australian men.

4 Conflicting discourses: attitudes to the ordination of women in the Anglican Church in Australia
Barbara L. Field

The Anglican Church in Australia is engaged in a continuing struggle, which now stretches back more than twenty years, over the issue of ordaining women to the priesthood. The arguments for and against the issue will not be dealt with in detail here but can be readily consulted in the works of such authors as Byrne (1988), Dowell and Hurcombe (1981), Franklin (1986), Giles (1985), Nichols (1990), Oddie (1984), Porter (1989), Ruether (1983), Russell (1974) and Wetherell (1987). The point to be explored in this chapter is that discourse analysis is a possible key to unlocking the deadlock in which the church seems to find itself over this issue of women's ordination.

Social meanings are produced within social institutions, and the language of each group which shares what it sees as common meanings is a discourse (Weedon, 1987: 34). To put it another way, a discourse is a perspective, a conceptual framework, a way of looking at things, and it has presumed shared meanings amongst those operating within and from the discourse. Foucault (1972: 49) theorises that a discourse is an *active, forming, constructing practice*. If, as Foucault proposes, a discourse *actively forms and constructs people's perceptions of reality,* the power of the concept is exemplified when applied to something as destructive as totalitarian discourses such as Nazism.

The fragility of the infrastructure of understanding and communication of meaning is discussed in Sless (1986: 20). When people in the Church debate the issue of the ordination of women, they appear not to be 'hearing' each other. They are using the same words such as 'priest', 'ordination' and 'ministry', but are not necessarily meaning the same things by them. As a way of analysing this kind of difficulty, Foucault's (1972: 31) concept of a 'discursive field' is helpful. He theorises that each social structure or institution that appears to be shaped by a single global discourse (such as the media, the law, the education system, the church) is in fact shaped by a discursive field (see Weedon, 1987: 35). There are discourses *embedded within* the global discourse and these can be in opposition to each other. The field of discourse by which the Church is shaped is made up of many, sometimes opposing, discourses, and these discourses all contribute to people's perceptions of the issue of the ordination of women. There is the overarching patriarchal discourse which subsumes the discourses of power and authority, theology and liturgy. There is also the discourse of subordination which subsumes the discourses of domesticity, equality, sex and gender. People construct their reality, and have their reality constructed for them, out of the discourses within which they are operating. This chapter will briefly examine how these discourses affect people's perceptions of the issue of the ordination of women.

In the debate over the ordination of women in the Anglican Church of Australia, then, the protagonists and antagonists are operating within and from the discourses that make up the 'field of discourse' that constitutes the church. Structuralists such as Saussure (1966) assumed that meanings changed *between* social worlds (i.e. discourses) but were fixed *within* them. A word such as 'priest' would be expected to mean the same thing to those within the Church, but might have a different meaning for someone who was a communist. Post-structuralists, on the other hand, see that, even within a discourse, meanings are not fixed (Weedon, 1987). I will be proposing that there are competing and opposing discourses within the global discourse of the Church and that, to understand the different reactions to the ordination of women from the various sections of the Church, we need to know the discourses from which people are arguing. Once their way of making sense of their own reality is understood in terms of competing discourses, people in the Church can begin to understand that in such issues as the ordination of women, they are not always hearing each other—they are not sharing meanings.

Before proceeding, there is a need to explain briefly one other theoretical term. *Semiotics* is the study of *how* messages are sent and received through signs (Greek *semion*: a sign). *Semiosis* is the *process* of sending and receiving messages. Some theorists such as Saussure (1966) see semiotics as concerned with signs in the form of words. Others such as Eco (1979), Hodge and Kress (1988) and Halliday (1975) see semiotics as dealing with social signs in all forms. They call this 'social semiotics' as opposed to 'semantic' or 'logocentric' semiotics. Here I am working with both, because the Church signals messages about gender positions not only in the words of its liturgy and its theology, but also in its architecture, its hierarchical government, its rituals and so on.

The study of semiosis shows that in any social sign system (verbal, iconic or kinetic) we can never guarantee that the message received will be the same as the one sent. People make sense of signs, and of their own reality, in terms of the the social worlds that they move in, and their social worlds are made up of different and often competing discourses. In the issue of the ordination of women, as in many other issues, people try to fit their opponents, and even those who agree with them, into their own discourses. The result is often misunderstanding and contradiction.

The field of discourse by which the Church is shaped contributes to people's understandings of all issues in the church and so to their understandings of the issue of the ordination of women. Various discourses will be examined separately for their effect on the debate over the ordination of women, but it must be remembered that the separation is an artificial one, as the different discourses are not wholly independent of one another.

Patriarchal discourse

Apart from a few notable exceptions such as the Celtic abbesses, the patristic women saints, the medieval mystics and saints and the missionaries of the nineteenth century, the Church has been a patriarchal institution for 2000 years. Patriarchy is the political structure which privileges men at the expense of women. Patriarchy, by definition, must have male power and female powerlessness in its structures. Patriarchal discourse is the over-arching discourse, in all of society as well as in the Church, that positions women as subordinate. It is so all-embracing and universal that it is taken for granted. A 'leader' to an article in the *Sydney Morning Herald* (6 July 1988: 45) said 'Everybody from the Prince of Wales to the porter has a wife and two children'. This would seem an ordinary-enough statement for our society, but it implicitly says that women are not 'anybody'.

The language of the Church is patriarchal, as will be seen below. Two examples will suffice here as illustrations. In the services for baptism and confirmation in *An Australian Prayer Book* (AAPB), the Anglican Church signals that the normal way to be human is to be male, and that to be female is to be 'other'. Thus the printed text of the central declaration of the baptism reads as follows: 'We receive this child into the congregation of Christ's flock and sign *him* with the sign of the cross, to show that *he* will not be ashamed to confess the faith of Christ crucified . . . ' (AAPB Baptism of Infants, First Order: 504). When a girl is being baptised, those present at the service have to do the translation from 'he' to 'she'. The italics are there to flag the pronoun so that the priest can change it if necessary. The compilers of the book appear to regard the male as the norm, and this thinking is conveyed to the congregation in the printed word.

Similarly, the text of the core prayer of the Confirmation Service says: 'Defend O Lord this your servant with your heavenly grace, that *he* may continue yours forever, and daily increase in your Holy Spirit until *he* comes to your everlasting kingdom' (AAPB: 514). Imagine the semiosis here on the 45 Year 8 girls who are confirmed each year in a local Anglican girls' school. The Bishop translates the pronoun to 'she', but the book has it frozen as 'he'. This kind of signalling, of male as norm and female as 'other', affects parishioners' perceptions of the maleness of priesthood.

The Church has always had an all-male, hierarchical government and it is within this powerful patriarchal discourse that women are asking for ordination—for access to leadership, power and authority. In any field of discourse, some of the discourses are more powerful than others. Those discourses which support the status quo are usually stronger than those which work for change. In the Church, a 2000-year history and tradition of male clergy strongly influences people's sense of who can and who cannot be priests. The discourse of Christian feminism is opposing the patriarchal discourse. This is discussed later in the chapter.

Discourses of power and authority

The role of the priest is one of authority and power within the parish and the wider Church. As things now stand, only males can be priests in the Anglican Church in Australia. If the Oxford English Dictionary definition of 'power'—'the ability to do or to act'— is adopted, women are seen as powerless to do or to act in any priestly function in the Church. The dictionary also defines power as 'control, influence and ascendency'. Women have little control, influence or ascendency in decision-making or policy-making in the Church because they cannot gain access to the seat of authority and power—the priesthood.

There are powerful silencing and marginalising strategies used against women. One of these is the 'guilt' strategy where the whole force of the God-given text of the church is used to make women feel unfeminine and unchristian if they aspire to leadership. Women are reproached for seeking power whereas men are lauded for doing the same thing. When women ask for ordination they are criticised for seeking power and status, whereas men are praised for wanting to give up their lives in sacrificial service to others. There is a great conflict of discourses here. Another marginalising and silencing strategy in the discourse of power is the 'humour' strategy where women and their efforts are trivialised. The New Zealand Papal Nuncio was quoted in the media as saying: 'A woman can no more be a priest than a pigeon can be a Christian' (*Sydney Morning Herald*, 13 November 1989: 10).

When women move out of their assigned subordinate position, patriarchal power is used to try to position them back in their 'proper place'. Jeremy Bentham's *Panopticon*—the 'all-seeing gaze' metaphor—is a concept of power that Foucault uses often (Foucault, 1979: 200). For women, the 'gaze' of subordinating power in the Church is that of (patriarchal interpretation of) God, of the Bishop and of priests—in short, of males.

The authority discourse is mixed up with the 'headship' discourse of fundamentalist 'Pauline' Christianity. This is a powerful discourse derived from the scriptures—both Old and New Testaments. In this teaching, God is the Head of Christ, Christ is the Head of the Church, and a husband is head of his wife (I Corinthians 11: 3). In the Church the ultimate authority and power belong to God. When a ruling such as this 'headship' doctrine is said to be God-given truth from the scriptures, it is very difficult to oppose it and remain an orthodox member of the community. Patriarchal interpretations of scriptures, such as the 'headship' passages of the New Testament (I Corinthians 11, Ephesians 5:22–3, Colossians 3:18–19, I Peter 3:1ff), are used as instruments of power to keep the status quo and to keep women in subordination. It takes great courage and resolution to defy this authority, but there are women who are gathering that courage.

These discourses of power and authority stand paradoxically alongside the discourses of liberation in the Church—besides the wholeness and freedom that is taught in the salvation and redemption discourses. In the Anglican Church in Australia, some male leaders acknowledge the full humanity and equality of all people, while at the same time blocking women from achieving wholeness and equality in ministry. They are working within two opposing discourses at the same time and yet are managing to experience themselves as coherent and rational. Post-structuralism helps us to analyse this situation by enabling us to see that there are multiple discourses where once only one was discerned.

The discursive field of ordination

The discourse of leadership—of ordination and priesthood—in the Anglican Church is powerfully informed by the 2000-year tradition of male priesthood. Catholic discourse within the Anglican Church sees ordination as a sacrament, in which God acts to consecrate men in the line of the apostolic succession to serve in the Church. Evangelical discourse within Anglicanism sees ordination as the prayerful and public setting apart or commissioning of a man for a particular work in the Christian community. In the catholic view, only men can be priests because Christ chose only men as his apostles; in the evangelical view, only men can be priests because only men can have authority over men. Although they agree in opposing the ordination of women, these two discourses have difficulty 'talking' to each other because they mean different things by words such as 'ministry', 'priest' and 'ordination'. They are speaking the same language, sending the same signals, using the same words, but they are a long way apart in meaning.

People who hold a more liberal view of ordination that would include women cannot 'talk' to proponents of either the catholic or the evangelical discourses, as they will find themselves holding different meanings even for words such as 'woman' and 'equality'. One silencing strategy used by the Church hierarchy is to say that women can usefully 'minister' in all kinds of ways in the church without being ordained. Women seeking ordination, however, see ordination as legitimising and authenticating their ministry—as, indeed do men seeking ordination. There are not shared meanings here about 'ministry'.

This kind of recognition of the fact that people are speaking from different and often conflicting discourses, and making different meanings of the same signs can lead to understandings of the different stances that people adopt in the conflict over the ordination of women. Such understanding may be a step towards a resolution of the problem.

Essentialist/naturalist discourse

Essentialist discourse on gender generally assumes that females have an innate tendency to caring and that males have an innate tendency to aggression. It sees women as different in personality as well as in biology. It claims that it is not natural for women to want to lead, or to be political, and certainly not to be priests. Research in the area is showing that there is no evidence for this essentialism (see Birke et al., 1980; Birke and Silvertown, 1984; Bleier, 1986; Keller, 1985; Rogers, 1988; Star, 1979). But as long as the essentialist/naturalist discourse is allowed to link caring nurturing qualities only to 'mothering' and so to the female sex, so the implication will be that males cannot have these qualities. Yet commonsense knowledge tells us that they can. Men can and do have qualities of gentleness, caring and self-sacrifice. And women can and do have qualities of leadership, strength and assertion. Some women who are accorded status and power in the world outside the Church, and who are leaders in their professions, find great conflict between the position the Church would have them assume and the position accorded to them by society.

Discourse of domesticity

The Church seizes on the essentialist/naturalist discourse to promulgate the discourse of domesticity—that a woman's place is in the home. The male sphere is public and the female sphere is private (Elshtain, 1981). This is the discourse that is most strongly signalled to congregations in patriarchal interpretations of the New Testament writings. The domestic tasks in the church—the cleaning, cooking, child-minding, flower-arranging, hospital visiting— are done by women. Indeed, if it were not for women who make up 65 per cent of Anglican congregations (Kaldor,

1987: 110), the Church would surely founder. Yet, on Sundays, the public leadership roles in most services are taken by men while women sit silently in the passive roles of onlookers.

Theological and liturgical discourses

The church by its very nature is steeped in God-talk—that is, in theology—the study of the nature and work of God. Much of that God-talk is of a masculine deity. There is an argument against the ordination of women that stems from this view of the maleness of God. In the iconic view of priesthood, the ordained priest is seen as representing, as imaging, God on Earth—and a woman cannot image a male. Some parishioners perceive an affinity between maleness and divinity. The thinking goes like this: Jesus was male, Jesus is God, so God is male. As long as Church teaching and preaching presupposes a male God, and as long as some members of congregations see the priest in some way as representative of God, then those people will continue to be unable fully to see a woman in the position of priest. The discourse sends the message that God is more like the man in the congregation than the woman and this gives the man the position of privilege and responsibility, making the woman subordinate. Elements of theological discourse, then, stand in the way of women's ordination. A patriarchal exegesis of the Bible is a strong part of the discourses of theology and liturgy. It is well documented by writers such as Fiorenza (1984) and Ruether (1983).

The liturgy is where the faithful gather to worship their God. In the Anglican Church people worship as a corporate act in psalms, hymns, prayers and Bible readings. It is in the language of the liturgy that we come up against what Kate Swift calls 'the semantic road-block of religion' (Miller and Swift, 1976: 71). There is a whole liturgical discourse that purports to be both male and female but which is solely male. The Church is out of step with most of the rest of society in that it still uses the generic 'man'. Women in the church knowingly or unknowingly (for such is the force of the semiosis) have to work at making the distinctions of when they are 'men' and when they are not; of when the pronouns 'he' and 'him' refer to them as women and when they do not; of when words such as 'sons' and 'brothers' include them and when they do not. This is a task that women do not usually have to do in the secular world and one that men never have to do. No matter how the above words are meant—generically or as specifically male—men are always included. What a woman has to do is a kind of subtraction sum in her head to decide whether she is included or excluded (see Griffith, 1989).

In the Anglican liturgy, women have to learn to see themselves as *included* in the word 'men' in the General Confession, 'Almighty God,

Father of our Lord Jesus Christ, maker of all things, judge of all men . . .'
(AAPB: 122) and in the words of the Nicene Creed, 'For us men and for
our salvation . . . ' (AAPB: 118), but as *excluded* from the word 'men'
when the priest preaches that 'only men can be priests'. They are assured
that the statement 'Christ died for all men' includes women, but they are
refused membership of the Anglican Men's Society! There was a time
when this 'translation' would have been easier for women to do.
Unfortunately for the Church, that time has passed. Equal opportunity
thinking has had a profound effect on the way both men and women view
our society. Women, especially young women, no longer see themselves
included in words like 'son', 'brother' and 'men'. Young businesswomen
talking with patriarchal members of the Church could find themselves not
sharing meanings on such a fundamental word as 'woman'. One coming
from a domestic discourse would see 'woman' as mother, nurturer, home-
body, while the other coming from a professional equal opportunity
discourse would see 'woman' as 'person', equal in every way to man.

I have already dealt with the invisibility of females in key parts of the
text for services of baptism and confirmation in the Anglican Church. The
typical Anglican is involved in these 'rites of passage' only occasionally,
so the effect of the positioning of females as 'other' is not as constant as it
is in the weekly liturgy. Here I will just mention the invisibility of
women in some of the hymns that are sung, week by week, in church—
mostly by women. In the following quotations from the *Australian Hymn
Book* (AHB), I use italics to highlight words which tend to make women
invisible:

Souls of *men* why do you scatter,
like a crowd of frightened sheep . . . (AHB, No. 72)

Widen our love, good Spirit, to embrace
in your strong care the *men* of every race (AHB, No. 328)

The *man* whose mind is stayed on thee
is kept in perfect peace . . . (AHB, No. 358)

We come unto our *fathers'* God (AHB, No. 387)

. . . thou my great Father, I thy true *son* (AHB, No. 455)

Jesus thou joy of loving hearts
thou fount of life, thou light of *men* (AHB, No. 420)

The problem is compounded in hymns where women are not only
invisible, but appear to be excluded from the scheme of salvation:

Lord Christ when first you came to *men* (AHB, No. 208)

Men are the *sons* of God and therefore *brothers* (AHB, No. 554)

Christ came to keep his Father's word
He raised *man* up from dark defeat (AHB, No. 211)

Blessed be the God who comes to *men*
with messages of grace (AHB, No. 289)

These are only examples of the vast number of hymns that use language which appears to exclude women. This results from the hymns' having been written at a time when there was no concept of sexist language and when male domination was the norm. The problem is not that they were written in the first place by those who were exercising whatever lights they had at the time. The problem is that in the last decade of the twentieth century the Church still uses these hymns, and that the semiosis of the discourse helps to position women outside the possibility of priesthood.

Not all women are angry about the exclusion. Many women do not even notice it. That is the point of semiosis—of signalling messages—as any advertiser will attest. The signalling to women that they are marginal, subordinate, even invisible, goes on unnoticed by many but still has an effect, Sunday after Sunday, in the language of the churches. It is the same process that works on us subtly through all the advertising in the media that seduces us into thinking that we need things that otherwise we would never have thought of.

The subordination of women is also signalled by the use of space in the liturgy. The French feminist Claudine Herrmann (1981: 87) speaks of the link between physical space and the discourses of power, authority, domination and hierarchy. For example, professional people such as lawyers, doctors and teachers, sit behind their desks—a position which distinguishes them and distances them from their clients. There are messages in the closeness that one can come to one in power. There are also messages in height placement. The architecture of Anglican church buildings sends messages of power and dominance to congregations. Those who are the leaders of the liturgy (mostly male) are placed in front of, separate from and above other participants (mostly female). By analogy with all of the other power/space situations we are familiar with, the message that is projected to all, men and women alike, is that men are 'public', important and powerful in the Church; women are private, marginal and powerless.

When women move into the space for leading the service (the chancel or the sanctuary) there can be resistance. A woman is seen as having no legitimate place there. The women wanting to be ordained are threatening to invade this male physical space in the church building. They are coming

out of a discourse of equality and freedom preached in Galatians 3:28—
'There is neither Jew nor Greek, neither slave nor free, neither male nor
female, for you are all one in Christ Jesus'—and are meeting an excluding
and powerful patriarchal discourse that blocks them from entering what
they see as a God-given vocation. There are many conflicting discourses
operating here. In the confusion, women who have a definite sense of
vocation to the priesthood are being frustrated (Field, 1989) and some
women are deciding to leave the church that appears not to be able to make
itself whole, let alone convey wholeness to its followers (Diesendorf,
1988).

Feminist and Christian feminist discourses

Christian feminists are seeking to transform the patriarchal discourses of
the Church which have been briefly outlined above. Such feminists work
from a position of relative powerlessness but their discourse is beginning
to be heard as part of the discursive field that shapes the church. People
mean different things when they claim that they are or they are not
'feminists'. Even the French radical feminist, Helene Cixous, had
difficulty labelling herself a feminist when she saw women who wanted
power in the patriarchal system that she was trying to eliminate calling
themselves feminists (Moi, 1985: 103).

There are three stages of feminism that Letty Russell (1974: 118ff), a
Christian feminist from the United States, and Julia Kristeva (in Moi,
1985: 12–13), a French feminist, agree on. The first is that of *liberal
feminism*, where women want to be able to have access to the professions
and to the power that men have held exclusively. Women seeking
ordination in the Anglican Church could be seen as being located in this
tier of feminism. The second is the stage of what Russell calls *'rage'*. It
shows frustration, despair and rejection of the patriarchy. Kristeva describes
this as 'women rejecting the male symbolic order in the name of
difference'. It is the radical feminist position. It leads, in the Church, to
the setting up of exclusively women's organisations such as Women-
Church. The third stage is one of *dialogue and co-operation*—of attempting
to shed the differences and recognising the humanness in each man and
woman. It is integrative—not oppositional and disintegrative, as patriarchy
has been over the centuries.

Feminist theory is struggling to transform patriarchy. *Christian*
feminist theory is struggling to transform the patriarchy of the Church. If
the starting point of feminism is the patriarchal structure of society, then
the starting point of *Christian* feminism is the patriarchal structure of the
Church. It follows then that Christian feminism is a politics directed at
transforming the existing power structures—indeed the very concept of
power—specifically within the church. Power is seen as 'empowering' in

feminist discourse. It is seen as power *for* not power *over*. The model is one of mutuality, connectedness, co-operation and inclusiveness. The Anglican Church in Australia is a long way from the ideals put forward by integrative feminism.

Conclusion

In the struggle to allow women to be ordained priests in the Anglican Church, people working within the patriarchal discourses of the Church are seeking to control and to maintain the status quo. Their model is still oppositional. Post-structuralism teaches us that systems and structures are problematic when dealing with the communication of meaning. The oppositions, conflicts and discrepancies within the field of discourse that shapes the Church must be analysed and recognised for what they are doing in the debate. This could be a first step in the process of unravelling the contributing elements to the struggle. What is necessary is a recognition of the *existence* of the often contradictory discourses within which people are operating, and an understanding of how people use and deal with each of the discourses. I have briefly outlined this first step to recognition—the achieving of an awareness of the semiotics and positioning power of the discourses that all are working within and that all are 'slipping' between. Perhaps this does not, as was suggested above, go as far as being a 'key to unlock the deadlock', but this awareness could, at least, be a step towards an unblocking of the communication process and this in turn could help both sides in the debate to begin to come to an understanding of the resistance to the ordination of women.

5 Inequality, belonging and religion in a rural community[1]
Ken Dempsey

A number of prominent sociologists of religion claim that conventional religion can meet a range of basic social-psychological needs that humans are finding it increasingly difficult to have satisfied in advanced industrial societies. Berger (1967), Wallace (1985) and Mol (1976) say that organised religion can fulfil the needs to belong, to experience love and support and to have the opportunity to exercise a degree of autonomy and influence that is rarely available in people's working lives or political activities. Berger argues that religious activity provides an important sphere for self-realisation: for affirming one's identity and for experiencing a sense of counting for something. Mol believes that organised religion can provide continuity in the sense of identity of individuals and an opportunity to make a commitment to a cause. Wallace and Mol affirm that religion can serve as a mechanism for integrating individuals into the community. These two writers argue that the churches have the potential to function in this way because they occupy an intermediate position between the individual and his or her family on the one hand, and the community on the other.

It is also commonplace for church leaders to reiterate the claim of St Paul that in Christ there is neither Jew nor Greek, neither slave nor free, neither male nor female (Galatians 3:28). Christians are called to live in a community which is not based on human values, but which is the creation of God: one in which God's love enables participants to be servants of one another (Galatians 5:13). Christians, of course, acknowledge that they live in an imperfect society and that therefore their relationships with one another will fall short of these ideals. Nevertheless, it is reasonable to expect that relationships among church-goers and within church organisations will be substantially different from those prevailing in 'secular' organisations and activities. One of the differences one would expect to find is strong resistance to the common practice of utilising the

63

attributes of class, age and gender to decide who associates with whom, who occupies positions of leadership, whose participation is restricted to subordinate or marginal activities and so forth. It is reasonable to expect active church members to relate to one another principally on the basis of their common faith in Christ.

In a study I have made of conventional religion in a Victorian rural community I have attempted to do two things. The first has been to establish whether the churches provide contexts in which basic human needs, such as the need to experience a sense of belonging, are met. The second has been to see if the structuring of relationships within the churches mirrors the structuring prevalent in the outside community, or whether the churches provide a distinctive alternative. For example, in conventional religious activities, are men and women of different classes and ages brought together as equals or, as in many secular activities, kept apart? The purpose of this paper is to present an overview of these findings. However, before doing so it will be helpful if I describe briefly the social and demographic character of the community and the methods I have used to gather data.

The setting of the study

The community, which I call Smalltown, has a population of 2700 people and services a farming community settled by a further 1050 people. Its population is ageing rapidly (15 per cent are 65 years of age or older). Two-thirds of its workforce are engaged in middle-class occupations.[2] Smalltown is a community where 'who you are' really does matter. Class, gender and age are good predictors of which positions people will occupy in the local structure, which relationships they will enter into and the quality and character of their daily lives. Being a woman ensures that one will almost certainly be in a subordinate position economically and socially, and often excluded by men from their activities (Dempsey, 1987; 1988; 1989b). Being old substantially reduces the likelihood of participation in more prestigious organisations and increases the likelihood of being economically impoverished, of occupying subordinate positions in many relationships and, much of the time, of having little opportunity for relationships with younger members of the community (Dempsey, 1990a). Membership of the working class virtually guarantees exclusion from the more prestigious and influential organisations and positions in Smalltown (Dempsey, 1990b).

It is plausible to argue that the elderly, the working class and women occupy a position of subordinate marginality in the Smalltown community (Dempsey, 1990b). Working-class elderly widows probably have less influence and lower status than any other sector of the community. On the other hand, upper middle-class men are able to enhance their public esteem and gain personal satisfaction by participating in prestigious organisations and exercising influence in economic activities and community administration. At the same time, Smalltown is a community where men and women of different classes have enough contact and awareness of common interests to produce a strong sense of attachment to the place and its people and a sense of a shared future. One of our interests is in seeing whether church activities facilitate the development of these powerful sentiments.

Smalltown possesses five churches. In descending order of size (based on active membership) these are: Roman Catholic, Uniting (comprised in this instance of the congregations of the former Smalltown Methodist Circuit and the Smalltown Presbyterian Church), Anglican, Church of Christ and Salvation Army. The primary focus of this report is on the two major Protestant churches: the Anglican and the Uniting. The Roman Catholic Church receives less attention because of my much more limited exposure to this denomination's activities and the reluctance of the parish priest to participate in the research.

The material I draw on for this paper comes from frequent interviews and conversations with the ministers, ministers' wives and lay people of Smalltown. More than 2000 interviews have been conducted since the first fieldwork trip was made to the community in 1973. I also have made use of as much participant observation as short but frequent trips to a community located some 250 kilometres from where I work permit. The present paper utilises data from the following surveys:

1 1973: A random sample survey of 443 households covering the issues of class, social mobility, religious and political beliefs and behaviour, relative deprivation, community identity and voluntary organisational participation.

2 1973: A survey of the town's secondary school pupils covering topics similar to those listed under (1) (N=350).

3 1974: A survey of religious beliefs and practices (N=130).

4 1982: A survey of church leaders and of ministers and their wives concerning the place of clergy and the church in the town (N=25).

5 1983–85: A survey of beliefs and relationships in the areas of class and status, of relationships between 'locals' and 'transients', and of the standing of churches and a range of other organisations in the community (N=179).

6 1983–85: A study of 485 friendships using data provided by a purposive sample of 175 community members.

7 1984–86: Semi-structured interviews conducted with 112 women and men to gain data on gender relationships and beliefs about the identities, roles and appropriate relationships of men and women.

8 1986–87: A study of the social characteristics of members and leaders of 40 of the town's 130 voluntary organisations and of the Anglican and Uniting Churches (N=2500).

Major issues to be addressed

In earlier papers I have focused on the decline in support for organised religion in Smalltown (Dempsey, 1983b; 1985b). Here I will update those reports but I will concern myself principally with the following questions:

1 To what extent do the Smalltown churches serve as contexts where people experience a sense of belonging, meaning and purpose?
2 To what extent do they serve as vehicles for integrating individuals into the life of the local community?
3 Do the churches mirror the hierarchical divisions of class, age and gender that are prevalent in this community or do they provide a context where those who are often segregated, subordinated or marginalised relate to one another as equals?

In dealing with these issues I will report on the level of support for the churches and their organisations, the perception community members have of the social standing and role of the churches in the life of the community, and the impact of conventional religion on friendship activities. I will also give a brief account of the activities which commonly serve as mechanisms for achieving a sense of belonging and purpose for members of this community.

Decline, self-realisation and integration

If the Smalltown churches are serving as mechanisms for self-realisation and for integrating individuals into the community, one would expect them to be retaining most of their membership, recruiting new members from younger age cohorts and receiving continued support for their various organisations. These generalisations seem reasonable ones to make in a community in which more than 85 per cent of members describe themselves as Christians and more than 80 per cent claim affiliation with a particular Christian denomination. The reality is that the organisational and numerical strength of the churches has been declining during the 1970s and 1980s. There are less resident clergy in Smalltown now than in 1973, the year in which fieldwork commenced. In 1973 Smalltown was the seat of an Anglican diocese. Financial problems resulted in its amalgamation with a neighbouring diocese. In the process, the town lost the bishop and his administrative assistant, who was also a clergyman.

Each year of the seventeen years this study has been in progress, the proportion of the local population attending worship has fallen. At the present time (1990) church-going is of minor importance in community life. Support for church organisations and Sunday schools has also declined. The Roman Catholic Church is, in 1990, easily the best supported of the town's five churches. Although Catholics comprise only approximately 25 per cent of the population, their church attracts more than three-quarters of the regular worshippers living in the community. Yet, Catholics are currently displaying a good deal of anxiety about their church's future. They are not fearful that it will disappear altogether, but that its importance to its members will continue to decline. Their anxiety stems, in part, from the fact that attendances at Mass are down about by 20 to 25 per cent from what they were in the early 1970s. But what makes them most anxious is the rapidly growing trend for young adults and middle-aged men to give up attending Mass altogether.

At the present time, Protestants comprise 66 per cent of Smalltown people claiming Christian affiliation. However, less than 10 per cent of Protestants are in church on any given Sunday. Church attendances have been falling in recent years. Seventeen years ago the Salvation Army and the Church of Christ were small causes, each averaging about twenty worshippers on any particular Sunday. In 1990 the numbers are less than this and these churches are struggling to survive. But undoubtedly it is the Anglican and the Uniting Churches that have experienced the greatest decline in support. About 40 to 50 people now worship in the Anglican Church on any particular Sunday, which is less than half the number in 1973. About 60 people attend Sunday worship at the Uniting Church, and this is less than half the combined attendance of the Presbyterian and Methodist churches in 1973. It was these two churches that joined together in 1977 to form the Uniting Church congregation in this town.

A further decline in attendance at worship is likely to occur because the elderly are disproportionately over-represented and the young under-represented among present attenders. Whereas those of 65 years of age or older constitute about one-sixth of the local population, they comprise about one-third of the worshippers at the Uniting Church and close to two-thirds of the worshippers at the Anglican Church. By contrast, less than 5 per cent of the people who are attending either the Anglican or Uniting Church on any given Sunday are aged between 20 and 30 years. Yet members of this age category comprise about 13 per cent of the community's population. Although children and teenagers constitute about a quarter of the community's population, they comprise only about 10 per cent of the worshippers at the Anglican and Uniting Churches. This meagre support from the very young is more disturbing for those concerned about the future of the churches than is the over-representation of the elderly. It also highlights the demographic impediment to these churches' ability to serve as catalysts for inter-generational relationships. These demographic characteristics exacerbate the tendency to keep the generations apart which has been built into the structure of church life in this as in so many other communities.

The Anglican and Uniting Churches, much more than the Catholic Church, have also experienced a marked decline in their organisational

strength during the last seventeen years. The pattern of this decline reflects
the disproportionately greater loss of appeal generally of these churches and
the diminution of their perceived relevance to the young. Over the last
decade the Uniting Church has lost its Couples Club and its Youth Club.
Each of these clubs was for both males and females. The Uniting Church
Sunday school is more restricted in age range and is about a quarter of the
size it was a decade ago. On the other hand, this church has gained an
additional women's organisation to bring its total to three. The new one
caters for middle-aged women, and the other two for women in their 60s,
70s and 80s. The Anglican Church has lost its two Girls' Friendly
Societies and its (Sunday) church school. Fifteen years ago the first two
had a combined membership of about 30, and 60 children were attending
the church school. During the same period its youth group disappeared.
Neither church has a mixed-sex organisation or a men's organisation of
any kind. Recently, the Anglican minister commenced a men's tea but he
abandoned the project after the third meeting, because of insufficient
attenders. Between them, however, the Uniting and Anglican Churches
have a total of four women's organisations. The ability of the churches to
provide a social milieu in which both men and women can enter into
equitable and mutually rewarding relationships has been reduced by a
decline in male participation in church worship as well as by the demise of
mixed-sex church organisations. In 1974 men comprised about one-third of
the regular worshippers at the Anglican Church. Now, on any given
Sunday, they comprise about one-eighth of the worshippers. Though the
decline in the support of male members of the Uniting Church has not
been as great, it has nevertheless been considerable. In 1974 men
comprised between 40 and 45 per cent of worshippers in this church, but
by the mid-1980s the proportion was down to between 30 and 35 per cent.

Community gossip chains and the churches' reputations

Smalltown possesses certain social and demographic characteristics which
facilitate the dissemination of information concerning any significant role
the churches are playing in the lives of their own members or in the life of
the community. Smalltownites proudly boast that theirs is a community
in which 'everyone knows everybody else'. This, of course, is not literally
the case in a population of nearly 4000 but there is an element of truth in
it. Two-thirds of its small population have lived locally for at least ten
years, and because all the major institutions are located in the immediate
community, multiple links rather than single-stranded ties are formed
between members. This means that many people who are neighbours also
belong to the same organisations, purchase their goods at the same shop,
send their children to the same schools, play sport together and so forth. It
is also relevant that it is a community where more than four-fifths of the

population claim an affiliation with a particular religious denomination and turn to that denomination to celebrate marriages, births and perform their last rites. Furthermore, Smalltown people, especially those of the middle class, pride themselves on their commitment to integrating newcomers into community life and working 'for the good of the community'. The churches draw most of their support from the middle class.

Given these structural and cultural characteristics, if a church is serving as a focal point of community identification and is providing people with a sense of meaning, belonging and being cared for, these things will be known, acknowledged and talked about, even by those who are not active participants in the particular church. Yet, during the course of this research project, there have been few signs that the churches, in contrast to a number of other voluntary organisations, are perceived as organisations which facilitate the achievement of psychological well-being for their members, demonstrate neighbourly care and support, or serve as mechanisms for integrating men and women into the life of the local community. The churches are certainly not perceived as organisations which overcome local injustices and bring into valued relationships the young and the old, men and women and members of the working and middle classes. Rather, many community members perceive them as anachronistic: as 'private clubs' for those people who 'like that kind of thing' or who are 'religiously minded'. They are not generally seen as organisations of widespread appeal or relevance.

Evidence for these judgements was gained in the mid-1980s during the course of an investigation of the relative social standing of ten of the community's voluntary organisations. A total of 175 respondents were asked to rank these organisations according to their standing in the community. There were two church organisations on the list: the Anglican Committee of Management (or Vestry) and the Uniting Church Ladies' Guild. No other organisation received a lower ranking than these two organisations. Many respondents failed to rank the religious organisations, often because they knew little or nothing about them or they did not know who belonged to them. By contrast, the organisations that most consistently received the highest rankings were those that were perceived as providing the most services for community members generally or for particular needy sections of the community, irrespective of religious affiliation. It is worth noting that 40 per cent of the respondents in this survey were regular church attenders themselves. They were, however, less likely to give the church organisations a high ranking than were non-attenders.

When participants in this survey were asked to volunteer the names of the organisations which they believed had the highest social standing in the community (rather than rank names from a set list), none of them nominated a church or church organisation. To realise the full significance of this finding it needs to be borne in mind that a majority of respondents equated social standing of voluntary organisations with the performance of charity or, at least, saw the latter as one of either two or three major contributors to social standing in this community.

Friendship and the relevance of religion

Convincing evidence of the lessening significance of conventional religion as a vehicle for integrating members into the community was revealed during a study of friendship behaviour. Information was collected from 175 respondents about 485 friendships. Some of this material is presented here for two reasons. First, because it is plausible to assume that if religious beliefs and activities are meeting fundamental social and emotional needs, the beneficiaries will talk about this to close friends; and second, given the propensity of human beings to choose as friends people similar to them in outlook, lifestyle and social characteristics (Bell, 1981), it is also plausible to expect friendships to be established and given expression in religious (here meaning church) activities if such activities are particularly salient to the actors concerned.

The information we collected during these interviews strongly suggests that conventional religion plays a very limited part in the friendships of the great majority of our respondents—including most of the church attenders in our sample. In support of this I offer the following points. First, respondents were unable to provide us with information concerning the religious affiliation of 20 per cent of their friends. Even church attenders were unable to provide the religious affiliations of 10 per cent of the people they nominated as friends. This was surprising given that the population of Smalltown is small and consists mainly of people who have lived in the neighbourhood for at least ten years. It clearly indicates that denominational affiliation is irrelevant to at least one of the close friendships of one in ten of those respondents who are church attenders. We also found that only 3 per cent of the friendships were established during participation in church activities; in only 4 per cent of the cases was a church or church organisation mentioned as a place where friends were usually seen; and in less than 2 per cent of friendships was a church, church organisation or religious belief mentioned as a topic of conversation.

To put these findings in a proper perspective, the following points need to be made. First, church and church organisations were the least frequently mentioned venues for seeing friends: they were outnumbered three to one as a place of contact by both non-church organisations and the hotel. Second, going to a church or a church organisation was the activity least likely to be mentioned as the one engaged in with friends: it was outnumbered seven to one both by attending non-church organisations and playing or watching sport together, and, twelve to one by such activities as attending a dance, a barbecue or eating a hotel counter meal together. Third, the church or church organisation was the least likely venue for a friendship to be established in the first place. Non-church voluntary organisations were three times as likely to be mentioned as places where friendships were established.

The meagre impact of conventional religion on friendship behaviour is highlighted by the following information. First, only 15 of our 175 respondents (9 per cent) made any reference to religion at all in the course of extensive discussions during interviews about friendship activities. Because of the way the interview was constructed there were about 40 opportunities for most respondents to make a reference. Second, those who did make a reference to religion or religious activities were hardly representative of the sample as a whole. All were church attenders and were over 40 years of age. Two-thirds of them were women and two-thirds were middle class. The modal group of respondents making at least one reference to religious activity consisted of widowed Protestant women of retirement age who had been members of one of the local women's church organisations for at least 30 years. Totally absent from the ranks of those making a reference to religion were men under 40, although they comprised 57 per cent of the male portion of the sample. Only one woman under 40 made a reference to religion, yet two-thirds of the women in the sample were less than 40 years of age. These findings underline once again the irrelevance of organised religion especially to men of all ages and to younger women. They also highlight the unlikelihood that the churches are able to serve as contexts in which age, gender and class segregation and inequitable relationships are overcome or at least put to one side.

The study of friendship did confirm findings from an earlier random sample survey of 182 elderly members of the community. This showed that certain older women, especially middle-class widows, were experiencing a sense of belonging through participation in church groups. These women stressed that their prime reason for participating in these groups was to meet with friends. Generally speaking, however, the evidence from the Friendship Survey suggests that the church attenders are as likely as non-church attenders to find their happiness and have their need to belong met in secular organisations and activities and, in those contexts, to find more friends among the non-church-goers than among the church-goers. It is therefore not surprising that church-goers often express a greater sense of identity with, and are more ready to make a commitment of time, emotional resources and money to, their Rotary Club, football committee or Red Cross organisation than they are to their church or one of its organisations. The former types of organisation, rather than the churches, are the contexts for their efforts to enhance their personal and public esteem and to achieve a sense of personal fulfilment.

One minister pointed out that the peripheral significance of the church in the lives of even active members was clearly displayed when a prominent member died. Members of the church were lamenting that person's loss—not to the church, but to important secular community organisations.The minister felt compelled to point out to them that the death would also be a serious blow to the life of the church. But they were quite taken aback by his comment and it was apparent from the expression on their faces that they did not really believe that the loss to the church mattered nearly as much as it did to other groups in the town.

Inequality and the churches

As I pointed out briefly in an earlier paper (Dempsey, 1983b: 28), social class profoundly influences the character of denominational religion in this community. Rather than generating cross-cutting ties between members of the middle and working classes, the churches tend to reflect and reinforce class positions. The Roman Catholic Church and the Church of Christ are partial exceptions to this generalisation. The Church of Christ draws its supporters mainly from the lower levels of the middle class (i.e. clerks, typists, salespeople, etc.) and from the working class, and the Roman Catholic Church from all levels of the middle class and from the working class. However, in both these churches lay leaders come disproportionately from the ranks of the upper middle classes (i.e. farmers, business people, professionals, etc.). In the Salvation Army and the Anglican and the Uniting Churches, the opportunities for cross-cutting ties to be formed between different classes are low, because each of these churches draws its active supporters mainly from the one class: the Salvationists from the working class and the Anglican and Uniting Churches from the middle class.

The middle classes comprise two-thirds of the population of Smalltown but three-quarters of Anglican and Uniting Church members. In 1987, only 40 of the 225 people (18 per cent) regularly attending[3] either the Anglican or the Uniting Church were drawn from the working classes, yet these classes comprise approximately one-third of community members. The chance of working-class men forming cross-cutting ties with members of the middle class are particularly slender, for working-class men comprise only 4 per cent of church members. The great majority of regular attenders are drawn from the farming and business classes. Working class male members are the poorest attenders at worship. Only 11 per cent of them attend at least once a month. Twenty-five per cent of upper middle-class men attend as regularly as this, as do 28 per cent of working-class women members. However, by far the best attenders are the upper middle-class women: 38 per cent of them attend at least monthly. The low rate of participation of the working class in these two churches decreases the churches' likelihood of helping to bridge class-based social inequality in Smalltown.

One's class position also significantly affects the likelihood of one holding a position of authority in church organisations. In the mid-1980s all members of the Vestry (the managing body of the Anglican Church) were members of the middle class, although one woman engaged in semi-professional employment was married to a working-class man. All but three of the 32 members of the Uniting Church Parish Council were also members of the middle class. The three exceptions were women: two of them were married to retired employee tradesmen and a third to a labourer. In both organisations all executive positions were held at this time by members of the middle class.

Gender combines with class to have a profound bearing on patterns of participation in church life and the range of activities available. There are no men's societies in these two churches. There are four women's groups associated with the Anglican and Uniting churches and in these middle-class women are greatly over-represented and working-class women under-represented. Occasionally a working-class woman holds an executive position in one of these organisations, but the organisations are controlled by middle-class women. What must be stressed, however, is that few of the members of the upper middle class who are prominent in town administration and in the community's more prestigious male organisations are, at the present time, active in either of these churches.

Age and gender inequality

Throughout their history, both the Anglican and Uniting Churches in Smalltown have deliberately utilised the characteristics of age and gender in the organisation of their activities. For example, Sunday schools have been for the young rather than for all ages. The women's organisations of the churches are age as well as gender homogeneous. At the present time, a majority of the members of the Anglican and Uniting Church women's guilds are 65 years of age or older.

Men have traditionally dominated the decision-making bodies of the Anglican and Uniting Churches. There is now, however, a greater amount of female participation in such bodies within these two churches. This participation has gone some way towards reducing gender inequalities of influence and power. It also needs to be noted that the elderly are over-represented and the young are under-represented among leaders, as well as worshippers, in both the Anglican and Uniting Churches. It is true that there is some mixing of the young and the old in the casual groups that stand around talking after church, but even in these informal contexts most interaction is between people of a similar age and of the same sex. In other words, the organising principles controlling so much of the social life of the town also seem to be controlling the life of the churches as well. In these respects at least, the churches appear to be epiphenomena of the community rather than focal points for a radically different lifestyle.

The part women play in keeping the churches going

The clearest signs of persistence of support for these churches come from women. However, this support is coming not from all women but from women of retirement age. These women have been the most regular attenders at worship and supporters of church organisations during the seventeen years this investigation has been in progress. In either the Anglican or the 'Uniting Church, only a handful of young female descendants (say those between 20 and 30 years of age) of families that have traditionally provided the core active membership of these churches are themselves today actively involved. Like their male counterparts, most left their church when they left Sunday school.

For those concerned about the survival of institutional Christianity in Smalltown, it is possibly the absence of younger women that is most worrying. Not only are the daughters and daughters-in-law of the present older female supporters largely absent from worship, but they have also elected to stay out of the churches' major women's organisations: the Church Guilds and Missionary Societies. It is only these organisations that have not experienced great fluctuations in membership or disappeared entirely. They have also been major money raisers for the churches, which are facing a growing problem of financial viability. Of course, the absence of the younger women renders it virtually impossible for the churches to serve as a context for women of all ages to work towards ending the inequality which they experience in family and public life.

Some of the older women are hopeful that when the young women are more advanced in years they will join the church organisations and ensure their continuity. This is probably a false hope, for there is a much smaller group of younger women actively associated with the church at the present time than when current older women were young themselves. Because this development is likely to have a profound bearing on the future of these churches and therefore on their ability to serve as contexts for equitable relationships and for the fulfilment of individuals' need to belong and to express themselves, it is worth considering them in some detail.

When the older women were in their 20s and 30s they were already locked into a routine of church attendance—usually twice on Sunday—and of active involvement in one or more church women's organisations as well as in other charity-type organisations in the town such as the Country Women's Association and the Red Cross. Throughout their lives the time away from home has been given over largely to activities which express, enhance and confirm familial roles: that is, roles in which they make use of their domestic skills. They are women for whom a sense of purpose and achievement in life has primarily been sought in the roles of wife and mother and somewhat vicariously through the occupational achievements of their husbands and the sporting, scholarly and occupational achievements of children. But they have also put their domestic skills to work for the benefit of a range of 'good causes', including their church and its organisations.

Many of the younger women, however, are ambivalent, even hostile, about exercising homemaking skills and engaging in wifely tasks. They are often dissatisfied with many aspects of their present lives, especially their marital relations. Yet they fail to perceive the churches as contexts in which their needs and aspirations can be even partially met. The churches are certainly not perceived as contexts for overcoming some of the shortcomings in their relationships with men, especially their husbands. For example, a church service of worship or social activity does not provide an opportunity to develop a companionate marriage if a husband absents himself from such activities. Similarly, the depth of friendship these women are looking for requires more than a few minutes' casual conversation after church or at a church meeting where many other people are present. Consequently, younger women in the town have institutionalised a practice of 'dropping in' on friends for a 'cup of coffee and chat'. They report that these occasions provide an opportunity to discuss mutual problems concerning child rearing and in some instances the difficulties of achieving a more fulfilling and equitable marriage relationship. The attitudes and ambitions they are displaying are not compatible with the subordinate and auxiliary roles women have traditionally played in church life. Rather, other contexts, other activities and other people seem to be offering them a greater chance of realising the needs that they are articulating. It is therefore not surprising that the younger Protestant women announce their intention of never joining church groups in which the older women predominate. Nor is it surprising that they absent themselves in increasing numbers from worship which neither their closest friends nor their husbands attend.

Concluding comments

It has been seen that support for the churches and their organisations has declined dramatically during the seventeen years this study has been in progress. Despite the church's oft-repeated claim that all men and women are equal in the sight of God, the Smalltown churches reinforce rather than challenge the inequitable relationships between the middle and working classes, between men and women and between the young and the old. It seems that within the churches, people give expression to external social ties and 'secular' values.

Not only do the churches fail to challenge inequalities and other injustices in this community (Dempsey, 1983b), but they also fail to serve as important mechanisms for the integration of many individuals into the life of the community and, it seems, to provide for most individuals a context in which a sense of usefulness and what Berger (1967) calls self-realisation can occur. Berger has argued at some length that while organised religion has been deprived of its traditional role of legitimating a society's political and economic activities, it retains its role of facilitating the achievement of a sense of meaning and autonomy in the private sphere of people's lives. In this sphere people can express themselves and find satisfaction, in part, through choosing friends and a marriage partner who share their religious convictions, through participation in a church of their own choice and in that church exercising some influence and finding a good deal of happiness. The data that have been presented strongly suggest that organised religion is functioning in such ways for a declining minority of Smalltown people.

Wallace (1985) also recognises the importance of basic human emotional and psychological needs being met. She observes that in a modern society there is a need for groups and activities that 'reverse the normal order' by providing contexts in which a sense of belonging and continuity in the midst of change can occur. 'Bring on the carnivals!' she cries: '. . . friendships where "the unusual may become usual" and small interests groups, religious or otherwise, where the "unbelievable is believable". . .' (Wallace, 1985: 31). Smalltown's churches seem to provide few carnivals. At least that is the conclusion one is brought to by an examination of the data gathered during this inquiry about the changing patterns of church attendance, decline in support for church organisations and the apparent irrelevance of church religion to much friendship activity and conversation. It is also corroborated by data presented in an earlier paper which showed that church lay leaders took little interest in the spiritual, educational and pastoral aspects of church life (Dempsey, 1983b). Indeed, it seems that for most Smalltownites the churches are failing to provide the social context in which they can experience their lives as making sense (Berger and Kellner, 1970: 50). My concern, in Wilson's (1982: 154–5) terms, is with their capacity to serve their votaries as total persons and not as role performers, and in so doing to help integrate those votaries into the local community. There seems little doubt that they are, at best, achieving such goals for a rapidly diminishing number of participants.

Smalltown has its carnivals, but they are much more likely to occur at family 'festivals', sporting functions, the activities of women's auxiliaries, the barbecues at which friends congregate and the nightly get-togethers of drinkers at the pub than to take place in the churches or their organisations. Such events are among the things that Smalltown people care passionately about. They are some of the things that help them to feel a part of this community and to regard it as a place where everyone is treated the same and all are part of one big family. These are the contexts for what Berger (1967: 369–78) calls self-realisation: not highly regimented contexts, but ones where people believe they can be themselves and find personal happiness.

Notes

1   I am indebted to Rae Ball for assistance with the collection of data for this paper and to Therese Lennox, Barbara Matthews and Beth Robertson for assistance with its preparation. I am also indebted to the J. E. Ross Trust, the Australian Research Council and the Research Committee of the School of Social Science, La Trobe University for financial assistance. Some parts of the paper were originally published in Dempsey (1989a), and are used here with permission of the Editor of *Sociological Analysis: A Journal in the Sociology of Religion* (official journal of the Association for the Sociology of Religion).

2   Class refers to the position individuals occupy in the economic and work system of this community. It is discussed in detail in Dempsey (1990b: Chapter 8).

3   That is at least once a month.

6 Social factors and individual preferences for images of God
'Tricia Blombery

If the ox could paint a picture, his god would look like an ox. (Xenophanes, 6th century B.C.)

Since the beginning of civilisation, humans have sought to explain, give meaning to and control the occurrences and events of their physical world. These explanations have frequently contained descriptions of super-human, super-empirical entities which may be revered as creators or primal causes, or may be seen as continually intervening in human lives and, hence, be worshipped in order to influence them to meet human needs. The nature of these gods varies between societies and between different historical periods of the same society.

Many of the concepts of gods have emphasised a human form and character or have been anthropomorphic at least to the extent that the god they portray is addressed, through the language of worship and prayer, as if human. Hume (1957 [1757]: 29) noted that 'there is a universal tendency among mankind [sic] to conceive all beings like themselves and to transfer to every object those qualities with which they are familiarly acquainted, and of which they are intimately conscious'. So strong is this tendency towards anthropomorphism that Stewart Guthrie (1980) includes it as an essential element in his definition of religion. However, there is a strong strain in Christianity which emphasises the 'otherness' of deity. Twentieth century theologians, striving to relate religion to what they regarded as a secular world, have preferred such concepts as 'absolute good', 'the ground of our being' or 'eternal spirit' in their images of God.

Origins of images of God

All religions, to some extent, reflect the ideas, values and images of the culture in which they are celebrated. Many attempts have been made to explain the diversity of gods. Sociologists have pointed out that the conceptions of the gods closely resemble the characteristics of societies and groups: agricultural people develop gods of sun and rain and ocean peoples worship gods of the sea; masters and slaves, the rich and the poor, the upper class and the working class all have very different views about God and human nature (see, for example, Weber, 1963; Swanson, 1960; Niebuhr, 1929).

In very general terms, it is possible to show how particular images of God have reflected the hierarchical structure of societies and their dominant cultural characteristics. As these have changed, new images of God have developed and to some extent supplanted the older images. For example, the emergence of a centralised, monarchical government in Judaism sees a shift of emphasis in the portrayal of Yahweh from a god dwelling in the wilderness to a potentate with a heavenly court. It is a short step from here to the image, favoured by the medieval Catholic church, of God as a feudal prince, a warrior and master ruling over human subjects and servants. Political struggles in Europe between royal despots and the emergence of a commercialised gentry, or middle class, saw another image, expressed by Wesley in his Good Steward sermon of 1768, of God as a just banker or benevolent employer of human servants.

One possible relationship between the characteristics of the gods and the characteristics of the society in which they are worshipped is explored by Robin Horton who states (1960: 217):

> If we assume that the gods of any population have become co-ordinated to individuals and the various levels of grouping that include them as a result of a process of selection based on perceived relevance to particular goals at particular levels of structural reference, we can expect to find 'written in' to the character of any god some implication of relevance in the particular social context where it has become fixed.

In developing his argument, Horton (1960: 224) focuses on the nature of interpersonal relationships in a society and concludes that 'The definition of a god's character ... bears in large measure the imprint of the communion strivings (for love, security, approval, etc.) of the individual ...'

This tie between images of God and styles of personal relationship is developed further by Christian (1972) when discussing changes in images of God at different times in the same society. He draws a parallel between the divine–human relationship and human interrelationships. In the past centuries of Roman Catholicism, divine–human relationships have been taught in feudal, monarchic and political images most analogous to relations on Earth which included an acknowledged imbalance of power. While God was essentially personal and loving, he was also transcendent and there was no place in the divine–human repertoire for peer relations. In the past 100 years, because of the decreased universal applicability of the power images, the Church has concentrated more on the family as a model for understanding the divine–human relationship (Christian, 1972: 173–4). Christian's point about the nature of divine–human relationships is expanded by Harvey Cox (1968). Speaking in a broader framework, he claims that in attributing particular characteristics to God, all cultures use symbols drawn from some aspect of social life. Thus changing family and political structures inevitably result in different symbolisations of God. Cox suggests that in modern society, where patterns of horizontal kinship and vertical authority are disappearing and being replaced by relationships of 'alongsidedness', God is met both in the I–Thou relationship which reflects authority and in the I–You relationship which reflects a degree of intimacy (Cox, 1968: 271–3).

Diverse images within the same society

While the theories discussed give some explanation of why particular societies have particular images of God, they make little reference to individual differences within the same society. Explanations for individual differences have come largely from psychologists. Some, like Gordon Allport (1950), have noted how people tend to emphasise supernatural features which reflect their own needs—if they are weak, then God is all powerful; if they are friendless, then God is a companion; if they need guidance, then God is all-knowing. Other psychologists have developed theories which assume that God-images are generalisations from images of parents (e.g. Freud, 1962) or self-images (e.g. Benson and Spilka, 1973). This type of thinking has been criticised because it 'abstracts people from the cultural context in which they live and individualises both the sociocultural milieu and theology' (Spilka, Addison and Rosensohn, 1975: 164).

Recent Australian research (Bouma and Dixon, 1986; McCallum, 1987) shows that over 80 per cent of the population affirm some degree of belief in an entity they label 'God'. A further 6 per cent affirm unbelief which, by implication, identifies a concept which they reject. Descriptions of God are many and varied. A sample of 90 interviews revealed over 40 distinct images (Bentley et al., 1986).

It is possible to suggest reasons for differences in images of God from the insights of sociological theory. The remainder of this chapter will look at different images held by Australian church attenders and, using age and gender as illustration, attempt to explain these individual differences from a sociological perspective. The data used are derived from over 6000 church attenders from 98 churches drawn from five different denominations across Australia (for details, see Blombery and Hughes, 1987). It was collected by the Christian Research Association in 1987 as part of the Combined Churches Survey for Faith and Mission.

Developing concepts of God

Functionalist sociologists such as Talcott Parsons see religious beliefs and values as part of the cultural system which is internalised by individuals as they learn appropriate guidelines for action and the expected standards of their society. The initial learning of religious beliefs occurs in early infancy as the child responds to the approval or disapproval of parents and other significant adults, copies their example and incorporates their ideas and values into his or her repertoire. As well as responding to parental influences, children's beliefs and ideas are moulded in terms of the values of the culture to the point where these values become part of them. Further socialisation is provided by the education system, the church, peer groups and occupational groups, which frequently reinforce previously learned patterns.

In modern society, religion is characterised by institutional specialisation. Each institutionally specialised religion typically consolidates beliefs, values and practices into a coherent model which includes a prescribed doctrine providing a coherent and explicit meaning system. In a religiously pluralistic society like Australia, there are a number of official models, each associated with a particular religious collectivity. Each of the specialist religious institutions mediates its official model to the individual adherent. This is done directly through its official teaching or indirectly (and usually more effectively) by exposing believers to certain ideas and ethics which are institutionalised in the norms and expectations of the group and reinforced by its sanctions. The church, or religious body, to which the person belongs is therefore an important source of religious socialisation.

Other theorists have criticised the functionalist account of religious socialisation because it suggests that the individual has no active choice but rather is caught in a one-way process, being pumped full of culture from diverse sources, by which personality is moulded. Peter Berger and Thomas Luckmann (Berger, 1973; Berger and Luckmann, 1971; Luckmann, 1967) have suggested that each individual's understanding of reality is socially constructed from his or her own experiences in the world. This process takes place in an ongoing, shared society. To some extent, social institutions impose predefined patterns on the individual. Humans adopt a 'world view' which can be used to 'make sense' of various elements of experience. Individuals' perspectives vary somewhat, because of different experiences of the society and such experiences are to a large degree mediated by the individual's status and position within the social structure.

Nor are the official models presented to believers consistent and uniform. In religiously pluralistic societies, such as Australia, the development of denominationalism, creating an institutionalised expression of social differences and divisions, not only allows choice between several competing official models, but also permits opting out of such religion entirely (Wilson, 1969). Different religious orientations may be reflected in separate religious collectivities or may 'interpenetrate' (Hill, 1973: 77), so that within a single institution there may exist distinct and sometimes competing orientations. It is therefore possible for members of the same broad religious group to have markedly different orientations. Demerath (1965) found that some members of the one denomination exhibited highly sectarian patterns of involvement but other members did not. A similar diversity is seen in the existence of charismatic congregations in many mainline churches.

Effects of position in the social structure

It is impossible in a single chapter to consider all the social experiences and influences which lead to preferences for different images of God. Undoubtedly denominational allegiance and teaching are of great significance. Important also are the ideal and material interests of the groups to which the individual belongs. These influences cannot be assessed in isolation, but must be considered in terms of the total society.

One approach to studying the structure of societies and its influence on the ideas of individuals is that developed by Mary Douglas (1970; 1975; 1982). Douglas has devised a four-way categorical schema to facilitate analytical consideration of social relations in any social context. The two dimensions she has formulated—'grid' and 'group'—represent two different ways by which society can 'grip' its members. 'Group' is 'the experience of a bounded social unit' (1970: viii) or, in a more recent version, 'the outside boundary that people have erected between themselves and the outside world' (1982: 138). 'Grid' refers to 'the rules which relate one person to others on an egocentric basis' (1970: viii) or the 'social distinctions and delegations of authority that they [people] use to limit how people behave to one another' (1982: 138). Group and grid exist together, and societies can be categorised on a fourfold model as being weak or strong on either dimension.

In terms of this schema, a social collectivity such as Australia exists as the linking together of constituent sub-groups of individuals bounded by multiple role reciprocities and relatively strong rules. The individual and the institutions are strong (strong grid) and not totally subordinated to the state (strong group) (Wuthnow et al., 1984: 127). This structure is represented in a religious approach where the cosmos is seen as 'morally neutral and basically optimistic' (Douglas, 1970: 137) and where there is a decline in ritualism and a tendency to see God as more intimate but diminished in glory and power (Douglas, 1970: 57). In such a loosely bounded, competitive society, smaller groups and individuals are differently placed with respect to the dimensions of grid and group, which categorise the social structure. It is possible to suggest different religious orientations which relate to specific groups of people.

In *Implicit Meanings* (1975), Douglas has identified grid with classificatory systems. As the rating for grid increases, so the classificatory system is increasingly shared and coherent over a wide range of experiences (Douglas, 1975: 218). In societies such as ours, where the lifestyle is individualistic, egocentric and competitive, those who are successful in society are more likely to accept the value system (Douglas, 1970: 160); their cultural vocabulary, including their concept of God, will favour the abstract and the instrumental and a God who is powerful but not interventionist. Their symbolism will express a high level of internal differentiation (Martin, 1981: 46) and religion will be a segmented part. By contrast, those who are less successful in terms of the society's expectations and values will have a cultural vocabulary which is expressive, emotional and personalised (Martin, 1981: 45) and an idea of God as one who, dethroned from the centre of power, loses majesty and becomes intimate, a personal friend who speaks directly (Douglas, 1970: 195).

The nature of the God-images found significant by each individual will vary, reflecting the particular person's degree of exposure to the 'objective' changes of society and his or her acceptance of the values implicit in the society. These individual estimates of personal power can again be assessed in terms of placement on one of Mary Douglas's dimensions. An individual's place on the group dimension can be seen in terms of how much pressure that person is able to exert over others and the extent to which his or her life is controlled by others (Douglas, 1975: 218). Those on the periphery of society—such as the young, the aged and women—have little say in many of the important decisions which shape their lives, and may perceive themselves as victims of an inequality which is random, unpredictable and unconnected with moral judgements (Douglas, 1970: 153). For these people, placed at the strong end of the group dimension, there is often a depressing sense of the unjust 'they' and their symbolism and religious world view emphasise a distinction between 'inside' and 'outside' (Martin, 1981: 45), where the inside is good and the outside is evil (Douglas, 1970: 143).

Relationships exist between particular images of God, people's assessment of the purposefulness of their life and their degree of control, and objective measures which will identify them as central or peripheral to the social mainstream. These relationships can be explored in terms of age and gender differences.

The influence of age on preferences for images of God

The relationship between age and religion has been explored chiefly with reference to religious affiliation and attendance. Here two major interpretations of age have been employed: age as an indication of a person's stage in the life cycle and age as membership of a particular birth cohort or generational group.

Age in terms of stage in life cycle

In Australian society, different status is given to people according to their age and stage in the life cycle. The individual is in a particular position in respect to the total society. This in turn influences how the individual perceives the world and his or her place in it in terms of power, status and personal freedom. The particular stage in the life cycle is also indicative of differing degrees of exposure to, and integration of the individual with, the wider society. Such influences are reflected in the different concepts held by members of different age groups in the survey. In part this is a function of age and maturity. As people grow and develop in their faith, as they explore their relationship with God, their images may broaden to encompass new religious experiences and understandings. Different concepts, however, also reflect a person's changing position in the wider society.

Age in terms of birth cohort

When people are considered in terms of their birth cohort they can be treated as being in many ways the same. They have distinctive shared historical contexts in that they grew up at the same time and have experienced, either personally or mediated through the influence and ideas of their parents, a similar social climate. This social climate may differ significantly in terms of its receptivity to religious appeals. For example, in the 1950s the climate was generally favourable to religion and religious values, and these prospered. In the late 1960s and 1970s the social climate became less favourable, and religion and religious values have declined. The 1980s have seen a continuing decline in the traditional mainline groups, coupled with a renewed vigor in fundamentalist and sectarian groups.

Table 6.1 Generational experiences

Born	Age in 1987	Common social experience
1900–16	over 70	World War I
1917–37	70–50	Great Depression
1938–47	49–40	World War II; Cold War
1948–62	39–25	Postwar affluence
1963–69	24–18	Vietnam War; counter-culture
1970 and after	under 18	Post-industrialism; nuclear threat

It is possible to identify six generational groups in Australia who will have shared or been influenced by some significant social experiences. These are listed in Table 6.1.

One possible influence of birth cohort comes from the different official models into which people were socialised as emphases within churches changed in response to changes within the wider society. The work of Cox (1968) and Christian (1972), discussed earlier, has expanded our understanding of the possible differences people from different age groups may have encountered in their religious education.

One of the most significant shifts, however, is that suggested by British researcher Bernice Martin (1981), who claims that since the end of World War II a major cultural change has taken place. Beginning in the 1960s as a radical 'counter-culture' movement among the cosmopolitan intelligentsia of the arts and politics, it has now become incorporated into the mainstream of social life. It heralded a whole new cultural style, a set of values, assumptions and ways of living, which has been termed 'the expressive revolution'. The 1960s movement 'countered' instrumentality and power, work and politics and championed individual and experiential dimensions. The shift in cultural norms can be seen as an increased attempt to realise the 1960s' goal of recovering the 'true authentic real self' which was seen to have been stolen or concealed by the established authorities (Foss and Larkin, 1986: 102).

The post-war cultural shift has been characterised in the churches as an increasing emphasis in the official teaching on the personal, the expressive and the experiential aspects of the Christian message. This can be illustrated by two examples. McSweeney (1980: 112), in discussing new theological trends within Roman Catholicism in Europe immediately prior to Vatican II, draws attention to:

> a marked shift of emphasis from Christ's divinity to his humanity; from the
> Church as an institution of salvation to the Church as community; from
> God's transcendence and otherness to his presence among men and in all
> creation; from the resurrection as a discrete event in the past and in the future
> to the kingdom already present in the world and in the process of fulfilment;
> from a moral theology of sin to a moral theology of human development and
> interpersonal relationships.

A similar trend within other churches can be seen in a move from more intellectual forms of celebration towards more experiential and expressive forms. This is exemplified both in the rise of new Pentecostal sects and in the development of charismatic elements in the mainline churches. These, too, are frequently a search for the real and the authentic, as groups seek to revive elements of an earlier tradition.

These changes in society and within churches form the background patterns and influences against which people's religious ideas are developed. People in different birth cohorts will share similar experiences, but these may be different from those in other cohorts.

Images favoured by different age groups

The survey results summarised in Figure 6.1 indicate that among the teenage age group in the churches, the deity is thought of primarily in personal terms. God is regarded as someone they can relate to as a friend. God provides constant love, support and help. This relationship is maintained through church services and fellowship groups which are valued for facilitating communion with God. Abstract images are rarely chosen by this group, and the idea of God as redeemer receives little support. In the choices of this group are reflected the adolescent emphasis and the need for a peer relationship. There is also a suggestion of the powerlessness this age group feels in still being dependent on others for many of the decisions which control their everyday lives and their minimal involvement with the wider society. God is thought of primarily as a person whose focus of concern is on the individual rather than in the wider world.

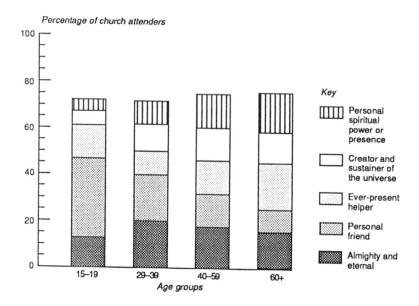

Figure 6.1 Image of God by age

In the 20–29 age group, there is an overall decrease in the proportion of people choosing individual person-focused concepts. The image of God as almighty and eternal has an increased importance in all denominations.

Redeemer is an important first choice for Baptists (15 per cent) and Pentecostals (20 per cent). There is greater emphasis on the non-anthropomorphic images of God as absolute good or as a spiritual power or presence. It is in this age group that many important decisions are made about career, relationships and general lifestyle. For many it is the beginning of an independent life away from their parents. It appears also to be a time of changing religious commitment. Twenty-three per cent of the people in this group have been connected with their present church for less than a year and a further 34 per cent have been involved for less than five years. For 30 per cent of this group, when they were of primary school age, their parents either did not attend church or attended only occasionally. Gender differences also begin to influence selection in the 20–29 age group. A significantly lower proportion of males than females are giving first preference to the personal relational concepts of friend and ever-present helper (27% : 45%). The increased social and professional involvement of males of this age is reflected in an increased emphasis on God's role as creator and sustainer of the universe.

In the 30–39 age group, personal relationships with God are still important to 32 per cent, but there is some evidence of a shift in emphasis from the intimate, peer relationship with God as personal friend (18 per cent) towards a somewhat more hierarchical, removed concept of God as ever-present helper (14 per cent). Among members of this age group the choices of image also reflect their increased involvement and status in the wider world, as was predicted in Douglas's work. While women express greater preference for relational images (35% : 25%), the increased emphasis on cosmic God-images is apparent for both men and women.

Among the 40–60 age group there is an increasing awareness of God as master and creator of the universe and as a spiritual force. When God is envisaged as personal, it is as a provider of help, support and comfort rather than as a close friend. Such images reflect the success and position of people in this age group who have risen to positions of responsibility within their careers and often within the church. They are financially more secure, their families are grown and will require less frequent day-to-day attention, and there are greater opportunities for leisure. This greater mastery of the world and confidence in their position is reflected in preferences for a bigger, less interventionist, more transcendent God.

The choices of the over 60s group are more like the emphases of the young age groups. In this age group, gender difference has a greater influence on choice than was evident in other groups. While the overall pattern is balanced between emphasis on individual (29 per cent) and cosmic (32 per cent) images of God, there is an increased preference from men (16 per cent) and women (22 per cent) for the image of God as an ever-present helper. A much higher proportion of men than women selected the image of God as creator and sustainer (20% : 14%). This swing back to more relational images is accompanied by a withdrawal from the wider world as people enter retirement. It is also, for many, a period of increased physical and financial dependence.

The above evidence suggests that individuals of the same age group, regardless of their denomination, tend to have similar images of the nature of God, and that these patterns of images will be different for different age groups. While there are gender differences within an age group, they are less significant than differences between age groups. The degree of exposure to and involvement in the wider society would also appear to be a significant factor influencing selection of image.

Although the above interpretation focuses on the influence of life-cycle factors, it is possible that generational factors also contribute to the observed differences. If those who are now in younger generations maintain their more egalitarian conception of God as they grow older, this would provide support for the theories of Christian (1972) and Cox (1968) that social relationships have become more egalitarian in recent times, and that images of God have changed accordingly. It is difficult to test this hypothesis with data collected at only one point in time.

The influence of gender on images of God

Our society has created two distinct sets of roles for men and women. Associated with these roles are stereotypes of interests, behaviours and emotions which are considered appropriate for either females or males. Traditionally, women are expected to be warm, expressive, nurturant and oriented towards the personal and the emotional. Their focus is confined to the domestic arena and the tasks, emotions and responsibilities associated with it. By contrast, men are expected to be instrumental and oriented towards the 'world', establishing careers and providing for their families. Men, supposedly are strong where women are weak; they are supposedly decisive where women are fickle; and they are supposedly coldly rational and instrumental where women are emotional.

Historically the church has been one of the most significant sources of these cultural definitions. The approved religious image of women in Western society is of the virgin/chaste bride/mother. The church has reinforced the importance of the woman's role as mother, caregiver and homemaker as an 'evangelical domesticity'. In religion, men have been given images of power and leadership. The language of the Bible and, of services and hymns, as well as the rituals and hierarchy of the church, has celebrated the authority and dominance of men.

While men and women may belong to the same religious group, the individual's religion is not necessarily a carbon copy of the group's entire official teaching. It is reasonable to suppose that a woman's religious experience, and what she holds most important in her religion, should reflect her personal situation, and that the values and characteristics associated with her idealised role should be reflected in her choices of God-image. In other words, a woman's version of a given religion will reflect those aspects of the group's total world view which speak to her own social situation. This would suggest that the values and characteristics of warmth, nurturance and expressiveness associated with the idealised role of woman would be reflected in women's choice of God images—that they would tend to perceive God in close personal terms. By contrast, men would prefer images which reflect God's power and involvement in creation. Similarly, based on Douglas's theories, it would be anticipated that the relative social status of men and women, as defined in terms of workforce participation, would be reflected in their choices.

Earlier studies (e.g. Vergote et al., 1969; Potvin, 1977; Nelson et al., 1985; Bentley et al., 1986) revealed a gender difference in the selection of God-images. These studies have shown women preferring warmer relational images and men selecting more abstract, distant images. The data from the present study, summarised in Table 6.2, likewise indicate that a significantly greater proportion of women than men select the close, personal images of God as ever-present helper, personal friend and comforter; and that a significantly higher proportion of men than women select the cosmic, distant images of God as creator and sustainer of the universe, redeemer (an image reflecting God's power and role as decision-maker) or beyond description. There is, however, no significant difference in the proportion of men and women selecting the image of God as almighty.

Table 6.2 Gender and selection of God-image

Image	Women %	Men %
Judge	1.8	2.4
Creator and sustainer of the universe	11.6*	17.0*
Ever-present helper	16.6*	11.9*
Personal spiritual power or presence	13.5	12.6
Personal friend	19.0*	13.5*
Comforter	4.1*	2.3*
Absolute good	1.5	2.3
Almighty and eternal God	18.1	19.5
Indefinable spiritual being	1.7	1.7
Redeemer	9.3*	11.5*
God is beyond description	2.3*	3.9*

*difference statistically significant, p< .05

These differences are more apparent when, after controlling for differences in the numbers of men and women in the total sample, one compares the gender composition of those who prefer any particular image.

Set out diagrammatically in Figure 6.2 are the results for those images on which significant differences were noted in Table 6.2.

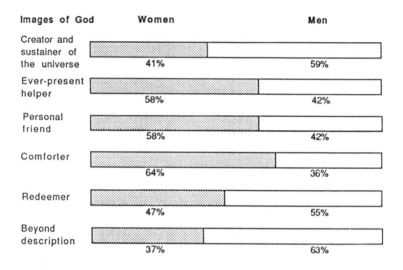

Figure 6.2 Gender and God-image, controlling for differences in the numbers of men and women in the total sample

The influence of women's workforce participation

A recent Australian study (de Vaus and McAllister, 1987) showed that where women are involved in full-time employment their religious practice more closely resembles that of men than that of women not working outside the home. If the significant influence on this difference in behaviour patterns is, as the researchers have suggested, employment status, it could be hypothesised that people of the same employment status will have similar God-images, regardless of gender.

To some extent, this is the case. There are no significant differences between the choices of men and women who are self-employed, unemployed or working part-time. There is, however, a significant difference between men and women employed full-time, and this conforms to the overall gender selection patterns. The explanation for this unexpected result rests on the occupational categories of the full-time workers. For those employed in lower status occupational groups, such as skilled trades, manual, clerical or rural work, administration or retail sales, there are no significant differences between men and women. Significant differences exist between the choices of men and women who are employed full-time in professional occupations involving work with people, and technical professions. Again the resulting patterns of choices are similar to those for the overall sample, with women preferring close relational images and men preferring more distant cosmic images. Perhaps this difference reflects the continuing imbalance of women in executive and decision-making positions.

Gender therefore has a significant influence on the selection of God-images. The pattern of differences confirms the findings of previous research into gender preference and also supports Douglas' and Luckmann's theories on the influence of structural placement on attitudes to religion. The influence of gender cannot be assessed in isolation, but must be modified with reference to employment status and occupational group.

Social factors and images of God

Age and gender are only two of the possible influences on individual perferences for particular images of God. Yet it is possible to see how being of a certain age or sex does make a difference due to the different life chances a person may experience owing to his or her perceived position within the social structure. Also significant in terms of these attributes are the social climate, especially the religious climate, that each individual has experienced. Similarly, factors such as education, occupation and employment status, all of which affect the individual's position in society, need to be considered.

The particular images different people find important relate to a multiplicity of influences. Some influences are direct and can be traced to the official teaching and religious orientation of particular denominational groups. The contribution of other influences is less easy to assess. They relate back to people's early experiences in their families, with churches and church people, to when and where they grew up, to their present place in society, and to the ideas they have of their own role and values as they live their life. No one of these factors determines which particular image a person will consider important, but each contributes. The building up of ideas is a continuing interactive process between the individual and the society of which he or she is a member.

There is ample evidence to suggest that social as well as psychological influences must be considered in investigating aspects of religion. A starting point for further research would be in the recognition of the primacy of a long religio-cultural tradition and the consideration of religious stereotypes and their cultural roots.

7 Types of faith and the decline of mainline churches

Philip J. Hughes

Between 1960 and 1990 there was a considerable decline in the size of most mainline denominations in many Western nations. An article in *Time* magazine (Ostling, 1989: 52–4) drew attention to the phenomenon in America. It noted that the United Church of Christ (which includes most Congregationalists) had shrunk 20 per cent since 1965, the Presbyterian Church 25 per cent, the Episcopal Church 28 per cent and the United Methodist Church 18 per cent. The Christian Church (Disciples of Christ) had contracted by 43 per cent, partly because of a schism. The five denominations had decreased by a total of 5.2 million people, while the population had risen by 47 million.

The trends in the mainline churches in Australia have been well documented (Harris et al., 1982: 229–93; Bouma, 1983; Kaldor, 1987). According to Australian Census statistics, the number of people identifying themselves with the Church of England or Anglican Church dropped from 3.9 million in 1966 to 3.7 million in 1986. The numbers identifying with Congregational, Methodist, Presbyterian or Uniting churches dropped from 2.2 million to 1.7 million in the same 20 years. During that period, the population rose by 38 per cent. These movements can be partly accounted for in terms of changes in birth rates and immigration patterns. Immigration from Britain, which had been the major source for persons of Anglican, Methodist, Congregational and Presbyterian affiliation, declined in the late 1960s and 1970s. At the same time, immigration from Catholic and from non-Christian countries rose. Between 1966 and 1986, Catholic affilation grew from 3.0 million to 4.1 million.

In the United States, decline in the mainline Protestant churches has been explained partly in terms of childbirth patterns. There have usually been greater numbers of children than older teenagers and people in their twenties attending churches. The churches expanded in the 1950s with the post-war baby boom, and one could only expect contraction as the children matured in the 1960s (Michaelson and Roof, 1986: 8). The growth in conservative churches and decline in liberal churches is partly a result of differences in birthrates. McKinney and Roof (1986: 44) reported that women from liberal Protestant churches had an average of 1.97 children, compared with 2.54 children for women from conservative churches.

The statistics from the 1987 Combined Churches Survey in Australia do not correspond exactly, for the survey asked for the number of dependent children at the time of the survey, rather than the number of offspring. The differences between the denominations were not as pronounced. Catholics had the highest number of dependent children, followed by Pentecostals and Baptists. Anglican and Uniting women had the lowest number, as shown in Table 7.1.

Table 7.1 Number of dependent children per woman by denomination

Denomination	Number of dependent children per woman
Anglicans	1.14
Baptists	1.27
Catholics	1.63
Pentecostals	1.48
Uniting Church	0.97

Source: Combined Churches Survey, 1987

While changes in the numbers of people identifying with the mainline denominations can be accounted for partly in terms of birth rate and immigration patterns, changes in the degree of nominalism cannot be explained in the same way. Table 7.2 shows that between 1960 and 1983 there was a considerable decline in the church attendance of those who have continued to claim allegiance to the denomination.

Table 7.2 Percentage attending church at least once a month in mainline denominations

Denomination	1960	1983	1987
Anglican	31	14	15
Catholic	69	44	42
Congregational/Methodist/ Presbyterian/Uniting Church	44	22	20

Sources: For 1960 and 1983, Kaldor (1987: 25)
For 1987, National Social Science Survey

The decline in church attendance is often attributed to a process of secularisation in Western societies. The nature of this process is far from clear. Indeed, the word 'secularisation' has been used in a multitude of ways, as Ireland (1988) has shown. Berger (1973: 113) makes a major distinction between the secularisation of society and culture and the secularisation of consciousness. Berger speaks of the secularisation of society and culture manifesting itself in the removal of religion from the institutions and culture of society, such as the areas of education, the arts and literature. The secularisation of consciousness is seen in 'an increasing number of individuals who look upon the world and their own lives without the benefit of religious interpretations' (Berger, 1973: 113). It is demonstrated in the lack of reference to God as people interpret the world and construct their lives within it. Wilson (1983), amongst others, associates the irrelevance of God in modern society with the development of science, industry and technology, which have hidden human beings from the mysteries of nature, and provided means for them to adapt the environment to their own needs rather than they adapting to the environment.

Can the recent declines in attendance and the increased nominalism in mainline denominations be accounted for in terms of such a secularisation of consciousness in our society? The first problem the theory meets is that the decline in attendance is not uniformly spread through our society. While some denominations have declined significantly, others have maintained their membership or expanded. The Baptist denomination in Australia, for example, increased its number of affiliates, according to Census data, from 166 222 in 1966 to 196 782 in 1986, an increase of 18 per cent. While this does not match the population increase, it demonstrates a pattern very different from that in some of the denominations mentioned above. Pentecostal affiliation has climbed significantly. In 1966 the denomination did not appear in the Census figures, but in 1986 it accounted for 0.7 per cent of the population. There is comparatively little nominalism in these denominations. According to the 1987 National Social Science Survey, around 60 per cent of Baptist and Pentecostal affiliates were attending church almost every week or more often. In the United States, conservative, fundamental and charismatic churches have boomed to the extent that some people have spoken of a religious revival (Ostling, 1989). The idea that 'religion' is in decline does not fit all the facts. The decline is much greater in some areas of organised religion than others.

There is also a resilience in some areas of religious belief and practice. Bouma and Dixon (1986: 166) reported from an analysis of the Australian Values Study Survey conducted in 1983 that 58 per cent of Australians describe themselves as religious persons. Seventy-nine per cent said that they believed that there was some sort of God. Two-thirds of them pray occasionally or more frequently. A simple description of Australia as a secular society cannot be maintained.

It might be suggested that some denominational groups, such as the Pentecostals, have grown only at the expense of the mainline denominations; in other words, that those who have switched to these groups mask the overall trend of secularisation. There is some evidence that a substantial proportion of people in the Pentecostal churches do have a background in other denominations. According to the data from the Joint Church Census in New South Wales, 39 per cent of people in the Assemblies of God said they had previous involvement with a church of another denomination. However, 18 per cent claimed that they had attended their present congregation for less than five years and that previously they had not been attending any church (Kaldor and Homel, 1988a).

Data from the Combined Churches Survey also provide evidence that the growth of Pentecostal churches is not altogether at the expense of mainline churches. Respondents were asked if their parents or guardians were involved in church life when the respondents were children. Thirty-six per cent of the Pentecostals came from families where there had been no church involvement at all. This compares with 22 per cent of Anglicans, 27 per cent of Baptists, 12 per cent of Catholics and 16 per cent of Uniting Church attenders.

Dean Kelley (1977) has attempted to explain why some denominations have grown while others have declined. He has argued that the different measure of success among religious groups is related to their ability to 'make meaning' of life for their members. The mainline churches, he says, have become relativistic and lukewarm. In that process, they have lost their ability to give people a clear sense of meaning in life. The conservative churches, on the other hand, have maintained a clear sense of meaning through demanding commitment and through a sense of absolutism and required conformity. Thus, they have proved to be more attractive.

Is it true in Australia that the mainline churches have become more relativistic? Have they, in fact, changed so greatly just in the last 30 years? Have not they always allowed more debate and more liberal ideas than some other groups such as the Baptists or Pentecostals? Can the exodus of people from the mainline churches in the last 30 years be explained in terms of changes in those churches over that period of time? Kelley's theories may be able to explain the attractiveness of conservative churches in comparison with liberal churches, but cannot explain why such a sharp increase in nominalism should have occurred in the latter over a relatively short period of time. The differences between the denominations with regard to changes in attendance suggest that these changes may relate to characteristics of the denominations or the ways in which they approach the Christian faith. In England, Robert Towler (1984) identified a number of types of faith through a content analysis of letters written to Bishop Robinson in response to his book *Honest to God*. Towler noted that people who held to different types of faith would regard the church quite differently. Perhaps an analysis of types of faith in the Australian context would hold the key to an explanation of the mainline decline.

Types of faith

The Combined Churches Survey, conducted by the Christian Research Association in 1987 (Blombery and Hughes, 1987), provided an initial opportunity to test these ideas. It was a national survey of church attenders in 98 churches of five denominational groups: Anglican, Baptist, Catholic, Pentecostal and Uniting Church. The survey contained detailed questions about a number of aspects of faith. Rather than asking people for a simple affirmation or denial of belief, it asked what was most important to them in their images of God and Jesus, in the Christian faith, in the ways the Christian faith operated in daily life and in the functions of the church and the clergy.

The data collected in the Combined Churches Survey were examined to see if patterns of responses to these questions about faith could be found. Various statistical methods were used in looking at the data, including principal components analysis. In checking patterns, scales were built and tested for internal coherence. Principal components analysis identified one major distinguishing factor in patterns of belief. This factor had two poles. The strongest variables distinguishing these poles were found in the responses to the question about the ways in which Christian belief is seen to be helpful in everyday life. At one pole, people saw faith as helping them in giving them access to a loving God. For this group, faith was personal and centred upon a relationship with God. At the other pole, people saw faith as helping them primarily by giving them a set of values for life. Among these people there was less emphasis on a personal relationship with God and greater emphasis on the way the Christian faith gives principles or rules by which to live and helps one to see the world. These two types of faith have been labelled 'access religiosity' and 'values religiosity'.

The access and values styles of religiosity can each be divided into two further groups, making a total of four patterns of faith. A description of these four patterns was first published in *Patterns of Faith in Australian Churches* (Hughes and Blombery, 1990). Figure 7.1 summarises the major elements in each pattern.

These four patterns were not exhaustive. Forty-two per cent of the sample scored highly in one or another of these four patterns, affirming the pattern in at least four of the five areas of faith considered. The other 58 per cent of the sample were checked very carefully. However, no other patterns which were distinctive in nature or widespread in adherence could be identified. In many instances it is appropriate to regard people as taking something from one pattern and something from another. The following sketches identify the patterns by pointing out major features and suggesting the connecting logic. They represent what Max Weber termed 'ideal-types' rather than specific individuals.

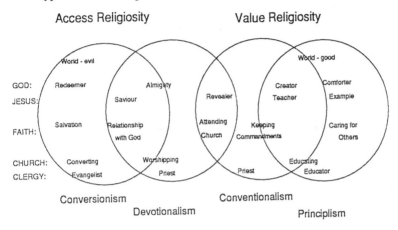

Figure 7.1 Major elements in patterns of faith among church attenders

Conversionists

The first of the two patterns of faith which came under the heading of 'access religiosity' revolved around the idea of conversion. At the centre of this pattern of faith was the experience of having been saved. The people who exemplified this pattern regarded the world as evil and saw themselves as having been saved out of the world. God was seen particularly in the role of redeemer and was significant to them primarily in saving them as individuals from the evil world. Jesus was important to them primarily as saviour: as a primary agent in God's act of redemption. The church was the gathering of the redeemed. It was constituted only of those who had had that experience of being saved from the world. The prime task of the church was the redemption of others, getting others to accept Jesus Christ as lord and saviour. They expected their clergy to lead them in this task. Many of them identified the primary task of the clergy as evangelism.

The church was also important as the centre of the social life of the conversionists. About 70 per cent of them said that they found all or most of their friends in the church. Members of this group felt that services of worship were important in providing guidance and help for daily living. These people stressed the need for a continuing personal relationship with God, whom they expected to intervene in the events of their lives.

The stark categories through which they saw the world and the church
were reflected in the ways in which these people interpreted the Bible.
They had a strongly literalistic view of Scripture and accepted the miracles
in the Bible as having happened just as described.

Devotionalists

A second group which emphasised personal access to God made much less
of the idea of an evil world and of God redeeming people from it.
However, faith was identified as a warm and personal interaction with God.
God was seen as almighty and as a personal friend or ever-present helper.
While Jesus was often referred to as saviour, there were few other
indications that a specific act of redemption was of primary importance to
them. Many identified Jesus as a friend.

Like the conversionists, these people saw God as involved in the events
of everyday life. God was their helper, and they valued God's intervention
in their daily lives. In their prayers, they would seek God's help and
guidance and would ask God to control their situations. They responded to
God appropriately with loyalty and devotion. The label which best
characterises their faith is 'devotionalist'. Church attendance was important
for them as a way of expressing their devotion. Indeed, for some of them,
it was the primary responsibility in the Christian faith. The clergy were
regarded with respect, and many would see them as performing priestly
functions.

In general, devotionalists accepted the traditions of the church that had
been handed down to them. Like the conversionists, they tended to have a
literalistic view of Scripture. But it was not their acceptance of tradition
which marked them off from other Christian groups. Their faith was based
not so much on cherishing the tradition as on a warm personal relationship
with God, involving daily access to God and response in devotion.

Conventionalists

A third group shared with the devotionalists an emphasis on worship,
attendance at services and an identification of the primary role of the clergy
as priestly. However, unlike the devotionalists, this group was of the
second major type in that it saw the Christian faith as helpful primarily in
giving values to live by and standards to hold on to. Many people in this
group identified the most important thing in the Christian life as keeping
the Ten Commandments. For these people, there was a divinely ordained
structure to the world. The Christian duty involved living in accord with
that structure. This meant keeping the Ten Commandments and, for many,
going regularly to church.

The warm, personal relationship with God which characterised the
devotionalists was not prominent in this group. God was considered to be
almighty, but there was little emphasis on having personal access to God.

Jesus was not seen primarily as saviour or friend, but as teacher, example or revealer. The members of this group maintained that the church existed primarily for worship. There was also some emphasis on the church as having the responsibility of teaching people the structure of the world and the corresponding Christian duties of life.

The identifying characteristic of this group was its emphasis on the rules, arising out of the view that there is a preordained structure cosmologically and morally. For the sake of a label, this group might be described as 'conventionalists'.

Principlists

It has been difficult to find a suitable label for the final group. Part of the difficulty arose from the fact that the group lacked precision in its characteristics. Various themes or emphases were found within the group. Unity was found in the fact that the members of this group identified the Christian faith as important to them in daily life because it gave them values to live by and standards to hold on to. However, unlike the previous group, this group identified those values and standards as principles rather than rules. The values were not contained in rules which were seen as part of a great moral structure of reality. The values were expressed in the form of simple principles which would generally promote a better life: that human beings should care for one another, or do to others what they would expect others to do to them.

There was a general belief amongst the members of this group that the world was basically a good place, and that human nature was basically good. In their view, people did not need redemption from the world. Rather they needed education to help them to live within it. If only human beings recognised the basic ethical principle of love, the world would be even better.

There were many conceptions of God found in this group. In general, these were less personal and more nebulous than the images held by those who emphasised personal access to God. God was seen as comforter, as creator or as a spiritual power or presence. Some could say no more than that God was beyond description. Jesus was seen as an example to follow or as a teacher. Jesus taught the basic ethical principle of love for one's neighbour. The church had the task of continuing to teach that principle and helping people to apply it in their lives.

Another theme within this group, frequently intertwined with the first theme, related to the idea of meaning. The Christian faith was seen as offering people an understanding of the world. Human life was seen as purposeful. The function of the church was identified as giving meaning, purpose and direction to life, particularly in times of crisis and at the boundary points in the life cycle. For these people, a major function of the clergy was that of counselling.

Among the principlists, there were those who saw the nature of faith in terms of social rather than personal ethics. For them, the most important thing in the Christian life and the primary function of the church was to work for social justice. The numbers who put the primary emphasis here were very small in our sample, although social justice had some importance alongside personal ethics for a wider group.

Types of faith and mainline decline

How do these patterns of faith which have been identified as being found in the churches today help to explain the decline in attendance at mainline churches over the last 30 years?

Figure 7.2 indicates that there was a strong relationship between frequency of attendance and faith pattern amongst the attenders who responded to the Combined Churches Survey. The principlists were the least frequent attenders of all the groups. In our sample of church attenders, only 8 per cent of the principlists went to church more than once a week, compared with 62 per cent of the conversionists and about 50 per cent of the devotionalists. Twenty-eight per cent of principlists attended less than once a week, compared with only 3 per cent of the conversionists and 5 per cent of the devotionalists. In short, most of the 42 per cent of the sample who scored high in one of the four patterns of faith and who only occasionally went to church were principlists.

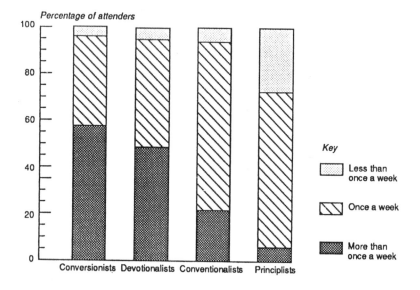

Figure 7.2 Church attendance and faith pattern

In the data from the Combined Churches Survey, differences in the nature of faith provided the best explanation for why some people kept to the fringes of church life while others joined the core (Hughes and Blombery, 1990: 61–80). The fact that most of the people on the fringe were principlists suggests that this may be a pattern of faith common amongst people who are nominal in their adherence to a denomination. It is not necessary, in the principlist pattern of thinking, to attend church frequently. One can maintain Christian principles and do the right thing towards other people without going to church every week. Affirming the great ethical principles of life may be desirable, but it is hardly necessary to do that on a weekly basis in a church service.

Preliminary data from the National Social Science Survey 1989 support the idea that those who do not go to church are more likely to be 'principlist' in their approach to the Christian faith and to see the faith as a way of life rather than as a personal relationship with God. Those who did not attend church identified God primarily as an indefinable spiritual being. Those who went occasionally placed the emphasis on God as creator. The regular attenders affirmed the image of God as redeemer more frequently than any other image. In the same survey, respondents were asked what was important in being a good Christian. In preliminary data, there was wide agreement that belief in God was at the top of the list. Those who never or rarely went to church said, secondarily, that one must keep the Ten Commandments. For frequent attenders, keeping the Commandments was some way down their list of priorities. They put the emphasis on 'having a personal relationship with God'.

In the Combined Churches Survey the reason most frequently given by principlists for attending services of worship was as an opportunity to share with other Christians. Many of the principlists who attended church in 1987, when the survey was conducted, did so not because they regarded it as essential for the maintenance of their faith, but because the church was the centre of their social lives. This was true for a much greater number of people two or three decades ago when, in many places, churches formed important social centres in their local communities. It was in churches that many people found their old friends and made new ones. Businessmen made their contacts. Younger people engaged in sporting or courting activities. Neighbours met. Indeed, many churches helped to maintain the social networks of their local communities. Over the past 30 years, the social reasons for attending church have become less applicable. In most places, but particularly in urban centres, many churches have lost their significance as centres of community life. That has been due not simply to internal factors within churches. Rather, the local community has ceased to have much importance for people. The churches have declined along with other aspects of local community life.

Increased mobility was one of the major factors which has led to the decline in the significance of local community. The last 40 years have seen considerable expansion in the ownership and use of motor vehicles. In 1950, there were 104.4 cars in Victoria for every 1000 people. In 1960, that had risen to 207.8 per thousand. By 1970, it was 312.2 per thousand and most people had access to a car. In 1986, the number had risen to 575.1 per thousand. For most people, it was no longer necessary to be able to walk to shops. Regional shopping centres could be developed. Many other kinds of services could also be regionalised. People could travel to see their friends and it became less important to form friendships within the local community. One could take advantage of the wide variety of sporting facilities available in the wider region, a variety with which the local community could not hope to compete. Sundays first became the day for a pleasant drive. In more recent years, ownership of weekender and holiday residences has increased. People employed outside the home spend very little of their time in their local neighbourhoods during the week, and some people go away at weekends.

Another factor in the decline of local community life was the advent of television. In 1956 the first transmissions began. In the 1960s it became commonplace to find televisions in the home. In the 1970s, black and white television gave way to colour. Television has provided something of a substitute for social activities in the local community.

A third factor is the involvement of women in the workforce. Married women were very important in local community life. They mixed with their neighbours, talking over the fence when they hung out the washing and down the street when they did their shopping. They were often involved in local community organisations. In 1947, only 8 per cent were involved in the workforce. By 1966, 27 per cent were engaged in the workforce and in 1986, it was 49 per cent. Most of those now involved in full-time home duties have either pre-school children or retired husbands. They do not have the same opportunity to engage in local community life. As married women have entered the workforce, they have tended to withdraw from church activities (de Vaus and McAllister, 1987). According to the National Social Science Survey data for 1983, 24 per cent of women involved in home duties attended church, compared with 16 per cent of women in full-time employment (Hughes, 1988b).

Some principlists have remained in the church and many mainline churches contain remnants of local communities. People who made social contacts at church 30 years or so ago and who have not moved from the area continue to attend, although their numbers are declining. Most of these people are now elderly. Indeed, they are hanging on tightly to their churches, because these are the last vestiges of the local community which gave them their social support and something of their identity. In some small rural districts, the church may still have an important role as a community centre. There are sub-groups within the community which revolve around particular youth groups or other social activities a church might organise. But the church, at best, offers only one amongst many centres for social life.

There are also some principlists who see the church as providing opportunities for them to express the Christian ethic in the community. The church is an alternative to Rotary or the Lions Club or other such organisations. Through the church, they feel they express their sense of citizenship and play a constructive role in the lives of other people. However, as the significance of the local community has declined, many principlists have ceased to attend churches. Or perhaps it is more appropriate to say that many people have decreased their frequency of attendance. Some people who formerly went about once a month are now attending once or twice a year.

The attendance of devotionalists at church has not been so greatly affected by changes in the significance of the local community. Their prime purpose in attending church was not to meet their neighbours. They attended in order to have 'communion with God'. They valued the personal relationship they had with God and found the service of worship an opportunity to reaffirm that relationship. Just as a close friendship needs to be maintained through regular communication, so they saw the need for the regular reaffirmation of their relationship with God. In worship, they would listen for God's guidance and direction. They would seek to hear what God had to say to them. This would direct their activities in the following week, or provide them with strength to cope with the events it would hold.

The attendance of conversionists has also not been affected by the decline in the local community, although they have valued the social life of the church. While they have found their friends within the church, they have never expected to find the local community there. Its absence was confirmation that they were different and were special. But they have continued to meet with other people who have had similar experiences of being saved from the evil world. The church has been important for their sense of identity.

Many conventionalists have also continued to attend church, for they have seen it as an important duty. However, according to our data, this group finds most of its support in rural areas and amongst the elderly. There are indications that it is declining in size and in significance. The mass media and multiculturalism are presenting alternative views of the world. It is not easy to maintain the sense of duty in going to church when surrounded by many others who do not share that sense of duty or the same view of the structure of the world.

According to the Combined Churches Survey, conversionists make up a much higher proportion of Baptist and Pentecostal church attenders than of attenders at Anglican, Catholic and Uniting churches. The Baptist and Pentecostal denominations have emphasised the conversion experience and adult baptism as conditions for membership. Principlists, on the other hand, make up a much higher proportion of Anglican, Catholic and Uniting church attenders than of attenders at Baptist and Pentecostal churches.[1] The Anglican, Catholic and Uniting churches have, perhaps unwittingly, encouraged this approach to the Christian faith. The very formality of the liturgy confirms the sense of worship as a celebration of the order of the universe, rather than as an occasion for personal messages from God to individuals. There has been a considerable growth in nominalism in these three denominations in recent decades.

While mobility and the increased segmentation of life that has accompanied it has led to a decline in attendance at mainline churches, it may have indirectly influenced the growth of conversionist churches. With the segmentation of life has come an increasing complexity. Each segment tends to have its own values and behaviour patterns. In each segment, one meets a different group of people. Segmentation provides the opportunity for people to have a much greater number of acquaintances. However, it makes it harder to have friends who share in life beyond that particular segment in which one meets them. In this complexity and changed nature of relationships, it becomes easy for people to fall between the segments. Life becomes too complex and it is hard to find fulfilling, intimate relationships. Conversionism offers very definite guidelines for life and a sense of certainty in a confusing world. It also offers a clearly defined sense of community in which people are committed to each other.

What about secularisation?

It has been argued that the recent decline in attendance of mainline churches between 1966 and 1986 can be explained in terms of the patterns of belief and changes in the nature and significance of local community life. It is not necessary to postulate any major changes in beliefs or a major development in the secularisation of consciousness in Australian society. This argument does not deny the possibility that processes of secularisation may be occurring in Australia and in other Western societies. Historians may well be able to point to long-term changes of consciousness which stem from the Renaissance, in which religious explanations of the cosmos and technologies for working within it have been replaced by scientific ones.

While the decline in church attendance among principlists may not imply a secularisation of consciousness, the growth in the conversionist sections of the church may be indicative of a secularisation of society and culture. The growing conversionist sections of the church seek some degree of disengagement from the wider society, which they see as being fundamentally evil. So, for example, many of them advocate the establishment of separate, Bible-based Christian schools that teach their own particular views. Bryan Wilson has argued (1982: 148–53) that it is the process of secularisation of society and culture which reduces spiritual systems to private affairs, to be treated like consumer items. The disappearance of religion from the local community is part of a disappearance of religion from public culture as a whole. As those members of the society who advocate religious principles become separated from supportive religious institutions, they lose the opportunity to express those principles in a communal way. There is a tendency for religion in Australia to become a concern of the private segment of life and of religious ghettoes. The growth of conversionism in Australian churches, rather than the decline of mainline churches, may be the most powerful indicator of secularisation in our society.

Note

1 This does not imply that principlists make up a majority of Anglican, Catholic or Uniting church attenders. It means, rather, that principlists make up a significant minority there, whereas they are hard to find among Baptist and Pentecostal church attenders.

8 Australian Pentecostalism in comparative perspective
Alan W. Black

The fastest growing churches in Australia are Pentecostal. According to Australian Census statistics, the number of persons associated with them increased from 38 393 in 1976 to 72 148 in 1981 and 107 007 in 1986. Such growth is not a uniquely Australian phenomenon. In most parts of the world, Pentecostal Christianity has been expanding rapidly in recent decades. One might ask why this is so, especially as some other forms of Christianity, such as in 'mainline' or 'oldline' churches, have not been expanding so rapidly—indeed, in many cases these churches have been declining in membership.

Before addressing this question, it is important to indicate what is meant by 'Pentecostal'. The adjective originally referred to an experience on the day of Pentecost, as recorded in the Acts of the Apostles, Chapter 2. On that occasion, the early Christians 'were all filled with the Holy Spirit and began to speak in other tongues, as the Spirit gave them utterance' (Acts 2:4). This was seen as a fulfilment of Jesus' promise that they would be 'baptized with the Holy Spirit' (Acts 1:5) and that they would receive power when the Holy Spirit came upon them (Acts 1:8). Pentecostals stress that this experience of the power of the Holy Spirit was not confined to the early church; it is equally available today and is evidenced not only in glossolalia (i.e. speaking in other tongues) but also in a range of other activities mentioned in the New Testament, such as the occurrence of miracles, supernatural healing, exorcism (i.e. the casting out of demons), prophecy and so forth.

The term 'Pentecostal' is thus a generic word to describe a particular style of Christianity. While it may sometimes appear in the official names of churches, such as the Pentecostal Holiness Church and the United Pentecostal Church, both of which are based mainly in the United States, it also applies to churches with other names, such as the Assemblies of God, Christian Outreach Centre, Christian Life Centre, Christian

Fellowship Centre, International Church of the Foursquare Gospel, Christian City Church, Christian Revival Crusade, Apostolic Church, Full Gospel Church and the like. Forerunners of modern Pentecostalism were present in Australia in the late nineteenth and early twentieth centuries, and some of the existing Pentecostal denominations, such as the Assemblies of God, trace their beginnings in this country to the latter part of that period (Chant, 1984). Until the 1970s, they had only a modest degree of success in attracting members. Then their rate of growth accelerated; additional Pentecostal denominations, such as Christian Outreach Centres and the Christian City Church, also emerged and expanded rapidly.

Like many reformist or revivalist movements in earlier times, Pentecostalism claims to have recovered the full measure of early Christianity. Like other fundamentalists, Pentecostals profess a very literal interpretation of the Bible, and they also stress the importance of being 'born again'. But they see the experience of the baptism of the Holy Spirit as quite distinct from, and usually later than, the experience of being born again, and quite distinct from the experience of baptism in water (which they also administer by immersion after people are born again, denying that any form of infant baptism is valid). Most Pentecostals maintain that the initial evidence of the baptism of the Holy Spirit takes the form of speaking in other tongues, which is thus a highly valued phenomenon. Nevertheless, some Pentecostal denominations (for example, in Chile or certain parts of Europe) believe that the baptism of the Holy Spirit is not always accompanied by this particular sign. According to Hollenweger (1986: 7), in many Pentecostal churches a large proportion of the members, and sometimes even some of the pastors, have never spoken in other tongues. I am not aware of any comparable figures for Pentecostals in Australia. Most, if not all, Pentecostal bodies here profess the 'initial evidence' doctrine, whereas 'charismatics' or 'neo-pentecostals' within mainline denominations are generally less inclined to regard this particular form of evidence as necessary. Nevertheless, the phenomenon of speaking in tongues is often routinised in Pentecostal churches, for example by making provision for 'singing in the Spirit' during their times of worship. This is not usually announced; rather, at a particular stage, perhaps after one of the quieter songs or choruses, the musicians improvise while each worshipper voices a series of sounds or words which may not belong to any Earthly language and which is different from those simultaneously being voiced by other worshippers, but which may harmonise with the music.

There are other respects in which Pentecostal worship is different from that found in most mainline churches. Commonly Pentecostal services— or meetings, as church members prefer to call them—last about two hours rather than one. They generally begin with about 30 minutes of singing, during which a mood appropriate to their style of worship is developed.

Although Pentecostals may occasionally sing traditional Christian hymns, they nowadays usually sing religious songs or choruses in a more popular musical idiom, the words being projected on to a screen and the music being provided by a modern type of instrumental group. Each song or chorus is generally sung two or three times before they proceed to the next. During such singing, the worshippers typically stand with arms upraised, and some may hand-clap or even dance spontaneously on the spot to the rhythm of the music. Further singing usually takes place during and at the end of the meeting.

At some time during the meeting, there is generally a period when anyone can contribute by telling of an experience he or she has had, speaking a word of prophecy or exhortation, engaging in glossolalia while others listen, or offering an interpretation of glossolalia. These activities are largely spontaneous, but there are unwritten norms as to what is appropriate or not. For example, it is generally assumed that at this point no more than one or two people will engage in glossolalia, and that they will not do so simultaneously. It is also considered desirable that, when a person has finished speaking in other tongues, someone else will offer an interpretation of what has been said.

In most Pentecostal churches, the Lord's Supper is celebrated each Sunday morning, though not with a printed liturgy and not requiring the presence of a person ordained to the ministry. The bread and the wine (or grapejuice) are usually distributed to worshippers while they remain in their seats. Preaching at Pentecostal meetings typically lasts about 50 or 60 minutes and is to some extent extemporaneous. Although the preacher has generally prepared by thinking about a particular theme or section(s) of Scripture, he—for the preacher is usually a male—expects that the Holy Spirit will inspire him with the words to speak. This is a time for communication in the vernacular rather than for glossolalia. Indeed glossolalic phenomena are unlikely to take more than a few minutes in any meeting.

After the preaching, if there are people present who may not have had the spiritual experience of being 'born again', they are strongly urged to have such an experience. The preacher may, for example, implore them to indicate their desire for spiritual rebirth by raising their hand while all are praying quietly. Then those who desire such rebirth are asked to come forward so that the preacher can pray with them and ensure that they are counselled by another believer. Often after this, especially in Sunday evening meetings, people seeking healing are invited to come forward. They are then ministered to in various ways. The pastor or other leader, invoking the name of Jesus Christ, may rebuke the evil spirit thought to be responsible for the illness, and order that spirit to depart. In some cases, the pastor or leader may then ask whether the person feels better, and he may repeat the treatment if necessary. While this is happening, other members of the congregation pray fervently for the person seeking healing.

After the pastor or leader has ministered as best he can to any particular person, the next person is dealt with. There are many variations on these procedures. For example, in Christian Outreach Centres the pastor will often announce a 'word of knowledge': God has told him that someone in the congregation has a particular form of illness (e.g. back pain or some form of kidney trouble) and any people in this category are invited to come forward to be ministered to. In the course of dealing with people who come forward with particular needs or seeking further spiritual blessings, Christian Outreach Centre pastors quite often proclaim, in authoritative fashion, an 'anointing' by the Holy Spirit which causes the person to fall backwards into the arms of another member of the congregation who is waiting to lower the person gently to the floor, where he or she can 'rest in the Spirit' or lie 'slain in the Spirit' for several minutes. This particular procedure would seldom, if ever, occur in some other Pentecostal churches. Such differences could be interpreted as arising from different perceptions of the way in which the Holy Spirit works.

Two other common features of Pentecostalism are worth mentioning at this point. The first is the high level of lay participation. Nearly all members attend worship at least once each Sunday, and many attend twice. There are opportunities for various instrumentalists, from pianists to drummers, and from guitarists to saxophonists, to be involved in musical accompaniment, which is an important element of many parts of the meeting. As already noted, neither the consecration nor the distribution of bread and wine in the celebration of the Lord's Supper is the exclusive province of clergy; lay persons may undertake these responsibilities. All members are encouraged to participate in singing (and not merely with their voices), praying, healing and speaking both publicly and privately about God's activity in their lives.

Another common feature of Pentecostal churches is the establishment of house church or home fellowship groups. These are small-group meetings, generally held mid-week in members' homes. Though their activities vary, they generally include a time of praise and worship, testimony about God's activity in members' lives, prayer, ministry to those with particular needs and some form of study or exposition of the Scriptures. Such meetings are seen as additional to, rather than a substitute for, larger-group meetings on Sundays. Though for occupational or other reasons some members might not attend the mid-week meetings, many others do, and this is further evidence of the high level of lay involvement.

Although I have outlined some distinctive features of Pentecostalism, it is important to note that in many of their beliefs Pentecostals are similar to the great majority of other Christians, especially conservative evangelical Christians. Thus they generally affirm the doctrine of the Trinity,[1] the humanity and deity of Jesus Christ, his virgin birth, his sinless life, his atoning death for the sins of the world, his bodily resurrection and his ascension to the Father's right hand. They believe that history will eventually—soon, some would say—culminate in the visible, personal and glorious return of Jesus Christ to reign upon earth. They also stress the power of God to transform lives and to give victory over evil in its various forms.

It is clear that in some respects contemporary Pentecostalism is not a new phenomenon. It is a recent expression of a tendency which has intermittently been evident in the history of Christianity. This tendency has been studied with great insight by Ronald Knox (1950) in his book entitled *Enthusiasm*. The term 'enthusiasm' comes from the Greek *en theos*, meaning 'God-possessed'. Another term which Knox suggests could be applied to the phenomenon is 'ultrasupernaturalism':

> For that is real character of the enthusiast; he expects more evident results from the grace of God than we others. He sees what effects religion can have, does sometimes have, in transforming a man's whole life and outlook; these exceptional cases (so we are content to think them) are for him the average standard of religious achievement. He will have no 'almost-Christians', no weaker brethren who plod and stumble, who (if the truth must be told) would like to have a foot in either world, whose ambition is to qualify, not to excel. He has before his eyes a picture of the early Church, visibly penetrated with supernatural influences; and nothing less will serve him for a model. (Knox, 1950: 2)

Something akin to Pentecostalism was evident not only in the early church at Corinth, but also in later movements, such as among the Montanists in the second century, the Quakers in the seventeenth century, the Methodists in the eighteenth century and the Irvingites in the nineteenth century. Pentecostalism also has some similarities to ecstatic forms of religion found outside Christianity (Douglas, 1970; Lewis, 1971). Nevertheless, contemporary Pentecostalism also has its own particular configuration of attributes.

Explaining the growth of Pentecostalism

Many explanations of the growth of Pentecostalism have invoked, in one form or another, the notion of deprivation. This term is used by Glock (1964: 27) to refer to 'any and all of the ways that an individual or group may be, or feel, disadvantaged in comparison either to other individuals or groups or to an internalised set of standards'. According to Glock (1964: 29), some form of deprivation felt by a significant number of people is a necessary but not a sufficient precondition for the rise of any organised religious or secular social movement. Further necessary conditions are that existing institutional arrangements seem incapable of overcoming the deprivation, and that leadership emerges with an innovative idea for building such a movement. Although Glock's paper does not specifically discuss Pentecostalism, he distinguishes between five types of deprivation: economic, social, organismic, ethical and psychic. He then considers the factors which influence the likelihood of there being a religious or a secular response to such deprivations, and the extent to which these responses eliminate or lessen the particular deprivations.

Other writers, such as Boisen (1939), Holt (1940), Kiev (1964), Calley (1964; 1965), Wood (1965), Gerrard (1970), Pattison (1974) and Anderson (1979) have applied deprivation theory more specifically to Pentecostalism. The fullest such study is Anderson's (1979) *Vision of the Disinherited*, an analysis of the genesis and development of Pentecostalism in the United States from about the turn of the century to the 1930s. He describes the early Pentecostals as people who came from marginal positions in American social, economic and religious life. Both the early leaders and the bulk of their followers were people from rural–agrarian backgrounds, poverty-stricken, sparsely educated, of low social status and suffering, both materially and spiritually, from the effects of modernity. They had generally experienced either the culture shock of moving to urban areas or, in the case of those who remained on the land, the difficulty of adjusting to the rural decay which accompanied the processes of urbanisation and industrialisation.

According to Anderson (1979: 229), the Pentecostal response to these experiences was 'a mixture of millenarianism and ecstasy'. Millenarianism involved a belief that the existing world was thoroughly wicked and beyond human redemption; that it would soon be destroyed by divine intervention and replaced by a new world. This response fitted well with the needs and aspirations of those whose experience of the present world was far from pleasant and who longed for a time when 'the first shall be last and the last shall be first'. In its origin, the word 'ecstasy' comes from *ek stasis*: standing outside oneself. The ecstatic element of Pentecostalism has been evident to some degree in the experience of conversion but supremely in the experience of the baptism of the Holy Spirit.

As Anderson (1979: 231) sees it, glossolalia was a symbolic expression of the early Pentecostals' highly unstable and chaotic social circumstances, conditions over which they had little or no control. He concludes (1979: 232) that 'Ecstatic-millenarianism was central to early Pentecostalism because the Pentecostals self-consciously sought to duplicate that aspect of the life of the early Church, but also because the early Pentecostals stood in much the same relationship to their society as the Apostolic Church had to its.'

Anderson (1979: 227) acknowledges that only a relatively small proportion of the socially and economically deprived in the United States in early decades of this century actually became Pentecostals. He contends that many people who did, including some who were neither poor nor socially alienated, were predisposed to do so as a result of some personal crisis, such as illness, divorce, occupational failure or the death of a relative or friend. If they happened to come into contact with a Pentecostal proselytiser at such a time, this was often sufficient to lead them into the movement. Before World War II, only the socially deprived were likely to have such personal contact with a committed Pentecostal. But, according to Anderson, it was the prior *religious* orientation of the socially deprived who became Pentecostals which most distinguished them from the much larger number of socially deprived who did not. The vast majority of Pentecostal converts came from 'emotional, evangelical, and revivalistic Protestant backgrounds or from the more crudely superstitious forms of Catholicism' (Anderson, 1979: 228). Only later, as they rose in the class structure through processes similar to those analysed by Troeltsch (1931), Niebuhr (1929) and Pope (1942), did Pentecostals succeed in attracting many persons from higher social strata. And, according to Anderson, the 'working poor' still make up a larger proportion of American Pentecostals than of mainline Protestants.

Deprivation theories of religious or social movements have been subject to criticism from both theoretical and empirical angles. Wallis (1975) has argued that generally the number of persons whom one might consider to be experiencing some form of deprivation greatly exceeds the number of those who join such movements. Consequently, some form of deprivation cannot be a sufficient condition in explaining their participation, a fact which, as we have already seen, both Glock and Anderson recognise. This latter comment does not, however, imply that either Glock's or Anderson's formulations of other necessary conditions are adequate; nor does it imply that a particular form of deprivation is necessarily operative among any or all of those who become Pentecostals.

Second, according to Wallis (1975: 361), 'it is hard to avoid the suspicion that a plausible type [of deprivation] can be invented to fit any and every social movement'. Frequently the indicators of various forms of deprivation are ill-defined or tautological. When participation in a movement which offers x is taken as evidence that the participant must previously have been deprived of x, it is obviously tautological to use 'deprivation of x' to explain participation in the movement. While such circular reasoning should certainly be avoided, the notion of deprivation is not necessarily tautological; it should, however, be carefully defined and appropriately applied if it is to be used at all.

Many proponents of the significance of deprivation speak of 'relative deprivation', because such significance relates largely to social actors' *perceptions* of their circumstances, particularly in comparison with those of significant others or with some internalised set of standards. Wallis contends that, although relative deprivation refers to a *felt* or *experienced* disparity, many of those who have used this concept look for evidence in terms of social actors' objective circumstances—rather than their perceptions of these—or in terms of the ideology of the particular movement. Glock's definition, however, allows for both a felt disparity and a perhaps non-perceived but actual disparity to be termed 'deprivation'. Elsewhere I have distinguished between these two connotations, regarding the latter one as an instance of 'situational strain' and the former as an instance of 'affirmed diagnostic-prescriptive ideas' (Black, 1976: 40–3). Circumstances are thus analytically separable from social actors' perceptions of those circumstances, even though empirically they are often closely linked.

Once one has made this analytic distinction, there is still the question of the significance one is to attribute to social actors' accounts of what their situation was prior to their joining a religious movement such as Pentecostalism. On the one hand, informants might not perceive that, say, economic deprivation or social deprivation played a significant part in their joining; on the other hand, they might point to some type of spiritual deprivation they had experienced. Indeed, it is quite common for people who have undergone some form of religious conversion or spiritual awakening to give testimonies of the 'I once was lost, but now I'm found' variety. Without dismissing these out of hand, it is important to note that retrospective accounts are generally shaped to some extent by the 'vocabulary of motive' prevailing within the particular religious movement. Whilst this does not mean that such accounts are necessarily false, it does mean that they need to be placed in their social context. Moreover, to test the significance of either particular circumstances or particular perceptions, one needs a matched control group. Many studies of conversion are deficient in this respect. One study with the necessary degree of methodological sophistication is Heirich's (1977) comparison between neo-pentecostal Catholics and other Catholics. Using various measures of recollected stress or stress-producing circumstances, Heirich found little evidence that such factors increased the likelihood of one's conversion to neo-pentecostalism. By contrast, social networks played a very significant part in such conversion, provided that one was already oriented towards a religious quest. The latter condition could perhaps be interpreted as evidence of a sense of religious or spiritual deprivation, though Heirich does not draw this particular conclusion.

That recruitment to Pentecostalism often occurs on the basis of existing social networks should come as no surprise to anyone who is familiar with church growth theory. The point is nevertheless worth restating, if only because some other theories, such as that Pentecostalism attracts predominantly the socially or economically deprived, do not appear to apply in either Australia or the United States at the present time. Whereas in its early stages Pentecostalism in both these countries attracted mainly people from lower social strata, the recent surge of Pentecostalism has attracted a much wider cross-section of the population. Although, compared to the population at large, Pentecostals in Australia have a slightly lower average level of education, income and occupational status

(Mol, 1985: 18, 89, 170, 173), the differences are not very great, and Pentecostals do not have a higher than average level of unemployment. Moreover, as Pentecostal churches have a much younger age profile than do the longer-established denominations or the wider population, proportionately more Pentecostals have not yet completed their education or reached their full earning potential.

The average level of education among regular attenders is nevertheless somewhat lower for Pentecostals than for the largest Protestant denominations, namely Anglican, Uniting and Presbyterian (Kaldor and Homel, 1988a). One occupational category which the Pentecostals have, however, been noticeably more successful in attracting than oldline denominations comprises persons who describe their occupation as skilled trades or craft work. According to my surveys of adult church participants in Australia,[2] 25.5 per cent of Pentecostal males fall into this category, compared with 10.8 per cent of Anglican males and 14.1 per cent of males in the Salvation Army. Likewise, 27.3 per cent of married Pentecostal females place their spouse's occupation in this category, whereas 17.9 per cent of married Anglican females and 17.4 per cent of married Salvation Army females do so. There is relatively little difference between these denominations in the proportion of participating males who describe their occupational status as that of manual or production process work (10.6 per cent for Pentecostals, 7.2 per cent for Anglicans and 9.1 per cent for the Salvation Army). The proportion of participating married females who describe their husband's occupation in this way is 10.2 per cent for Pentecostals, 11.3 per cent for Anglicans and 21.7 per cent for the Salvation Army.

As was noted by Gerlach and Hine (1968; 1970), the ability of contemporary Pentecostalism to attract persons from a fairly wide cross-section of the population is aided by its relatively decentralised or segmented structure. The predominant mode of leadership is charismatic (in the broad sense of that term) rather than bureaucratic. This provides opportunities for individual initiative, including openings for persons who may lack the formal educational qualifications required for ordained ministry in oldline churches but who feel a strong sense of divine empowerment and calling to Christian ministry. The segmented structure is reflected in the development of several varieties of Pentecostalism, each with its own emphases and potential to appeal to a particular section or sections of the population. Even within the one Pentecostal denomination, the stress on 'openness to the Lord's leading' allows for considerable local autonomy and variation. The net effect of all of this is a much greater degree of dynamism and flexibility than is possible in most oldline denominations. At the same time, the various local units and segments of Pentecostalism are parts of a larger network created and sustained by personal ties between members and between leaders, by shared core beliefs despite some diversity, and by fairly similar styles of worship.

Other features found by Gerlach and Hine (1968; 1970) to be important in the expansion of Pentecostalism are the following:

1 face-to-face recruitment by committed lay members, using pre-existing links of kinship, friendship, neighbourhood, or other forms of close positive association;
2 a strong stress on personal commitment resulting from an identity-altering experience, a bridge-burning act, or both;
3 a belief system which offers certitude, empowerment, a strong sense of identity, and a way of accounting for both good and evil (one could add here that this particular aspect may be one of the reasons for Pentecostalism's attraction to skilled tradespeople, who are generally accustomed to thinking in black-and-white 'how to do it' terms);
4 a measure of real or perceived opposition from the society at large or from existing institutions.

It should be noted that, with the partial exception of the last point, each of these conditions refers to inherent features of Pentecostalism, rather than to broader contextual factors. Gerlach and Hine (1970) discern similar features in some other social movements, such as the Black Power movement in the United States in the 1960s. One must continue to ask, however, whether there are any contextual factors which influence the likelihood of the emergence or the expansion of any particular type of social or religious movement, such as Pentecostalism. The reference by Gerlach and Hine to 'real or perceived opposition' alludes not simply to what Pentecostals sometimes term 'spiritual warfare' (i.e. a struggle with hostile supernatural forces) but also, on occasions, to a degree of conflict between Pentecostalism and other social institutions or sections of society, including other religious denominations. For example, Pentecostals generally oppose what they see as various forms of moral permissiveness, such as pornography, premarital sex, gay liberation and the practice of abortion. Likewise, they are aware that some of their own activities, such as glossolalia or the (re)baptising of adults whom other denominations consider to have already been validly baptised as infants, are frowned upon by such other denominations. As they do not regard the baptism of infants as valid, Pentecostals deny that they practise rebaptism. They admit, however, that some of their practices and emphases are different from those within what they sometimes refer to as 'denominational churches'. This, they say, is because these churches have lost some of the essential characteristics of the early Christian church.

Pentecostalism and contemporary culture

Although Pentecostalism involves a reaffirmation of some relatively unfashionable—one could even say pre-scientific—thought forms and practices, and although it involves a deliberate rejection of some aspects of contemporary culture, in other respects it is closely attuned to that culture.

Writing shortly after the turn of the twentieth century, Max Weber noted the increasing rationalisation of more and more areas of life in modern society. By this he was referring to the systematic formulation and application of principles which could be relied upon to produce predictable outcomes (Kolegar, 1964; Gerth and Mills, 1948: 51–2). Indicative of the process of rationalisation are trends such as the growth of science, of technology, of bureaucracy and of professionalism. The process of rationalisation has also affected churches—for example, in the modification of former beliefs in the light of science, in the development of bureaucratic organisational structures and in the professionalisation of the ministry. In some respects, Pentecostalism represents an antithesis to such trends. In particular, it rejects those scientific theories which appear to be at odds with a literalist reading of the Bible; it eschews the bureaucracy and formalism which it perceives in oldline churches; and it disclaims particular forms of professional exclusiveness accorded clergy in various denominations. On the other hand, Pentecostals show a marked readiness to employ modern technology for religious purposes, to deliberately apply theories propounded by church growth theorists and to accept norms of rationality in most areas of their lives. McGuire's (1982: 212) comments about neo-pentecostal Catholics apply also to most other Pentecostals:

> Although members of such religious groups appreciate nonrational styles of cognition in certain aspects of life, they desire and utilize rational modes in other aspects. They would be upset if the airplane in which they were riding were piloted by a person in a trance, if the job for which they had applied were allotted by divination, if the judge for their court case were not interested in rational evidence but intuited the resulting decision. Thus there is an interesting tension between believing that the supernatural realm does impinge on the events of everyday life (including safe arrival from a journey, getting jobs, and winning court cases) and, on the other hand, the overwhelming lack of certainty as to whether any given situation is so influenced (that is, 'of the Lord').

Furthermore, the day-to-day self-discipline encouraged by their religion typically makes Pentecostals reliable workers in their various occupations. E. P. Thompson (1968: 406) said of the early Methodists: 'Sabbath orgasms of feeling made more possible the single-minded direction of [their week-day] energies to the consummation of productive labour.' Much the same could be said of today's Pentecostals.[3] The emotional and spiritual gratification which Pentecostalism offers in its meetings and through its fellowship serves as a counterbalance to the instrumental rationality and discipline demanded in the world of work.

Bernice Martin (1981) has argued that in recent decades, especially during the late 1960s and the 1970s, the Western world experienced a significant cultural change which, following Talcott Parsons, she terms 'the expressive revolution'. This revolution began as a counter-cultural movement involving a relatively small number of middle-class radicals committed to ideals of individualism, self-expression, self-determination, and the welcoming of perpetual change within society. Such Romantic ideals were opposed to Classical principles of formality, rationality, hierarchy, ritual and tradition. Eventually many of the Romantic values became woven into the fabric of our culture, although by the mid-1970s it was clear that the techno-economic and political orders were going to make only limited concessions in this direction. According to Martin, the main vehicles through which the revolution occurred were the youth culture and rock music, and its most lasting effects have been in the fields of leisure and cultural consumption.

Insofar as it opposes moral permissiveness and upholds patriarchy, Pentecostalism is at odds with the expressive revolution. But in many other respects it is in harmony with that revolution. Indicative of this are its stress on self-validating experience; informality in dress, forms of worship and interpersonal relationships; spontaneity, immediacy and instant (religious) gratification; anti-intellectualism; some degree of ecstatic or expressive disorder; involvement of the body; excitement and novelty; the use of popular rather than classical musical forms; and, in characteristics such as these, a deliberate contrast with more conventional religious institutions.

Another way in which Pentecostalism differs from some such institutions lies in its anti-sacerdotal rhetoric. Pentecostalism proclaims that charisma is not confined to the few: it is available to all. This emphasis is consonant with the anti-hierarchical and anti-ritualistic aspects of the expressive revolution. Whereas authoritative speech in many secular and some religious contexts is reserved for those duly trained and authorised, Pentecostalism provides opportunities for the untrained and unauthorised to declare, pronounce and direct (Fenn, 1982: 119). On the other hand, there is a form of spiritual elitism in the implicit and sometimes explicit claim that those who have not received the baptism of the Holy Spirit as evidenced in glossolalia are second class Christians. Pentecostals have not eliminated ritual requirements; they have simply substituted one form of ritual for another. Moreover, many Pentecostals invest their leaders with an authority far greater than that accorded by members of other Protestant denominations to their own clergy. In my surveys of adult church participants, I found that 77.2 per cent of Pentecostals agree with the statement that 'God gives various church leaders authority over other members'. Among Anglicans and members of the Salvation Army, the only denominations for which I have comparable information, the corresponding figures are 39.6 and 52.8 per cent respectively. It should be noted that the exercise of authority over Pentecostal members depends heavily upon their consent; it is not absolute. Nevertheless, the belief in divinely ordained authority serves as a buttress to a form of hierarchy. Lacking constitutional limits, such authority can become quite potent and, on occasions, somewhat arbitrary. Disputes over authority can also be reasons for division within the Pentecostal movement.

There are other aspects of the human condition in contemporary societies to which Pentecostalism appears to be particularly attuned. It promises clear direction, moral and spiritual power and a sense of community in the face of the moral ambiguity, powerlessness and absence of community felt by many in our society. In these respects Pentecostalism is fairly similar to some other religious movements which have also been growing in recent decades, such as the Jehovah's Witnesses. An important factor in this growth is the strong sense of meaning and belonging which each movement, in its own particular way, provides (Kelley, 1972; Mol, 1976; 1985). Pentecostalism, which has had the fastest rate of growth, is especially success oriented. Its general mode of operation, including its stress on the individual believer's being open to the leading and empowerment of the Holy Spirit, both encourages and provides scope for a form of spiritual entrepreneurialism. The 'prosperity doctrine' taught by many Pentecostals appeals to those who wish to be materially as well as spiritually successful.[4] My surveys show that 80.2 per cent of Pentecostals believe that 'the Christian who gives one-tenth of his or her income to God will certainly prosper financially'. This belief is based mainly upon their interpretation of a few verses in the last book of the Old Testament: Malachi 3:8-10. The distinctive emphasis given to this prosperity doctrine by Pentecostals is clear when one finds that only 15.6 per cent of Anglicans and 42.4 per cent of members of the Salvation Army believe likewise. Whether tied to a prosperity doctrine or not, many growing churches teach the duty of tithing (i.e. giving one tenth of one's income to the church). In addition to being one indicator that people's religious commitment is more than a token one, tithing makes resources available to develop, sustain and expand Pentecostal churches. Such churches can maintain a higher ratio of pastors to people than is possible in oldline churches. This fact, coupled with the strong Pentecostal emphasis upon outreach and pastoral care by lay persons, means that Pentecostals are much less likely than members of oldline denominations to feel forgotten or uncared for by the pastor or by other church members. Pentecostals are also more likely to feel that they have a vital part to play in the life of their church.

Another distinctive element of Pentecostalism is its emphasis upon supernatural healing. Whereas only 19.4 per cent of Anglicans and 27.8 per cent of members of the Salvation Army believe that 'if people have sufficient faith in God, every illness can be healed miraculously', 65.6 per cent of Pentecostals endorse this proposition. Although this might seem to be an anachronistic belief in the light of the unprecedented achievements of science and technology in the modern world, there nevertheless remains a range of human ailments for which there is no satisfactory medical treatment. Some of these, like AIDS and certain forms of cancer, are life-threatening and have clear organic characteristics. Others are not necessarily life-threatening, and they may have much vaguer symptoms. The body's self-defence and recuperative mechanisms enable a large number of ailments to be overcome without any form of medical intervention. A person's attitudes and behaviour can also be important factors in the process of healing, whether aided by medical intervention or not. The persuasiveness of an authoritative person, the emotional catharsis of religious conversion or spiritual awakening, consequential changes in lifestyle or relationships, relief from stress and confidence that healing is now occurring can all assist in the healing process, especially for ailments that are not life-threatening.[5] Reports of supernatural healing or an improved condition occur with sufficient frequency among Pentecostals to convince them that God still performs 'signs and wonders'. When an earnestly desired healing does not take place, they have various ways of accounting for this (see, for example, Wimber and Springer, 1986: 159–78).

Concluding comments

Douglas (1970) has argued that ecstatic or 'effervescent' forms of religion such as Pentecostalism tend to be reflections of social situations which are somewhat anomic or unstructured. By contrast, Lewis (1977: 12) maintains that 'the ecstatic style of religiosity is typically a response not to lack of structure, but to an oppressive excess of it'. It would be an over-simplification, however, to regard contemporary Pentecostalism in Australia as predominantly an ecstatic religion. Nor should Pentecostalism here be interpreted simply as a reflection of an unstructured social situation or as a compensatory response to an oppressively structured social situation. Contemporary society is characterised both by a relatively high degree of structuring in the work sphere, and a much less structured situation in the sphere of leisure and cultural consumption. In its present forms of worship, Pentecostalism reflects many of the characteristics of popular culture, at the same time compensating for the processes of rationalisation, regulation and perhaps impersonality in the techno-economic order. Nevertheless, Pentecostalism's black-and-white belief system and its strict code of personal morality generally mesh with the 'culture of control' which dominates the techno-economic order, while they are also a reaction against the scepticism and moral ambiguity that are evident in many areas of life. So, for example, Pentecostalism's reassertion of male authority is part of its attraction to those who lament the blurring of traditional gender roles.

Pentecostalism in Australia has generally toned down or moved away from some of the more ecstatic elements such as convulsions, trance-like states, uncontrolled shouting, jumping, rolling on the floor and similar phenomena found among some of the early Pentecostals as well as among some Pentecostals now in Africa, Latin America and parts of Asia, or in ethnic minority situations in various countries (Boisen, 1939; Bloch-Hoell, 1964; Anderson, 1979; 1987). For most Pentecostals in Australia, even the definitive experience of glossolalia has become routinised or ritualised: a case of 'organised spontaneity'. There are nevertheless some variations in style and emphasis from one Pentecostal church to another. The older Pentecostal denominations, such as the Assemblies of God, are now generally less sensational in the style of their meetings than are some of the newer ones, such as Christian Outreach Centres or the Christian City Church. The ethos of these newer groups of churches is a reflection not only of the personal orientation of the founder of each particular group but also of the fact that these churches have not yet proceeded so far down the path of institutionalisation and the routinisation of charisma.

Notes

1   The United Pentecostal Church is an exception at this point (Chant, 1984: 205).
2   Here and in later paragraphs I draw on the results of a survey questionnaire sent to every fifth adult on the membership lists of fifteen Pentecostal churches in New South Wales. Seven of these churches were Assemblies of God, five were Christian Outreach Centres, two belonged to the International Church of the Foursquare Gospel, and one was a Christian City Church. For comparative purposes, similar data were collected from representative samples of Anglicans and members of the Salvation Army. The Anglicans were drawn randomly from within nine parishes in the Diocese of Sydney and ten parishes in the Diocese of Newcastle, giving approximately equal numbers from each diocese. The Salvation Army sample was drawn randomly from available corps directories throughout New South Wales and the Australian Capital Territory. There were 500 usable questionnaires returned by Pentecostals, 263 by Anglicans and 320 by members of the Salvation Army—effective response rates of 69 per cent, 64 per cent and 62 per cent respectively. Additional information on Pentecostal churches in Australia is contained in Black (1990b).
3   For an insightful comparison between early Methodism and contemporary Pentecostalism in Latin America, see Martin (1990).
4   This might be another part of the attraction of Pentecostalism to skilled tradespeople, especially if they are self-employed. Further research is needed on this.
5   For a discussion of the work of non-medical healers and comparisons with medical practitioners, see Easthope (1985).

9 By what authority? An analysis of the locus of ultimate authority in ecclesiastical organisations
Gary D. Bouma

As religious groups cope with change in membership, the application of faith to life, the definition of central beliefs, questions of liturgical innovation or new structures, the issue of authority becomes very important. As such issues as the ordination of women, new forms for the prayer book, difficult issues such as questions of the right to life, lifestyle and the right to die with dignity are raised and discussed, appeals will be made to various types of authority. While each type of authority is evident to some degree in any church, different denominations of the Christian church and different sub-groups within these denominations appeal to one type of authority more than another. Moreover, each denomination has one type of authority base which is ultimate in the sense that it is the final court of appeal, the ultimate arbiter of disputes.

All organisations have a cultural aspect which can be seen clearly in the legitimations given for the existence and purpose of the organisation or in the arguments marshalled for or against change in the activities or structure of the organisation. While, in the day-to-day administration of an organisation, a variety of authority styles may be employed and various pragmatic considerations may serve adequately to legitimate decisions, the ultimate principle of legitimation or the locus of ultimate authority is seen most clearly when an organisation is under threat or when what is considered to be a major change is suggested. When there is serious conflict in an organisation, it is possible to observe the legitimations to which the several factions appeal to support their views, and the bases of ultimate authority which are invoked in order to settle disputes.

Ecclesiastical organisations typically emphasise one of three distinct types of legitimation or authority. Elsewhere (Bouma, 1991) it is argued that these styles of authority are related to different modes of religious transcendence, since the appeal to authority is always an appeal to

121

something which transcends the group or organisation. Whether these three types exhaust the range of observable bases of legitimacy is not known. These three forms can be distinguished and observed in Christian religious organisations. Once the three types of authority are identified, existing denominations can be located within a triangular space using each type as one of the points of the triangle. In addition, tensions between dominant sub-modes of authority can be identified and historical trends noted.

The issue of authority in formal organisation has not received much systematic attention from sociologists since Weber. Such issues as ultimate authority and ultimate legitimation in organisational life have received even less. Most sociological analyses of formal organisations focus on structural aspects of the organisation to the neglect of cultural aspects. The question quickly shifts from what form of authority is used to the question of where the exercise of control is located. The discussion of authority quickly becomes a consideration of legitimate power, precluding a consideration of differences in types of legitimation, or loci of authority. Although authority and legitimate power are related, they are analytically distinct. The distinction is fundamentally that between a structural analysis of an organisation and a cultural analysis.

The major source of data for this chapter is the author's experience as a religious professional in eight different denominations in four different countries. This experience has included service under each of the three main types of ecclesiastical authority. While it was not planned in advance as a participant observation study of the operation of ecclesiastical organisations, this has in fact been the result. Participating in the debates of various ecclesiastical governing bodies—synods, presbyteries, parish or diocesan councils, etc.—as well as attending committees, advising planning boards and engaging in the ministry of these different denominations is one of the best ways to begin to assess differences among religious groups. In addition to my personal exposure to these data, the perceptions have been corroborated by student reports (for twenty years students in my sociology of religion classes have been required to attend and report on a variety of religious services) and by lengthy discussions with clergy groups, sociologists of religion and parishioners.

Weber on authority

Weber (1947: 328) delineated three types of legitimate authority—rational, traditional and charismatic—depending upon the basis of their claims to legitimacy. Such claims may be based on:

'1. Rational grounds— ... a belief in the 'legality' of patterns of normative rules and the right of those elevated to authority under such rules.'

In fact, the ground of rational authority is reason, a belief that reason transcends human affairs and provides a source of objective or trustworthy legitimation. Appeals are made to reason to arbitrate disputes, to legitimate decisions and to authenticate action. In this case, Weber identifies one of the styles of authority but quickly moves to an analysis of one of its manifestations—law and the lawful exercise of power.

'2 Traditional grounds— ... belief in the sanctity of immemorial traditions and the legitimacy of the status of those exercising authority under them.'

Traditional authority is grounded in a belief in the sanctity of the ways things have been done by the organisation. Present action is guided by, judged according to and legitimated by reference to the past. Proposed changes are opposed because 'we have never done such a thing before'.

'3 Charismatic grounds— ... devotion to the specific and exceptional sanctity, heroism, or exemplary character of an individual person ... '

The ground of charismatic authority is in the emotions, in the subjective feelings of persons. Charismatic authorities have their authority, like other authorities, because it is given to them by others. In the case of charismatic leaders, it is because of the responses they evoke in others. Charismatic leadership is only one example of the operation of charismatic authority. When appeals are made to feelings, to subjective states, to the emotions, in order to defend action, to legitimate a claim or to oppose change, a charismatic authority style is being used.

Weber's discussion of authority proceeds in terms of systems of imperative co-ordination, rather than systems of legitimacy. That is, he quickly moves to the structural implementation and location of authority rather than completing his discussion of the cultural location of these three styles of authority. Thus rationality becomes legality and an appeal to law rather than an appeal to reason as the basis of authority. Similarly, traditional authority is described in terms of traditional structures of imperative co-ordination rather than cultural systems in which appeal to tradition is used to legitimate claims. Charismatic authority is described in terms of charismatic leaders as opposed to a cultural system in which reference to feelings and emotions is used to legitimate decisions, actions and instructions. Weber elaborates this typology with respect to the emergence of bureaucratic formal organisation and emphasises the tendency toward rational–legal bases of organisational authority in the formal organisations emerging at the beginning of this century.

While Weber's typology is given frequent credal assent in sociological analysis, it has not been used to analyse the cultural locus of authority in organisations. This may have been due to Weber's preoccupation with rational–legal authority. Moreover, Weber seems to argue that with the emergence of modern capitalist industrial society there has been a major, unidirectional shift from traditional to rational–legal bases of authority, with occasional eruptions of charismatic authority. This assumption is not uncommon among students of modernisation and formal organisation. This tendency has lead to an impoverished use of Weber's insight into the fundamental types of authority. More recently, the assumption of a unidirectional, irreversible shift towards rationalisation in processes of modernisation has been subject to increasing criticism.

In fact, Weber's three types of authority base (reason, tradition and emotion) provide a very useful basis for analysing authority in formal organisations, particularly those formal organisations which deal with the development, promulgation and application of meaning. They are particularly useful in the analysis of the authority styles of different denominations of the Christian church. While they may also apply to other organisations, only their application to denominations of the Christian church is explored here. Others have indicated that the typology developed here could easily apply to other religious groups as well.

Three types of ecclesiastical authority

The formal organisations of Christian denominations are usually classified into one of three distinct types: episcopal, presbyterial and congregational. While it will be argued that these correspond to Weber's three types of authority, the terms refer to the structure of governance in the organisation rather than to the location of authority itself. Locus of authority refers to the source of ultimate legitimation in the organisation, to a cultural aspect of organisational life rather than a structural one. To what does the organisation refer to legitimate itself, to explain the actions of its officials, to settle disputes or to describe what it does when it is undertaking its most important activity?

Weber's 'traditional authority' is most characteristic of 'episcopal' ecclesiastical structures. Power and authority are vested in bishops. Conflict is resolved by reference to tradition. Obedience is a key element in submitting to this authority: obedience to superiors, to the way things have (always) been done, to the wisdom of the ages. The focus of worship in an episcopal ecclesiastical organisation relying on traditional authority is on the sacraments, which are seen to be objectively valid independent of any personal characteristics of the priest or recipient. The chief duty of the Christian in this system is to receive the sacraments at the hand of a correctly ordained celebrant who correctly and objectively dispenses grace through the sacramental system. Major issues faced by this type of organisation include *how* to do the sacred things and *who* is to be allowed to do them. Central concern will be with orthopraxy, doing the sacred things correctly (i.e. the way they have been done in the past).

The most significant contemporary issues facing episcopal ecclesiastical organisations relying on traditional authority, those raising the most dust, will centre on the liturgy—new words for the Mass, the language of the Mass and the ordination of women. Disputes are settled by reference to tradition. Cranmer argued that he was returning to the practice of the early church and the wisdom of the early church fathers in order to legitimate his changes to the Latin Mass. The defenders of the new Australian Prayer Book argued that it more faithfully set forth the traditional liturgy of the church. Those who oppose the ordination of women argue that the church has not done so for nearly 2000 years, so why start now. The fact that those in favour need to find another basis for their argument than tradition may help to explain why the ordination of women has proceeded first in those denominations employing a different form of ultimate authority. It is interesting in this context to note that one of the current developments in women's spirituality and understanding of Christian faith is the rediscovery of the role of women in the church over the past 2000 years and attempts to reconstruct the views and actions of Jesus and the early church with respect to women. Was Paul in competition with female missionaries? Did Jesus have female disciples? Did the early church have female leaders, including deacons and priests? Were abbesses bishops? Did they celebrate the Mass? If any of these questions can be answered in the affirmative then there exists a 'traditional' basis for the contemporary argument in favour of the ordination of women.

With the Protestant Reformation/revolution of the sixteenth century, two new loci of authority emerged. While they had probably existed in the church beforehand, they emerged at this time as organisationally distinct bases of ultimate authority. These new loci of ultimate authority were required on the one hand to legitimate the revolt against the traditional authority and episcopal organisation of the Catholic church. On the other hand they were needed to provide the basis for internal control and legitimation for the new denominations formed. While both of these new forms may be seen as early as the sixteenth century, the nineteenth and twentieth centuries have witnessed the fullest effloresence of these types of authority to this time. While early in this century it could be assumed, as was particularly the case in centres dominated by Protestant scholarship, that these new forms would come to dominate ecclesiastical organisation, this assumption is far less clear now.

The first of these alternative loci of authority is rational–legal authority. In their revolt against traditional authority, Protestants appealed much to reason, to correct interpretation of sacred texts and to right belief in order to legitimate their demands for change. If one were to reject the authority of the bishop it was necessary to find another basis of authority than tradition. Reason as an objective or transcendent means for judging the correctness of interpretation of the sacred texts was claimed to be a higher authority providing an ample basis for disagreeing with and even disobeying the bishop. Similar arguments were heard among those who revolted against the monarchs of the time.

The form of church polity which was developed among these new denominations relying on rational authority has been labelled 'presbyterial'. The means of governance is the presbytery—a regional body comprised of clergy and lay delegates from local congregations. Clergy appointments are ratified by the presbytery, candidates for ordination are examined by the presbytery and ordained by the presbytery. Decisions are taken by majority (or greater) vote after careful debate concerning the theological and Biblical bases for the several possible courses of action.

In this system the chief duty of the Christian is to believe correctly, to subscribe to the right theology. Orthodoxy is the key issue; heresy, wrong thinking, is the greatest danger. In a rational/legal presbyterial denomination the sacraments are symbolic acts with quasi-legal contractual (covenant) connotations. All action is legitimated by appeal to the Scriptures and the creeds. Deviants are dealt with by heresy trials. Those found to hold heretical beliefs might subsequently establish another denomination centred on variations in theological interpretation.

In a denomination characterised by presbyterial church order and reliance on rational/legal authority, clergy are selected and ordained primarily on the basis of proper training in theology. Academic degrees from the right places are important. While in a denomination characterised by traditional authority, respect is given according to position, in a rational/legal authority system respect is earned by virtue of the demonstrated ability to think, argue and teach. The ability to use reason skilfully in the interpretation and application of the sacred texts and creeds is paramount. Denominations in this tradition emphasise preaching as the central element in worship and treat the rewriting of creeds as the most important kind of change. While those in traditional authority structures may make changes in their prayer books and missals, those in a rational/legal system fight over creedal changes. In this context it is interesting to note that the basis of union drawn up for the formation of the Uniting Church in Australia is a doctrinal statement.

Debates in rational/legal presbyterial denominations take the form of arguments over interpretation of scripture and creeds. In conservative circles this takes the form of proof-texting from the inerrant Word of God, while in liberal circles it takes the form of higher Biblical criticism, form criticism and socio-historical contextual interpretation. The issue of the ordination of women centres more on their fitness to preach. Will they be heard with authority? The debate is settled by reference to scripture, confession and theological argument. Those against appeal to the scriptures, citing in particular certain of the seemingly misogynist statements of St Paul. Those in favour appeal to the more inclusive and irenic passages of St Paul and argue that reason is to be used in the application of sacred texts to contemporary life and that any sense of social justice which has its roots in the teachings of Christ by logical extension requires the ordination of women. The use of reason as an ultimate basis of authority is clearly evident.

The third type of authority is charismatic authority. Whereas the first challenge to the traditional authority of episcopally ordered denominations was based on an appeal to reason, the second challenge is based on an appeal to emotion, subjective feeling. With the rise of Methodism in the eighteenth and nineteenth centuries, and the philosophy of Schleiermacher and others, emphasis on feelings as a basis for authority emerged. There had been elements of this in the pietistic elements of the Protestant Reformation. For an institution relying on charismatic authority, the ultimate test is 'does it feel right': what is the subjective assessment (gut feeling) about this issue? Is the right emotion evoked? Is the emotional response what it should be? If it does not feel good or right, then it is not. The charismatic leader is one who evokes in followers the reaction of trust, the right emotional response, a willingness to give over responsibility, a feeling of being in the presence of someone who has notable personal qualities.

The management structure associated with charismatic authority is congregational. The local congregation is the seat of decision making. It owns its own property and hires and fires its clergy. The pastor serves at the will of the congregation, which determines the terms of employment and pays the salary directly, so long as the goods (right feelings) are produced. The local congregation may delegate certain responsibilities to regional boards, but it retains the right to determine its own pattern of belief, worship and ministry. Clergy are selected on the basis of the reaction they evoke in the congregation. Do they show the signs of the spirit?

Services of worship in a denomination characterised by charismatic authority are conducted to evoke an inward, subjective, emotional response. There is much use of music, dynamic presentations and creation of mood. The chief duty of the Christian is to feel: to feel convicted of sin, to feel the release of salvation, to feel good, to feel at peace with God, to be in touch with a subjective, inward certainty. There is much criticism amongst those in charismatic denominations of the dead formalism of traditional liturgy or of the cold 'head' religion of rational/legal denominations. The sacraments in this tradition are neither objective nor symbolic, but evocative acts and stamps of approval—you have shown your faith and thus feel good.

Issues in denominations characterised by charismatic authority tend to centre on persons. Is that person fit for the job? Does that person qualify? The issue of the ordination of women is decided on whether particular women have the required gifts of the spirit. In the nineteenth century it was among denominations characterised by charismatic authority that women were first allowed to be clergy. There was no tradition to overcome, nor was it necessary to devise rational arguments; it simply felt right.

Thus among ecclesiastical organisations there can be seen to be three sources to which appeal for ultimate legitimacy is made: tradition, reason and emotion. In general, episcopally governed religious organisations like the Catholic, Orthodox and Anglican Churches locate ultimate authority in tradition. Denominations with presbyterial systems of government such as the Presbyterian, the Uniting and the Reformed Churches rely on rational authority. Finally, denominations following a congregational system of government such as Pentecostal assemblies, Adventist, Baptist and Holiness groups are examples of churches which rely on charismatic authority.

It is probably true that the most effective leadership in any ecclesiastical organisation will employ all three types of authority. Certainly aspects of each can be seen to operate in many situations. This, however, should not cloud the issue of the location of ultimate authority. Ultimate authority is invoked to settle disputes, or to legitimate what is done that is different from other denominations, or to describe what the organisation does when it is undertaking the most important thing it does. Thus, while effective leadership may require the use of all three, each denomination and tradition will regard one style as ultimate.

A large number of other distinctive features of denominations cluster around these three types of authority. For example, architecture follows authority style. Whereas the central feature of a church building in a denomination characterised by traditional authority will be the altar, and in one characterised by rational/legal authority will usually be the pulpit, in a church building of a denomination characterised by charismatic authority it will usually be an organ or a platform. Charismatic congregations will have the latest sound systems, and ample provision for choirs, musical ensembles and the like.

Similarly, the body is treated in different ways in each tradition of authority. In charismatic services there will be room to move, to be expressive, to join the feeling. Indeed it is almost as impossible to sit quietly in a charismatic service as it is to move at all in a presbyterial one, while all movement in traditional liturgical services is carefully controlled and highly symbolic. In services of worship characterised by rational authority, listening to the sermon is all-important. The body is immobilised in long straight pews before the pulpit. The sacrament of communion is brought to the worshipper. At most the worshipper will stand to sing the hymns. There is more movement in traditional liturgical services. The worshipper moves from the pew toward the altar to kneel in order to receive the sacrament. These actions signify an obedient movement toward the mystery and a submission before the mystery. The long nave and deep sanctuary of the traditional church, indicating mystery and that there is more and more still beyond what can be seen, develops in architecture the idea that the object of faith is beyond the limits of the mind. Contrast this with the flat back wall of the typical church building in a denomination relying on rational authority. In rational services of worship there is little emphasis on mystery, and emotion is suspect. What you see is what you get.

Table 9.1 delineates characteristics commonly associated with each type of ultimate authority.

Table 9.1   Related characteristics of ecclesiastical organisations

	Locus of ultimate authority		
Characteristic	Tradition	Reason	Emotion
1 Basis of authority of clergy and leaders	Properly ordained and installed	Properly trained	Evokes right feeling
2 Basis of respect	Position	Ability to think, argue, teach	Ability to evoke feeling
3 Title of religious professional	Priest	Minister/ preacher	Pastor
4 Central element in worship	Sacrament	Sermon	Mood/music
5 Central architectural focus	Altar	Pulpit	Platform/ organ
6 Action of leader	Dispense grace	Preach	Evoke feelings
7 Response sought from people	Acceptance of grace	Assent to orthodox beliefs	Feelings of being saved
8 Theological primacy given to	The Father	The Son	The Holy Spirit
9 Salvation comes by	Receiving the mystery/ obedience	Believing the right doctrine	The experience of being born again
10 Treatment of the body	Ritual movement	Rigid restraint	Free to move
11 Polity	Episcopal	Presbyterial	Congregational

Weber's three types of authority are useful in delineating differences among ecclesiastical organisations both now and through history. This typology corresponds with a number of other commonly observed characteristics of denominations of the Christian church. Given the way other differences cluster around the three loci of ultimate authority, it becomes clear that differences in locus of authority are fundamental differences. Authority in organisations is a major issue. Co-ordination and control need to be legitimated. The overall purpose and administrative style of an organisation require powerful legitimation in order to maintain effectiveness. This is all the more true in ecclesiastical organisations, particularly as they increasingly become voluntary associations. Differences in locus of ultimate authority are more basic than type of administrative order, architecture or theology. These differences are related to differences in transcendence, differences in the way in which religions perform their most basic task, that of sacralisation, relating the now to the eternal, the everyday to that which is beyond, the passing to the abiding. In history the selection of a 'new' locus of authority was the precondition to the rise of the denominations associated with the Protestant Reformation and indeed was the factor which forced the separation of the movements associated with that reformation from the Catholic Church. Rational and charismatic loci of authority began as, and continue to be, 'protest' styles of authority.

Toward a dynamic triangular typology

To this point Weber's typology has been applied to ecclesiastical organisations and found to be a of sensitising heuristic value in organising some concepts pertaining to the ecclesiastical structures of Christian churches. Two further developments of this typology are possible at this stage. First, the typology developed using Weber's types to differentiate three very different loci of authority can be transformed into a dynamic typology by using the three loci to define a triangular space in which each point of the triangle represents one of the three styles of authority. Secondly, the typology can be further clarified by locating in this triangular space specific examples of ecclesiastical organisation.

The three loci of authority are each unique and distinct from the other two in such a way that, when taken together, they define not a continuum between two points but a triangular space within which specific instances of ecclesiastical organisation can be located. While all three loci of authority are identifiable in any denomination, one will be relied on to provide the ultimate base of authority. Denominations are classified in Figure 9.1 on the basis of the ultimate authority which is relied on.

The Catholic and Orthodox churches are the clearest examples of denominations locating ultimate authority in tradition. The Anglican

Church is located between traditional and rational loci because there is a continuing tension between these two authorities in Anglicanism. It is closer to the tradition corner of the triangle because that is the mode of authority resorted to in the final analysis. The Reformed and Presbyterian Churches are the most familiar Australian examples of churches relying on rational authority. The Mormons and Christian Scientists are added because they are 'religions of a book' and rely on reason for settling disputes.

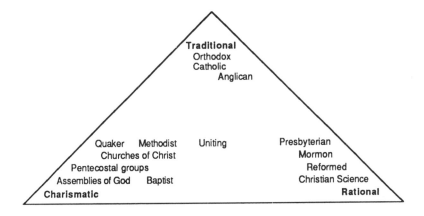

Figure 9.1 A triangular typology of the locus of authority: locations of specific denominations

The Assemblies of God and other Pentecostals are the clearest examples of denominations (or groups of congregations) relying on charismatic authority. The Quakers are placed here because of their reliance on the 'inner light', the witness of the spirit within each member. Disputes are settled only when all members feel the same way, not by resorting to rational argument and debate, or by reference to authority, but through quiet individual meditation. The Methodists were one of the first major denominations to rely on charismatic authority. John Wesley was a charismatic leader who emphasised the feeling aspects of conversion and was not ashamed of enthusiasm. Subsequently there have been tendencies towards traditional authority (in some countries Methodists have bishops) and towards rational authority, but these are devolutions from the initial genius of Methodism. Similar reasons apply for the location of the Baptists and Churches of Christ.

The Uniting Church is located mid-way between charismatic and rational authority because it is a merger of denominations which have relied formerly on these two bases of authority. Issues of authority and decision making are being worked out at this time.

The typology can be used to identify tensions and trends within denominations as well. Australian Anglicans provide a very useful case in point. The Anglo-Catholic wing of the Anglican Church maintains commitment to traditional authority. Evangelical Anglicans, in particular 'Sydney' style Anglicans, tend very much towards the use of rational authority. In the Sydney diocese, the traditional authority of the bishops is used to enforce doctrinal and liturgical conformity. Meanwhile, the charismatic movement has introduced a strong leaning towards charismatic authority in some Anglican congregations. As a denomination, traditional authority is still the type of ultimate authority relied on.

The larger culture within which any denomination operates will also have a tendency to favour one sort of authority. Britain and the Commonwealth have tended to favour traditional authority. Reason and emotion continue to be 'protest' styles of authority. In contrast, the United States favours charismatic authority. The largest denominations are charismatic in authority structure. In the broad sweep of American history there was a general shift from the traditional to the rational until the Revolution, rational until World War I and charismatic since. Australian culture poses an interesting mix. Part of the Commonwealth and still related to the monarchy, Australia (particularly under Menzies) has tended toward the affirmation of traditional authority. However, Bob Hawke is nothing if not charismatic, making appeals to the feelings of the electorate to win support for his policies. He leaves the rational to Paul Keating.

Three styles of ultimate authority have been delineated following Weber's initial insight into the nature of authority in organisations. Ecclesiastical organisations can be seen to rely predominantly on tradition, reason or emotion as ultimate bases of authority to arbitrate disputes, to legitimate the activities of the organisation and to either promote or resist change. These styles of authority are related to other features of ecclesiastical organisation and have potential application to other organisations as well.

10 Radical subjectivity in 'self religions' and the problem of authority[1]

Rachael Kohn

Amidst the efflorescence of religious activity in the 1970s and 1980s, the human potential movement attracted the attention of many sociologists of religion eager to explain the social significance of its putative emphasis on the self. For sociologists, the movement's overriding concern with enhancing the individual's potential for personal fulfilment raised obvious questions about its social value. While some saw the movement as little more than spiritual hedonism, others regarded this interpretation as simplistic. Various alternative explanations attempted to set the movement, with its unmistakably Eastern-influenced ideals, in the context of modern Western societies in the period of late capitalism. Let us look at some examples of this work.

Donald Stone (1978), a principal researcher in the San Francisco Bay Area study of the 'new religious conciousness', noted the portability of beliefs in which divine authority resides in the self instead of an external entity. In identifying certain common features of these religions—their experiential emphasis, pragmatic approach and open organisational pattern—Stone argued that they function positively in, if not actually mirroring, a society which is itself organised along these lines.

An elaboration of this view was offered by Frances Westley (1978), who analysed the human potential movement against the backdrop of Emile Durkheim's prediction of a 'cult of man'. This was Durkheim's term for the type of spirituality that he thought would become prevalent in a modern world increasingly atomised by speciality and demystified by science. Taking Silva Mind Control as representative of 'cult of man' spirituality in which a preoccupation with self-perfection and self-reliance is paramount, Westley sought to show that its ideals were in keeping with those of the educated middleclass in modern society, whose professions require ever-greater specialities. Westley extrapolated from the socio-economic situation to the personal sphere, concluding that this population would naturally seek a parallel 'uniqueness' (her interpretation of

Durkheim's use of 'speciality') in its religious life. Individualism is thus an all-pervasive quality in both public and private life.

The most prolific of sociologists in the area of new religious movements, Thomas Robbins, has taken a perspective somewhat different from the above in that his conceptualisation of society emphasises its technocratic, impersonal and utilitarian aspects. Thus he has frequently argued for the personally restorative effects of these groups. In 'Getting Straight with Meher Baba' (1972), Robbins and his co-author Dick Anthony contrasted the impersonal social sphere with the intensely personal, over-loved and over-indulged family setting of middle-class America. The disjunction between the two environments, they argued, created problems at the age of maturity, resulting in the drug-users and dropouts of the hippy generation.

Meher Baba, famed for his 'Don't Worry, Be Happy' optimism, effected two important, if diametrically opposed, changes in his followers. First, as the living embodiment of love, he provided a unique setting for an 'expressive community' to which former drug-users and dropouts flocked, in refuge from the impersonal and instrumental relationships of a technocratic society. Second, as the yogi famous for disciplined obedience to his vow of silence, Baba encouraged a sense of 'inner detachment', a feature common to Buddhist and Yogic practices which, the authors note, 'makes the impersonality of technocratic vocational routines less oppressive'. Thus, while arguing for the ameliorative effects of the movement, Robbins and Anthony also understood it as preparing individuals for the conditions of modern society.

Paul Heelas (1982), a social anthropologist who examined several groups in the human potential movement, also invented a term to describe their salient feature. He used the concept of 'self religion' to characterise groups 'which exemplify the conjunction of the exploration of the self and the search for significance', together with an 'obsession for perfection'. Heelas, like the aforementioned theorists, also viewed the groups he studied, such as Kerista, The Farm and Rebirthing, as naturally emanating from the privileged lifestyle of modern middle-class America, in this case of Marin County, California.

His explanation for the genesis of such groups, however, became more specific in a later work by Heelas and Kohn (1986). There he drew a direct line from the popular cathartic psycho-therapies of the late 1960s and the 1970s to 'self religions', by noting the increasingly spiritual concepts and explanations which the therapeutic groups employed, a propensity that Donald Stone (1976: 96) also noted in his earlier survey of the human potential movement. Heelas explained the trend to 'self religions' as resulting from the deeply traumatic, indeed transformative, experiences which these therapies induced, but for which clinical language was inadequate if not entirely unsatisfying. Heelas's work on 'self religions' is by far the most interesting and plausible of those cited so far but, like the others, he also took the emphasis on, if not the elevation of, the self in these groups as an accepted fact, to be understood as a reflection of these same emphases in the social milieu from which they emerged.

Whether or not one agrees with the logic of the arguments proffered—arguments which add sociological sobriety to Tom Wolfe's 'The Me Decade' and Christopher Lasch's *The Culture of Narcissism* (1979)—I believe that the fundamental weakness in the analyses of the purported relationship between such groups and society is the fact that they are based on unqualified claims about the extraordinary empowerment of the self as indicative of the group's *nature*. What is frequently apparent, on close examination, is the utter impossibility of the follower ever achieving, or even acknowledging, that empowerment in his or her lifetime.

In contrast to what has been advanced about the human potential movement, I shall argue that the promotion of the self as an absolute value is powerfully undermined by contradictory messages from the leader. One might protest that the teaching itself and not the leader is to blame for the discrepancies or contradictions in statements about self-empowerment or self-enlightenment, but that objection is squarely ruled out when one considers the claims leaders make about *their own* achievement of it.

The problem of authority

This paper focuses on three 'self religions', the Da Free John movement, Scientology and *est* (now known as The Forum), which have become established in Australia. Da Free John's movement, called the 'Johanine Da'ist Communion', was founded in 1972 in a two-room storefront in Los Angeles. As noted in Da Free John's (1983: 759) major treatise, the movement 'has grown to become an honorable sacred institution' of which there are seven regional chapters of its educational branch, called the 'Laughing Man Institute', located in the United States, Europe, Australia and New Zealand. The movement has been operative in Australia since 1974, and currently has 85 financial members, with its community now located in Melbourne.[2] Scientology began under the name Dianetics, which L. Ron Hubbard, its founder, originally held to be a science. In 1955 he redesignated his organisation as a religion under the title of the Founding Church of Scientology. Scientology was introduced as Dianetics to Australia in the early 1950s, first in Melbourne and later in Sydney. Officially recognised in a High Court decision in 1983 as the Church of the New Faith, it has seen thousands of people take its courses.[3] The term *est* is an acronym for Erhard Seminars Training, begun by Werner Erhard. The movement has been offering courses in Sydney since 1982, and was renamed The Forum in 1985. It claims to have inducted about 9000 or 10 000 Australians in its courses.[4]

The definition of 'self religion' follows that of Paul Heelas, though I have further specified four common emphases on the self in the teachings of the three groups under consideration. They are:

1 the individual's inherent godliness, which has enormous 'transformative' power;
2 the satisfaction of the individual's mental, physical, and material desires;
3 the individual's freedom from established forms of authority and their imposed moral requirements; and
4 the individual's power and freedom to pursue his or her own interests.

Explicitly or implicitly, this new dispensation teaches the deleterious effects of authority. The authority attacked is sometimes particularised, as in the case of Scientology's continued barrage on the psychology establishment,[5] but more often than not, the teaching contains a generalised attack on any form of authority that is seen to either cripple the ego or prevent the introspection that leads to empowerment or happiness.

Locating authority in the individual, however, does pose a serious problem for the leaders, who would wish to gain an audience and remain the preferred if not the only teacher of the Truth to their followers. This phenomenon is well known to anyone who has read Max Weber on the paradoxes of sectarian religious leadership. The point that I wish to make here, however, is that the authority granted to individual followers is not unrelated to the force of authority exercised by the leader. Indeed, I contend that where radical subjectivism is encouraged among followers, radical authority will be exerted by their leader. This obvious contradiction within the group requires some subtle, if not at times jumbled, discourse or preaching by the leader, which will be explored in this paper.

The self as authority or radical subjectivism

In his tape-recorded lecture 'God Is Not In Charge', Da Free John hammers away at the 'Semitic belief' that God will somehow take care of us. To the parent–child concept of God as 'the Father' or 'the Protector' he juxtaposes the historical tragedies of our time, and concludes that 'apart from our own gestures in that direction, there doesn't seem to be much protecting going on'. Not only is the belief in God the Father an ineffective prophylactic against hardship, but those whose lives are relatively enjoyable are often entirely without a belief in God. The West has been 'propagandised', according to Da Free John, to adopt this infantile attitude, as it cannot be proven, for example, that Christians, Jews, Zoroastrians or Muslims experience in their lives any more or less intervention by some superior being, either before or after belief.[6]

No change, asserts Da Free John, can be discerned apart from 'whatever you may manufacture in your own life by changing your behaviours and getting others around you to change their behaviours'. What must be rejected is the Biblical presumption 'that if you align yourself to God, then God, who is external, omnipresent, and all powerful will make things happen for you, while you live and after you die'. After asking his audience if there is any concrete evidence to support such a belief, Da Free John asks, alternatively, if we are not 'involved in a matrix of possibilities in which there is no other'. 'In other words,' he asks, 'is there any option but self responsibility . . . ?' He then enjoins his audience to 'enter the *real* consideration—of self, of life, and of the divine . . . and develop the characteristics of a life that is being spiritually transformed, *not* by the one cause that is in charge of everything, because there isn't any such force'.

Yet Da Free John does not deny the existence of God, only the Western conception as he has crudely portrayed it. As he understands it, 'the world inheres in God, certainly. There *is* only God.' However, the only direct action of God is through 'an entity, being, or consciousness that has thoroughly transcended itself and is in a state of absolute conscious, self-radiant unity with the transcendental being'. Thus a transcendent entity exists, according to his view, but is directly known only through one who has experienced what, in traditional Buddhist terms, is known as enlightenment. Nature, normally a sign of God, is given only inferior status as God's mechanical dimension and, in what amounts to Da Free John's reiteration of Buddhist belief (that is, of the Wisdom or *Prajna* school), it is nothing compared with the subjective dimension through which God is directly operative, that is, 'through the knowers of God, the adepts'.

A similar condemnation of Western beliefs is found in L. Ron Hubbard's lecture 'My Philosophy' in which he dismisses the received wisdom that has 'regarded [philosophy] as a subject for halls of knowlege or the intellectual' and 'denied [it] to the man on the street'. In this fairly brief talk, Hubbard does not actually disclose the details of his complicated belief system, first outlined in his book *Dianetics, the Modern Science of Mental Health* (1950) and its sequel *Science of Survival* (1951), but he does expose his hostility toward established authority—those 'selfish scholars' who, in their greed for power, reject people (like himself) who 'break down the walls of mystery and let the people in'.

The three principles of Hubbard's philosophy are that:

1 wisdom is meant for everyone;
2 it is capable of being applied, and
3 any philosophical knowledge is only valuable if it is true and if it works.

All three principles reflect his emphasis on the individual dimension. The first is explicit; the second and the third imply individual application and assessment and are manifestly practically oriented. The elevation of the individual over institutional authority is further underlined by Hubbard's characterisation of 'the common man' as one who is committed to the truth through his sincere wish to 'understand things', in contrast to the 'holy places [which he came across in Asia] where wisdom was great but hidden and given out only as superstition'.

His own struggle against 'the establishment' is recalled, if only in a telescoped fashion, as an example of what opportunities of self-advancement lie before the individual who challenges authority. Blind and lame after the war, Hubbard worked his way back to fitness and strength against all odds and despite a continuous refrain of 'no hope'. 'Abandoned by family and friends', Hubbard portrays himself as 'using only what [he knew] about man and his relationship to the universe' to embark on a course of study (we are not told of what), which, as he pointed out, was 'quite a trick when you cannot see'. As a result, in less than two years, Hubbard 'bought an entirely new life', as he put it. Summing up the lesson of this fantastic tale of personal struggle, Hubbard holds out a promise to his followers: 'There is a way to freedom. The old must give way to the new. Falsehood must be exposed by Truth.'

Elsewhere, Hubbard elaborates on the constituents of this Truth, which demand that at the centre of every individual existence lies the life-task of purification.[7] In this system, as described in the 'bible' of Scientology, *Dianetics,* and in later in-house publications where it was considerably elaborated, the individual's consciousness stores up in a mental 'bank' the accretions of life's emotional and physical hurts, not as mere memories but as actual entities. These entities, which he named 'engrams' (noting their strictly scientific biological meaning)[8], accumulate not merely at the point of conception but from previous lives, an idea Hubbard borrowed from the Brahmanic belief of *karma*. 'Engrams' are stimulated by similar subsequent experiences or thoughts, and this duplicating phenomenon constitutes the 'reactive mind'. Condemned to repeat the engrams *ad infinitum*, the only hope of escaping their negative influence is to discover, confront and clear them away in a series of counselling courses devised by Hubbard.

The pathway towards 'clear'[9] is thus one of self-discovery. It is not quite the drama portrayed by Hubbard in his own biographical sketch, but it is one which entails much the same emphasis on a singular, self-centred path, which is poised against both the religious and the scientific establishments and must proceed amid the din of 'cat calls', as he terms any criticisms of his ideas.

Just as L. Ron Hubbard evolved an elaborate belief system, replete with science fiction motifs that owed much to his being a principal contributor to the magazine *Astounding Science Fiction*, so too did Werner Erhard develop his seminar training, known as *est*, by borrowing heavily from his expertise as an encyclopedia salesman for the companies Parents and

Grolier and as a leading trainer in personal assertiveness for a company called Mind Dynamics.[10]

Erhard's early interest in self-development courses, such as those of Dale Carnegie and Norman Vincent Peale, later developed to include the self-image psychology of Napoleon Hill and the psycho-cybernetics of Maxwell Maltz. As his official biographer put it, Erhard searched 'for a new self image', but what he 'actually found was a sort of religion' (Bartley, 1978:62). Originally, Erhard admitted, 'It was a religion of self motivation and self reliance' (Bartley, 1978: 62), but it later expanded to include many ideas from Zen Buddhism, which Erhard considered 'the *essential* one ... of all the disciplines that [he] studied, practised, [and] learned'. According to his account, '[Zen] built up in me the critical mass from which was kindled the experience that produced *est* ... While the *form* of Zen training is different from the form of the *est* training, we come from similar abstractions.' (Bartley, 1978: 121)

Erhard's training in self-image and self-promotion intersected with Zen at the point of 'the search for the Self' or, more accurately, the search for the powerful, creative and untroubled self. Erhard had learned from Maltz the concept of 'engram', also popularised by Scientology, which conveyed the idea that past experiences are destructive when remembered (even unconsciously) because they create self-criticism and guilt. To function at the optimum level is to live without the intrusion of memory, in the *here and now*. This outlook is central to Zen teaching, which Erhard learned from a leading American Buddhist, Alan Watts, whose many books turned this philosophy into the popular catchcry of the hippie generation, 'Be here now!'

In a tape-recorded talk entitled 'Creation', Erhard drives home the notion that people are out of touch with themselves because they are determined by received concepts and not by their experiences. This condition is ongoing, due to the inability of people to distinguish between concepts and experiences. Thus, when they think they are experiencing love, for example, they are in fact experiencing only the concept of love. Making the distinction, Erhard argues, is necessary if one is to live authentically, with 'aliveness', as he puts it, and with 'real self expression'. By making the distinctions, people are able to 'create a context' to do what they wish, and thereby break out of the 'vicious circle' of a life constituted of mere symbols and not real experiences. If one were to choose a motto among Erhard's sayings, it would have to be the following taken from that talk: 'To know yourself as a context creator is to transform the quality of your life.' This philosophy turns on a concept of the self, which is described as any one or all of a number of ontological states, such as 'appropriate action', 'just being there' or (in the Taoist sense of *wu wei*) 'non-action'. The true self also implies a mental state in which neither will, nor prejudices, nor what Erhard calls 'positionality' can be seen to interfere with action.

Bartley compares Werner Erhard's view to that of Nietzsche, in which a pure self, unalloyed with the trappings of traditional thinking, only needs to be awakened in order to realise its power. Thus, Bartley (1978: 214) distances Erhard from conventional morality and accepted definitions of good and evil as well as social reform. He asserts that 'Werner combats those elements of our culture and institutions that are characteristic of the Mind state and thereby [he] comes into conflict with all defenders of the Mind state.' The extent to which traditional concepts loosen their hold on a follower of *est* was apparent to Donald Stone (1976: 103), who noted that 'a psychiatric social worker [who had] formerly used terms like God to explain suffering and the source of happiness and love', 'subsequent to *est* training . . . did not use these terms so often, sensing that she is god in her universe and the creator of what she experiences'.

It should be apparent, at this point, that all three leaders—Da Free John, L. Ron Hubbard and Werner Erhard—advocate a world view that regards true knowledge as immanent, and that considers tradition, whatever its content, as false because it is external and received. They also avoid referring to the psychoanalytic corpus, which clearly influenced some of their teachings and methods, as well as to the Eastern traditions, Hinduism and Buddhism, whence many of their leading ideas are drawn. These include the reducibility of the phenomenal world to illusion, the rejection of the conscious mind in favour of a pristine self and the elevation of the self as co-extensive of God. All three leaders also offer to anyone the promise of empowerment, bliss and happiness as the rewards of realising one's true self.

The prisoner of consciousness

When that most popular articulator of Eastern mysticism, Krishnamurti (see note 1), whose influence in the West spanned more than 40 years, proclaimed to an audience at the University of San Diego that his aim was to set people absolutely and unconditionally free, he followed with a thumping admonition to his listeners on how they were fundamentally deluded and, despite their good intentions, were bound to place obstacles before themselves. Among these obstacles were the following: finding a teacher, seeking enlightenment, virtue, morality, etc., and undertaking a practice toward that end.

Krishnamurti thereupon exhorted his listeners to discard notions and concepts in which, for example, moral order or even the techniques of meditation are understood according to a blueprint laid down by 'some authority'. He urged his listeners to adopt a view of learning that is 'not learning from another, but learning by observing what is going on in yourself'—a process that is 'not possible if there is any form of prejudice, conclusion, or formula, according to which you are observing'. Thus, according to this view, observation, guided by ideas, concepts or theories, is antagonistic to 'self knowing'.

If this seems an easy proposition, Da Free John underlines the difficulty through an engaging joke in which a traveller in the English countryside asked a farmer how to get to London. After some thought, the farmer answered, 'You can't get to London from here.' In the same way, asserts Da Free John, 'you can't get to God as *this self*—'the self of gross experience', which is 'the conventional notion of your existence'. Da Free John refers to both the physical body and the mental self as the 'Body–Mind' while, in contrast, God and the 'Divine self' are not to be understood as objects, and are therefore beyond seeking or knowing in the conventional sense.

Like Krishnamurti, Da Free John repudiates 'knowledge' derived from sensory experience. He also echoes Krishnamurti when he rejects causality, where the individual (as Body–Mind) is seen to pursue 'the game of spiritual practices', as he cynically puts it, and 'at the end of a sequence of actions' is said to realise God or the Divine self, which are synonymous in his view. While Da Free John allows the limited use of terms in their conventional sense, he warns that from such a perspective one can be neither free nor happy. Ultimately, he declares, the 'me of awareness must surrender to the point of realising its identity with the Divine Being' a process he also calls 'dissolution or ecstacy'—the dropping away of 'self illusion' or self-consciousness.

Da Free John contrasts the state of dissolution to what he terms the 'egoic' preoccupation in which people take their Body–Mind seriously, and mistakenly think 'that's who [they] really are', a 'separate personality', where 'attention locks into particularities', with a 'mind [that] turns in on itself so many millions of times'. This mental activity, which Da Free John depicts as a downward spiral, is the opposite of realising the Divine Being, which is 'clear, patently obvious, incontrovertible, beyond knowledge, and beyond certainty'. Therefore, he concludes, it is simply 'the obvious' and 'there is no arguing about it'.

If, in Da Free John's view, there is no arguing about what constitutes enlightenment, from L. Ron Hubbard's perspective every measure is taken to prevent such arguments from occurring. For the extent to which the intellect and accumulated knowledge are relegated to the netherworld of utter futility is never more apparent than in his writings, despite the promise of extraordinary intellectual, not to mention supernatural, gifts once the highest state of 'operating thetan' is achieved. As already noted, the 'reactive mind', in response to engrams, is condemned to repeat in automatic fashion the actions which produced physical and emotional pain in the distant past. To reveal these myriad engrams imprinted on the soul, or 'thetan', Scientology recruits are immediately subject to readings by an 'E-meter', a form of galvanometer. While the recruits' responses to questions are invariably presumed to be deceptive, the machine, in contrast, is held to be infallible—in the words of Hubbard, 'it sees all, knows all. It is never wrong' (Wallis, 1976: 116).

Among the numerous methods of revealing engrams, or 'auditing' as it is known officially, a process not unlike Arthur Janov's 'Primal Scream' is frequently described, in which an individual is 'talked back' to the earliest unconscious prenatal memory, to be followed by 'memories' from past lives. Yet Hubbard warns against heeding the 'analytical mind' of either the auditor or the recruit. In the case of the auditor, diluting Dianetics with some practice or belief of yesteryear, as he calls all non-Dianetic thinking, is interdicted. With regard to the recruit, the auditor is instructed to ignore his analytical mind, which 'should have no force in [the auditor's] computations' (Hubbard, 1950: 282).

It has also been noted by Bainbridge and Stark (1980: 130) that Hubbard prohibits the independent creation or evaluation of a person's 'clear' state on the grounds that the auditing processes are impossible and even dangerous if undertaken alone. Roy Wallis (1976: 125), on the other hand, has pointed out that the hierarchy of states of 'clear' and 'operating thetan' is maintained among Scientologists through a controlled and guarded release of information about the elaborate cosmosological belief system and the role of the thetan in it.

The thorough-going suspicion in which the 'analytic mind' is held by L. Ron Hubbard is matched by Werner Erhard, whose entire auto-didactic philosophy disavows any attachment to concepts. When asked in an interview how, for instance, est deals with the failure to meet goals, Erhard protested that he had none: 'I don't have a vision. I'm not selling some ideal. I don't know where I'm going. I know where I'm coming from. And I think that the people on the staff know where they're coming from.' (Anthony, Ecker and Wilber 1987: 129) He followed this comment with a critique of motivation in general (presumably towards articulated goals) in which he asserted that 'It teaches you that you're not [something] . . . [it] reinforces that you're not. Even achieving that towards which you were motivated seals the fact that you are not [that something].' Tellingly, Erhard ridicules intelligent people, 'particularly people who wear their intelligence on their coat sleeves', concluding that 'underneath it, you find invariably that they are intelligent to avoid being stupid' (Anthony, Ecker and Wilber, 1987: 129). Intelligence, in this case, is fraudulent.

Erhard's caricature is not aimed merely at deflating the PhDs and professionals, who are among his severest critics. It is, more practically speaking, aimed at the elimination of rational standards against which his teaching might be evaluated. 'Creating the context' for something, such as the elimination of hunger in the world, an est undertaking known as the Hunger Project, is the aim and, as Erhard concluded: 'Therefore you cannot fail.' Yet exhibiting a characteristic, if perplexing, fluidity of thought processes, Erhard responded to the interviewer's repeated question about the possibility of failure by saying, 'Yes, you can fail—no you *know* you will fail in the objectives. That's part of the expression of a context of succeeding ... Failure doesn't destroy anything ... as a matter of fact, it forwards things ... Errors are important. They're how you get there. *Mistakes are the path*' (Anthony, Ecker and Wilber, 1987: 130).

An observer would readily conclude that the contradictions here, which deny failure and then assert its inevitability, which deny goals and then imply or concede their existence, are designed to escape any logical assessment. Less ambiguous, however, are Erhard's closing comments to his interviewers, in which he reveals the greatest tragedy befalling his followers. '*It's a really interesting thing*,' he wondrously exclaims. 'The one thing that burns people out is when they think they'[ve] *got* it. It's amazing. It starts to happen *exactly* that moment when they figure they have it made, they have it together, they *understand* it now. At this point it's so deadly, it's really sad.' (his emphases) Erhard then warns of the immediate downfall of those who take leave of him: 'They may go on to be very successful, but their success never has the quality of making a difference again' (Anthony, Ecker and Wilber, 1987: 131).

The inescapable conclusion to be drawn from the teachings outlined so far, beginning with the influential yogi to the West, Krishnamurti, is the paradoxical nature of the idea of the functioning, enlightened self, which, by its very nature, is said to elude conscious apprehension, affirmation and, most importantly, evaluation. Indeed, because the true self and the conscious or analytical mind are taken to be diametrically opposed entities, the followers, insofar as they retain a functioning intelligence, are condemned to a life 'just below the angels', forever in the shadow—outside their Divine Self.

The leader as supremely enlightened

Such a pessimistic outlook would be well nigh impossible to live by were there not concrete evidence of enlightenment. Apart from the changed lifestyles which augur the imminent spiritual transformation—or perhaps encourage it—the single most important sign of enlightenment is the leader. In so far as Da Free John, Hubbard and Erhard admit to their enlightenment, they open up the possibility for their followers to experience it as well—a situation which could spell the demise of the leader's role or claim to authority. Thus all the leaders espouse beliefs which rule out the possibility of individuals' acknowledging their enlightenment, while nonetheless implying their own. This is achieved by presenting the realisation of the Divine Self as a psycho-spiritual conundrum, a 'Catch 22', if you will, and/or as an ever-receding goal beyond an endless series of courses. The latter is especially true of Scientology, which has spawned numerous sub-states of purification, and also of *est*, which holds out a series of advanced courses intended to improve functioning in all areas, even in losing weight!

Da Free John, on the other hand, has kept his followers guessing about his next incarnation and ready to respond to a course of ever-changing demands on them. He has transformed his persona several times (appearing as a long-haired hippy, then as a shaven headed, half-naked monk) and suddenly altered the course of his financial undertakings. The small group of followers in Sydney, for example, ran a large bookstore which Da Free John abruptly closed in 1988 without mentioning a substitute venture. In an interview with me, the only reason for the closure that the group leader could identify was that change was the condition necessary for sustaining detachment, and he accepted the closing of the bookstore—his source of livelihood—on those grounds. By way of such tactics, which impose on followers an endless series of challenges that pre-empt the likelihood of experiencing the calm, or alternatively asserting the powers, which are said to be forthcoming from the teaching, the leader is able to maintain his supremacy without actually declaring it.

Modesty, however, is not usually a strong point of religious leaders. Da Free John, for example, whose title is Heart Master, refers unmistakably to himself as 'the adept' who 'appears' and is recognised as one through whom God is directly operative. 'Such adepts,' says Da Free John, 'being free of self, free of the limiting self imposition of their own mechanical influence, shows [sic.] the condition in which everything inheres, and are [sic] creatively, spontaneously active'. 'So,' he concludes, 'it is the adept . . . that is the sign of God'. In these words we can readily see that Da Free John's mercurial behaviour is appropriate to the spontaneous adept, for it is the sign of God.

Da Free John further explains the scope of his behaviour, which would appear to an outside observer as authoritarian, in a warning that 'when an adept appears, he certainly must criticise. But there isn't any negative intention—there isn't any intention at all, simply the self-radiant personality of the adept. And you, as you are, experience the radiance of that force.' Here Da Free John unambiguously differentiates between the 'adept' (himself) and 'you' (his followers), who by implication are not adepts. Lest his behaviour appears incongruous, Da Free John also notes that among the magnificient qualities of the adept—'love, bliss, [and] happiness'—there also figures 'playfulness' as well as all the other characteristics of human beings. This wide array of behaviours stems from the fact that he enters into a 'conjunction with beings as they are'. 'That,' says Da Free John 'creates the play . . . You, therefore, determine what the play will be.' In this way, he not only renders all his behaviour—his weaknesses and frivolities—beyond his followers' judgement, but also holds his followers responsible for it.

Closing his talk, Da Free John concludes: 'So this is your Spiritual Master . . . In the midst of your trials . . . you will discover that the

Spiritual Master was never anything but the Great One . . . [he] seems to be a particular someone, other than yourself, and yet somehow intimately unified with yourself. The Spiritual Master, like a laser force, fine, one pointed transmission, imposition, transforms everthing, makes transformation possible. You'll clearly discover that the Spiritual Master is the Living One Incarnate.'[11] In these words, Da Free John significantly undermines the notion of the entirely self-enlightened state, which all followers are promised, for he pointedly states that as Spiritual Master he unifies with his followers and makes their transformation possible.

His own most recent transformation was of momentous significance. In July 1990, Da Free John announced that he was the last *avatar*, or manifestation, of Vishnu, bringing an end to the dark age (of 'materialism and scientism' as one of his devotees explained) and inaugurating the spirit age. Accordingly, Da Free John's name was changed to Da Kalki.[12]

When we consider the more consciously scientific American product, like Scientology, the leader's claims to divinity are to a larger extent implicit. Certainly the greater levels of functioning described and devised in the course work presuppose that their creator has already attained them. Encomiums of praise are forthcoming from various celebrities and printed in Scientology's in-house magazines, with Hubbard's myriad extraordinary accomplishments listed. These include 'Explorer', 'Administrator', 'Artist' (the latter comprising writing, composing, screenwriting, directing, photography and cinematography, and codifying a philosophy of art), 'Author of Fiction', 'Humanitarian' and, finally, 'Friend to Millions'. Probably Hubbard's transfiguration into a latter-day Moses as well was effected when he set down for his followers a 'modern, practical and workable moral code, based on common sense', which he published as *The Way to Happiness*.[13]

In comparison to L. Ron Hubbard's pretentions to patriarchal status, Werner Erhard projects a 'regular guy' image. He kids around a lot and has an unmistakable penchant for the stand-up comedian, Philadelphian street-talk *schtick*, which is a peculiarly intimate brand of repartee. But he is also tall, handsome, possessed of a liquid voice and is a good story teller. An analysis of his talks reveals a pattern of one or two positive statements broken by one or two (usually devastating) negative ones, followed by a joke and a highly modulated, seductive laugh. As his interviewers pointed out, his magnetism is legendary among those who have taken his courses or heard his tapes, and they exhibit 'slavish adulation' for him (Anthony, Ecker and Wilber, 1987: 125). This is corroborated by my personal impressions from course graduates, who referred to Erhard only in superlatives.

About his enlightenment, however, Erhard is predictably slippery. When asked whether *est* training provides in two weekends what Zen would call enlightenment, Erhard answered unequivocally, 'Yes' (Anthony, Ecker and Wilber, 1987: 112). He then explained his answer by saying that enlightenment actually takes no time at all. (This is similar to a Buddhist position, in which enlightenment is regarded as one's true nature, *a priori*.) Later in the interview, however, Erhard retreated from this position, for in response to the question 'They were enlightened already, right?', Erhard exploded: 'No, no, no, no. They were not enlightened until they got into the training. Now remember, I didn't say that was true. I said, I want you to entertain that possibility.' (Anthony, Ecker and Wilber, 1987: 118).

Pressing him for an answer to whether he held his sort of enlightenment to be the same as that in the 'spiritual traditions', Erhard answered in a riddle: 'Those who know don't tell, and those who tell don't know.' Dick Anthony recalled that, when he went through the course, his trainer *did* seem to think they were the same, but Erhard countered with another conundrum: 'Well, I have never said that, nor would I say it . . . Nor would I say the opposite was true.' When he finally referred to himself as enlightened and one of the interviewers exclaimed, 'We got you to say it!', Erhard then deflated the comment by saying, rather obscurely, that he 'really did a better job when [he] was kidding' (quotations are from Anthony, Ecker and Wilber 1987: 114,118). As in Zen, enlightenment is presumed but never unambiguously stated.

Conclusions

The three leaders considered here all stand at the apex of the human functioning that their teachings promise to all followers. Not surprisingly, Da Free John's singular message of spiritual unification with the Divine Self is as elusive as Transcending the Self is enigmatic. Yet, his self-descriptions as an 'adept', the 'Spiritual Master' and, finally, the 'Incarnate One' are, by contrast, boldly declared. The other two leaders are more specific regarding the features of the promised perfection, with various levels of atainment and diverse areas of increased functioning outlined in the numerous courses which they devise.

Neither Hubbard nor Erhard is in particular need of bold assertions of his divinity or enlightenment, since it can be presumed that they possess the qualities which they demand of their followers, and in their biographies both are shown to have exhibited extraordinary talents, skills and achievements, from the moment of their earliest discoveries and despite lowly beginnings. While Da Free John's is the most radically subjective form of knowledge and consequent expression, Hubbard's and Erhard's can be discovered through course work, which provides a range of objective proofs or, put another way, constructs an endless series of controlled opportunities to manifest the prescribed enhanced functioning.

For all three, the onus is on the individual to be 'at cause' in all matters from spiritual transformation to material success, but the extent to which followers are guided through the steps in a uniform fashion by trained personnel is far more evident in Scientology and *est* than in Da Free John's local chapters. In the latter, the local group leader holds a singular and highly unstable post, where the objective proofs of self-transcendence are neither set down clearly, nor presumed to be constant (Da Free John, 1983). As mentioned above, Da Free John cultivates a kaleidescopic image and thereby ensures a continuing state of uncertainty in his followers—a key factor in maintaining absolute authority.[14]

In a short section on 'Transpersonal Experience[s] as Shortcuts to Power', Donald Stone (1976: 111) made a passing observation that the human potential movement's optimism about human nature assumes that the power gained must be entirely benevolent. As he puts it, 'if there is magic, it must be white magic'. There is no doubt that this comment applies equally to the leader's assumption of power, although it is often plainly stated as emanating from a 'universal love' of his followers, as Da Free John states, or from a paternal desire to bring happiness to all, as L. Ron Hubbard avers, or from an unsuppressable desire to share the key to 'authentic living' with humankind, as Werner Erhard claims. Herein lies the key paradox of all three movements, and many of a similar ilk, for although their foundation belief is that higher functioning results from the radically subjective experience of gnosis, devoid of intellectualising concepts, the leaders have all produced an astonishing amount of printed and taped materials designed to convey to followers, uniformly and precisely, their intricate revelations and instructions. In all three cases, courses on the gnosis are given, although Scientology and *est*, by virtue of their larger audience and wealth, have produced many more than has Da Free John.

This apparent contradiction has dogged the more iconoclastic and antinomian movements in Buddhism (as well as other religions) for centuries, and it revolves around the problem of authority in the transmission of a teaching, a problem that is exacerbated when the teaching is transmitted broadly. Sociologists of religion have been familiar with this contradiction ever since Troeltsch included the 'objectification of grace' among his criteria for the 'church type' as against the subjective experience of it in the 'sect type', and viewed them as dialectically related.

More recently, analyses of groups in the human potential movement have taken account of other expressions of this objectification (although not necessarily recalling Troeltsch), such as the 'commercialisation' or 'commodification' of the gnosis, as well as the 'professionalisation' of the staff. Wallis (1986a: 180) explained these developments as a consequence of the failure to form successful communitarian groups, which in turn makes the commercialisation of the gnosis preferable to disappearance. This interesting thesis depends on establishing that these groups did have communitarian aims, which Wallis did not do, and I think could not do for many such groups. Some of them, like *est,* never had communitarian aims, and others, like Da Free John, regard communitarian and commercial aims as compatible.

Other sociological works dealing with a *mixture* of new religious movements, including Christian ones, have looked at their financing as a distinct concern, requiring little explanation other than that borrowed from the study of social movements. Called resource mobilisation theory, this holds that organisations, as such, are committed primarily to survival and secondarily to their ideals, with the concerns of the former exerting influence on the latter (Bromley and Shupe, 1979; Bromley, 1985; Richardson, 1982).

In these studies, the financial concerns of a religious movement imply, if they do not necessitate, a system of authority, not unlike that which Bainbridge and Stark (1980) observed in Scientology, as the conflation of the access to the gnosis on the one hand with the exercise of power on the other hand, in what was a constructed and controlled hierarchical arrangement of states of 'clear'. It should be apparent that such a vertical arrangement of access to gnosis is antithetical to the putative individualism of the human potential movement. Indeed, claiming it was too authoritarian, Wallis (1986a: 158) confined Scientology to the margins of the movement, although elsewhere in the same article he admitted that the definition of criteria for inclusion in the human potential movement was problematic.

Wallis's position obscures the extent to which individual authority in the human potential movement is thwarted by various means. We see, for example, the forceful expression of authority in a leader like Da Free John, who calls himself God, while we witness authority of equally great proportions in two leaders, such as Hubbard and Erhard, who are believed to possess superhuman, extraordinary powers or characteristics. While Scientology and, to a lesser extent, *est* are said to be authoritarian in their structures, Da Free John is at least as powerful in his personal declarations of divinity. Even his writings are not didactic but impenetrable and consciously idiosyncratic, with a lack of punctuation and eccentric use of the upper case.

A preoccupation with only organisational mechanisms of authority misses the extent to which radical authority may inhere in the teachings of 'self religions', is appropriated exclusively by leaders and is imposed by them within or outside of a communitarian context, and in ways that are sometimes subtle and sometimes crude, but always extreme. For if there is one thing to emerge from my preliminary study of 'self religions', it is the feeling that followers express of their own puniness next to the leader, their own failure to achieve ideal functioning compared with the ease, the power and the success of their leaders. By virtue of the fact that followers in any of these groups never achieve the status accorded the leader, let alone fill the position he occupied, even in the case of his death as in Scientology, it is clear that the leader's supremacy is inviolable, and immune from takeover by the keen and the able followers.

This observation leads me back to the phenomenon of commercialisation, which has been identified as one of the key characteristics of the human potential movement groups, implying a consumer-centric ethos of personal autonomy and free choice. A closer look at the three groups discussed here, however, reveals that the 'commodification' of the gnosis did not occur at the expense of the leader's absolute authority; indeed, if anything, it reinforced that authority by quantifying it in ever-burdensome fees. We do not see, for example, the mushrooming of self-governing denominations, only the careful establishment of uniformly patterned and tightly controlled franchises, analogous to the planting of McDonald's hamburger outlets. Regular contact with the parent organisation and the leader is not only expected of all followers, it is vitally necessary to their advancement up the ranks or, put another way, towards their enhanced functioning.

What we have seen is that 'self religions', based as they are on the suppression of the conscious, analytical mind on the one hand, and the unification with, or the approximation to, the Divine Self (which is embodied only in the leader and in no other human or conceptual form) on the other hand, constitute a situation in which authority does not reside in the self, but absolutely and unquestionably in the leader.

Notes

1   I wish to thank Arlene Harvey of the Linguistics Department, University of Sydney and Ian Dunn for making some materials relating to the groups discussed in this paper available to me. Sources of information used include not only the printed publications cited in the text or notes, but also tape recordings of Krishnamurti ('The Essence of Being'), Da Free John ('God Is Not In Charge', 'You Can't Get There From Here' and 'The Ultimate Mudra'), W. Erhard ('Creation' and 'Celebrating Your Relationships') and L. R. Hubbard ('My Philosophy').

2   Colin of the Melbourne community gave me this information on 3 July 1990.

3   Information provided by Frank of the Scientology/Dianetics centre in Sydney on 2 July 1990. Sydney offers higher level courses than Melbourne, after which one must proceed to Florida for the advanced courses.

4   Catarina of The Forum (*est*) gave me this information on 26 June 1990.

5   The Citizens Commission on Human Rights, established in 1969, is Scientology's organisation for 'investigating and exposing psychiatric violations of human rights'. Its publications include *Freedom, Independent Journal* (Church of Scientology, publisher) and *Information*

Letter. In the latter, no. 1, 1987, see 'How Psychiatry is Making Drug Addicts Out of Australia's School Children'.

6 Da Free John's comments on the world religions can be found in the course handbook called *The Basket of Tolerance: On the Seven Schools of the One and Great Tradition of God Talk* (6 March 1988: 9), in which the mythological elements of the great traditions are discussed as provisional ways of thinking to be outgrown.

7 *The Purification Rundown* (pamphlet, 1978) is one of the courses offered, although it is devoted to the physiological dimension of this general preoccupation in Scientology. See also L. R. Hubbard's *Purification, An Illustrated Answer to Drugs* (pamphlet, 1986) and his *Purification, the Route to Clear Thinking* (pamphlet, n.d.).

8 The term 'engram' was coined by the British biologist Sir Charles Sherrington and the neurophysiologist Sir John Eccles.

9 In *Dianetics, the Road to Clear* (pamphlet, 1965) L. R. Hubbard outlines the basic course of Scientology.

10 Both of these companies had major legal actions brought against them for unethical business practices, although Bartley (1978: 177) assures his readers that Erhard had nothing to do with them.

11 Such claims, as in the appearance of avatars or the myriad manifestations of the Buddha, are not uncommon in overtly Eastern-based traditions, stemming from the belief in metempsychosis or reincarnation. Meher Baba was also given to such declarations: 'I am the Highest of the High', 'the Divine Beloved'. 'There is no doubt of my being God personified . . . I am the Christ. I assert unequivocally that I am infinite consciousness.' (Needleman, 1972: 75)

12 Peter of the Melbourne community conveyed this information to me on 7 September 1990.

13 See, for example, *L. Ron Hubbard, The Man and His Work* (pamphlet, 1986) by The Friends of L. R. Hubbard.

14 Roy Wallis (1986b) has analysed the manipulative aspects of charismatic authority in the Children of God. The precariousness of this form of 'unorganised gnosis' was brought to my attention when the local leader of a Da Free John chapter asked me why it was that Jewish followers were always troublemakers—asking hard questions, and challenging the leader's activities. One, apparently, brought a legal action against the 'Spiritual Master'. The inquisitiveness, so valued among Jews in their own tradition, clearly did not translate to one in which verity was embodied in a person, who therefore remained beyond question. Indeed, Jewish tradition rewards and celebrates the questioning student and regards the one who 'wits not to ask' as below even the simple minded.

11 Aboriginal religions in time and space
Tony Swain

History has been one of the victims in the study of Australian Aboriginal religions. It has often been convenient to forget that everything known by Europeans about Aboriginal religion has been recorded since invasion. Maddock (1974: ix) opens his valuable portrait of Aboriginal society with the reminder: 'one has . . . to add L. R. Hiatt's observation that anthropologists in Australia have moved behind the advancing frontier to A. W. Howitt's observation that the frontier in Australia has been marked by a line of blood'. Entire communities were murdered, or died of introduced diseases; many 'tribes' were severely reduced before researchers ever encountered them. It is estimated that the population in the South-East of Australia had been culled by a staggering 96 per cent a full generation before the first serious ethnographic accounts of the region were produced.

Yet until the 1960s, virtually every report was written about the alleged nature of 'traditional' Aboriginal societies. Scholars simply ignored the reality that the people they consulted lived on missions, stations and government reserves and maintained a radically transformed culture. To a large extent they also downplayed the fact that, at the time of colonisation, Aborigines in the north of the continent were, and had been for some time, in constant contact with Indonesian and Melanesian peoples, who had undeniably added to the Aboriginal cultural heritage.

In this chapter I provide a brief region-by-region overview of Aboriginal religions, in each case highlighting the history of the area and the effects of that history upon religious dynamics. A general thesis to emerge is that if we seriously acknowledge time and history, we will be able to observe, first and foremost, some radical changes to the Aboriginal understanding of space. In particular, contact with outsiders has constantly placed pressure upon Aborigines to overlay their exceptionally pluralistic and site-based traditions with beliefs and cults which transcend social, spatial and ideological boundaries. Increasingly, Aboriginal religious life acknowledges spiritual transcendence co-joined with a pan-Aboriginal social base. Principally, this can be understood as a process of permeating (if not actually dissolving) the multitude of spiritual borders that Aboriginal traditions had constructed across their lands.

This article also serves as a convenient summary of research into religious change throughout Australia and the unique religious features of the major Aboriginal cultural blocs within the continent. The areas I have demarcated to some extent follow drainage basins, owe something to language family distribution, and are close to the classification system used by the Australian Institute of Aboriginal Studies, but ultimately are designed to suit my own understanding of the accounts we have of Aboriginal religions.

Figure 11.1 Cultural blocs and language groups mentioned in the text

Due to the poverty of the data, I will say nothing here about religion in

Tasmania and the South-West. I begin with the Desert regions, as these have been the most isolated from contact with outsiders and, I believe, reveal much of the nature of pre-contact religions. I then consider Cape York and the Central-North, where Melanesians and Indonesians respectively transformed Aboriginal cultures prior to the further impact of colonisation and a colonial Christianity. Next, I swing back to the South-East, the seat of invasion, before looking at comparable effects in the adjacent Lake Eyre region and the Kimberley region on the other side of the continent. Finally, I make some concluding observations on the interaction between historic time and sacred space in the ongoing procession of Aboriginal religions.

The Deserts

While bordered east and west by regions which had lost much of their pre-contact religious life, the Deserts were to some extent havens for Aborigines precisely because of their distance from the coasts upon which newcomers landed, and their inhospitability to European economic pursuits. Yet even here it is impossible to speak of people unaffected by alien lifestyles. The exception proves the rule. When, a few years back, a handful of Pintupi who had never before seen whites were encountered, the event was so unexpected as to attract considerable media attention.

Within the Desert itself there have also been degrees of outside influence on religious life. Towards the very heart of the continent there were, from an early date, not only the overland telegraph line and the station that was the embryo of what is now Alice Springs, but also the Lutheran Mission at Hermannsburg which, whilst recording useful material, at the same time prohibited the performance of Aboriginal ceremonies. Under such a régime, change was inevitable. In other areas, reflected in studies such as Meggitt's (1962) work on the Warlpiri or Tonkinson's (1978) on the Mardudjara, the authors can claim to have witnessed traditions showing minimal signs of outside influence, but such contexts do not prevail today. Missions, mining companies and European bureaucracies have become ubiquitous.

I follow the academic custom of separating the Western and Central Deserts, but the division is not absolute. A Western bloc can, nevertheless, be demarcated by its common linguistic and cultural core (Tonkinson, 1978: 6–8). The Pitjantjatjara belong to this region, but their northern neighbours, the Aranda, differ from them in some important ways. From the Aranda to the Warlpiri—via whom Central-Northern cultural elements passed into the Desert—lie the approximate reaches of the more heterogenous Central Desert cultures.

Desert religious conceptions, in my view, represent the essence of Aboriginal religion throughout the continent, but in other regions historic processes have overlaid the general pattern with new motifs. We thus find apparent 'contradictions' or 'redundancies', as shown below: the spirit of the dead goes to a site-based home but *also* to the Land of the Dead (Badu, Heaven, etc.); myriad ancestors transform the world but there is *also* a transcendental or quasi-transcendental figure beyond this process (All-Mother, All-Father, etc.). The 'Desert' understanding of the cosmos can thus be seen in non-Desert areas, barely below the surface of new tides of religious thought.

Desert ontology is fundamentally pluralistic: there are no pre-eminent ancestors, nor are there any people with access to more than a small segment of the eternally world-sustaining Dreaming powers. The whole consists in the fabric woven of independent threads, yet even this image is too formal and lends itself to the misunderstanding of a universally acknowledged blueprint. Not a geometric grid but an organic pattern of Dreaming pathways criss-crosses the landscape. It is readily acknowledged by Aborigines of the Western Desert that no one knows the full body of their Law. While some stories, like that of the *Wadi Gudjara* or Two Men, transverse this area and thus link communities together, it is nonetheless understood that people are custodians only for that segment of the Ancestor's spiritual forces which have been localised in their country.

Ritual in this area serves to link living people with the Ancestral order to maintain a balance which can endure. The people spiritually associated with a site at which Dreaming beings are (*not* 'were') manifest perform ceremonies (re-)actualising sacred events and thus ensuring the balance of those parts of the cosmos for which they are responsible (Tonkinson, 1978: Chapter 5). Rites of passage affirm that human beings are ontologically identical with Ancestors. The Ancestor's spirit essence, which is fixed in the country, causes pregnancy and birth as it becomes incarnate in a woman. Later, novices are inducted into the meaning of their true identity. Finally, death is a return of spirit essences to their rightful place and no general Land of the Dead is recognised. One might rather speak of a restoration to the Lands (in the plural) of the potential for life.

The Central Desert, while boasting some of the most influential studies of Aboriginal religion, and considered in some scholarly circles to be almost synonymous with Aboriginality (have not the Aranda words *tjurunga*, *intichiuma* and *Altjiringa* found a universal application?), is in some respects anomalous. This is especially true of the Aranda. Their 'conception totems', which recruited members of 'lodges' in terms of the place where the mother first felt the pangs of pregnancy, were to some extent at odds with the principles of patrilineal inheritance found elsewhere in the Central Desert. Some scholars, such as Hamilton (1982), have argued that there has been a shift from place-based to patri- rights in the Desert over time, but it is impossible to provide absolute proof for such assertions.

To the north of the Central Desert, the Warlpiri provide another variation on Desert themes. While remnants of fertility cults have entered the Western Desert via the Kimberley, the Warlpiri *Gadjari* (see below) is far more conspicuous in this regard (Meggitt, 1966). Yet while ritual symbols of women's procreative powers are explicitly evident, the mythology of the Mother has been replaced among the Warlpiri by the story of two males known as the *Mamandabari*, who traverse a wide range of Warlpiri country and whose exploits can only be recalled in part by the people of any one site-based descent group. In this sense *Gadjari* has been transposed into a typically Desert segmentary religious key.

In the main the spiritual aspects of the life cycle in the Central Desert are of the same kind as those found in the Western Desert. Among the Warlpiri with whom I have worked, the *kuruwarri*, or life essence deposited in the landscape by an Ancestor, is lodged in a woman who passes near the site. These *kuruwarri* are the source of all fertility, animal and human, and a major part of ritual is to ensure their balanced continuation. Unlike the Aranda, however, this conception Dreaming does not determine lodge affiliation, which is regulated by patrilineal descent, and their patri-spirit or *pirlirrpa* is revealed to them upon initiation (Meggitt, 1962: 206–8).

Not all Desert ritual is of the *intichiuma* (Warlpiri *banba*) or cosmic balance ('increase') type. *Gadjari* and initiation ceremonies have already been mentioned and there are also relatively widespread cults associated with celebrating the activities of various ancestors. The serpent *Yarapiri* is an example. He emerged from Pitjantjatjara country and among the Warlpiri is associated with fire ceremonies. A further class of ritual is the public ceremony ('corroboree') which, despite its entertainment value, is nonetheless of religious significance. The Warlpiri *purlapas* belong to this class and are often said to be revealed to individuals by Ancestral Beings while they are dreaming. In more recent times God has been counted among these Ancestors, and Christian ceremonies and icons have come to play a significant part in Warlpiri and neighbouring religious life (Swain, 1988).

The relationship between Christian and other beliefs and practices is often a complementary rather than competitive one, and Desert Aborigines will maintain that they uphold 'two Laws'. In my analysis of Warlpiri Christianity I argued that, although at one level it can be seen to relate to problems attributed to specific white influences (alcohol, etc.), it is more basically related to the problem of white ontology and an understanding of land and space which does not recognise eternal worldly boundaries. Most fundamentally the Warlpiri have married a ubiquitous, universal Being (God) to the Aboriginal principles of plurality, a development we can recognise as having occurred long ago in various different ways in the north and South-East of Australia.

Despite the impact of Christian missions in the Deserts, especially upon the Aranda at Hermannsburg, very little has been done to investigate recent religious innovations. With the exception of my paper on Warlpiri

Christianity and Glowczewski's study of *Julurru* among the northern Warlpiri (see below), and a few notes by F. Rose (1965: 90–1, 100–1) on possible cargoistic beliefs in the Central Desert, new religious movements in this area remain an uncharted topic.

Changes to and within traditional religious life in a post-colonial context have, however, received some attention. For the Western Desert, Tonkinson (1970) has examined what happens to an Aboriginal culture when the people are removed from their lands, showing how the all-important spiritual contact with sites is maintained despite enforced breaches in physical proximity. Others have briefly considered the effects the colonial presence has had on initiation ceremonies and other specific, but fairly circumscribed, issues of religious change, but considering the extent of transformation of traditions in this region—the type of change F. Rose (1965) hints at and Tonkinson (1974) provides the context for—the dynamics and history of religious life have been sadly neglected, perhaps because this is the region which tends to attract researchers searching for that unicorn of Aboriginal studies: Aborigines totally untouched by the non-Aboriginal world.

Cape York

Turning now to the region with the most ancient contacts with outsiders, it becomes readily apparent that there are strong affinities between the religion of the Melanesian Torres Strait Islanders and that of the Aboriginal people in Cape York Peninsula, links which were maintained in the past by trade routes and which are preserved today by a shared experience of government and church.

Thomson's account of religious life among the Koko Ya'o, for instance, has several points of convergence with Haddon's interpretation of the traditions of the Western Islanders. Haddon had recorded beliefs concerning the Culture Hero *Kwoiam* (1934), who had travelled to the Islands from Australia. Thomson, in turn, relates the Cape York narratives of *Shiveri*. *Shiveri* is furthermore structurally almost identical with *Iwai,* a crocodile who, amongst other things, was the inspiration behind the initiation ceremonies of the area (Thomson, 1933: 488). According to Thomson, these cults, which share with those of the Islanders and Papuans a great deal of unique (by Australian standards) ritual paraphernalia (e.g. drums and shelters resembling Melanesian clubhouses), migrated to Australia long ago and have evidently overlaid more ancient traditions which approximate those to be found elsewhere in Australia. *Iwai* had not only been incorporated into the 'totemic' order (to adopt Thomson's choice of term) but had been regarded as *Tjilbo*, an honorific meaning 'old man', among the Ancestral Beings.

The recognition of Ancestors to whom all people are spiritually linked is one of the most common Aboriginal responses to radically different classes of strangers. The All-Fathers of the South-East and All-Mothers of the north are discussed below in this regard. The Heroes of Cape York never become fully transcendent beings, however; that is, they were denied the status of being everyone's spiritual parent, with whom all humans thus stood in a single unified relationship. Because the Hero cult, despite its wide cultural significance, was localised within one clan, Thomson saw it as being largely brought within the normal 'totemic' scheme. McConnel (1936: 88), who worked further to the south with the Wik-Mungkan, went so far as to say the Hero cults were entirely in accord with religious systems elsewhere in Australia and hence largely indigenous in origin, but in arguing this she was unduly reluctant to recognise the important modifications to belief and practice highlighted by Thomson.

In the Cape region, the spiritual affiliation linking people and land was once again largely patrilineal. Ancestral Beings and the potent essences giving rise to all life were also associated with these patri-places. *Iwai* himself was a part of this order, although his association was apparently more with abstract principles (e.g. 'sexual licence') than specific species (Thomson, 1933: 503). Rites were performed by the people of a land to either increase *or* decrease species populations, thus indicating the presence of cosmic balance ceremonies comparable with those of the Desert. In Thomson's data, however, another 'aberrant' feature appears. Despite the patrilineal association between Ancestors, sites and living people, a person's own spirit does not emerge from that land. There were, apparently, no 'spirit children' associated with sacred sites which impregnated women, but rather the *ngorntal* was linked with the mother's country, and what Thomson (1933: 493ff) calls the 'personal totem' was consequently not inherited immediately upon birth. Thomson suspected an older stratum of matrilineality being conflated with a later, Islander-influenced, patrilineality. Certainly there are conflicting principles at work, but as McConnel (1936: 455–6) found patrilineality in the areas further to the south—along with the more typical Desert-like arrangement in which a conception is understood to result from the implantation of a spirit essence from the father's land's sacred centre (*auwa*)—it is more likely that it is matrilineality which can be ascribed to Islander influence. (For a detailed analysis of the Hero cults, see Swain, n.d.)

By the time of the earliest ethnographies, Cape York culture had already been affected by white Australians. While missionaries were relatively late to arrive, Seligman (1916) reported that he was greeted in 1908 by an Otati 'Bible Story', while various ethnographers have been presented with myths of the respective origins of blacks and whites. Some have argued that the latest wave of aliens has had little impact. Others, like Sharp (1952), predicted total disruption and no possible future but civilising and Christianising. Both views, of course, are naïve.

Christian belief and practice have been accommodated in Cape York, yet this Christianity has unique forms clearly revealing the persistence of tradition. At Yarrabah there has been a spate of visions and deliverance rituals with their roots in both Christian and Aboriginal domains (Hume, 1988); the Yir-Yiront have achieved cosmological and ritual accord between pre-European attitudes and those which have resulted from contact (Taylor, 1988); and among the descendants of the people with whom Thomson observed Islander influence, new attempts are now being made to establish harmony between initiation into the cults of the Heroes and initiation into the Christian church (Thompson, 1988). As in Desert regions in recent times, there is clear evidence in Cape York of an accommodation between localised traditions and the pan-Aboriginal—indeed pan-human—principles of Western Christendom.

Central-North

If the Islander-inspired Hero cults are the most conspicuously unique aspect of religion in Cape York, then in the Central-North of Australia, and particularly in Arnhem Land, the fertility cults of the All-Mother, which were at least partially developed from contacts with Indonesians, are a defining feature.

Among the Yolngu in eastern Arnhem Land, religious belief and practice are ordered by two exogamous moieties. The *Yirritja* moiety's traditions dwell on the various classes of strangers to come to this area. Europeans and Japanese are among the recent groups, but before them were the people of Badu in the Torres Strait (Berndt, 1948) and, in particular, the Macassans from southern Sulawesi, who sailed on the monsoons to Australia's northern coast in search of trepang (see Berndt and Berndt, 1954). According to Yolngu accounts, however, there was an even more ancient class of trepang collectors called the *Baijini*. They are said to have brought their families to Australia, built stone houses and established a rice-based agriculture, but no evidence, historical or archaeological, has yet been forthcoming to suggest who these people might have been.

The explicit references to these newcomers in Arnhem Land religious life are of two main kinds. First, they are the subject of extensive song cycles, which have yet to be published, and of a large class of myths (e.g. Maddock, 1988). Second, they are tied in with Aboriginal conceptions of the soul. This includes their representation in ceremonies celebrating the affiliation between individuals and their spirit land, and also particularly in mortuary ritual. Although the *birrimbir* (soul) is said to return to the 'clan well' (Warner, 1958: 447), it is also claimed to travel to the Land of the Dead. In the *Yirritja* moieties' case this is Badu, and the rites for the departure of the soul replicate the Macassan praus setting sail for Sulawesi. Sculptures identified with Dutch custom officials are also used as funerary posts.

The All-Mother cult itself also has clearly alien elements. The Mother, right across the coast of a Central-North Australia, is said to have come from a land to the north, and in Arnhem Land some people quite explicitly name her home as Macassar (Berndt and Berndt, 1951: 113). In the famous *Djanggawul* song cycle when the All-Mothers and their brother are getting close to Australia's coast, they smell the *Baijini* on the land and later find these light-skinned trepang gatherers already well established in their stone house (Berndt, 1952a: 101–2). Analysis of the available ethnographies and comparisons with traditions from southern Sulawesi provide a strong case for the Mother cult in Australia being a post-Indonesian phenomenon which possibly developed as recently as the early eighteenth century (Swain, 1991).

The Mother is the heart of the cults in Central-North Australia. Most widespread is the *Kunapipi* ('Womb') which appears to have begun in the Roper River area (Berndt, 1951: xxviii), spreading to the north coast and also westwards, from whence it swung both to the north where it was documented as *Punj* (Stanner, 1959–1963) and south into the Desert where it is referred to as *Gadjari* ('Old Woman') (Meggitt, 1966).

The *Kunapipi* ritual varies considerably under local conditions. Away from the coast the significance of fertility symbolism diminishes, and in differing coastal areas it has become attached to various myth cycles. In east Arnhem Land, for example, it is associated with the story of the *Wawalag* sisters, a narrative which also sustains the *Djunggawon* and *Ngurlmag* rituals in that region. The *Kunapipi* rituals symbolically replicate, among other things, the swallowing of the sisters by the python *Yulunggur*, and the life-giving properties of their wombs. These are instances of the commonly paired ritual metaphors of subsumption (swallowing, killing, etc.) and giving birth; of death and life.

The womb is a central image to other cults in northern Australia. The *Dua* moieties' *Narra* rituals focus on the myth of the *Djanggawul*. The grounds represent the womb, and the sacred poles (*rangga*) are brought forth from the shelter in a manner parallelling the birth of the first people from the Mother (Warner, 1958: 340ff). The western Arnhem Land *Maraiin* are closely related to these *Narra*, although naturally linked with different mythic constellations.

The All-Mother traditions, as the name implies, have provided a vehicle for establishing a pan-Aboriginal and spatially continuous order in Central-North Aboriginal Australia. For reasons I will not pursue here (see Swain, 1991), the transcendent Mother did not unduly disturb the pre-existent localised religious base. But not all northern cults are associated with images of motherhood. Berndt (1974, fasc. 3: 3) notes that the *Yirritja* moiety *Narra* are primarily associated with the myth of *Laindjung* and *Banaidja* which emphasises male principles, while Stanner (1959–1963: 55) says the myth of *Kunmanggur* and *Tjinimin* symbolically competes with the All-Mother's 'mysterious female power'. In more recent times, the most prominent male mythic figure is the Christian God. There is currently a very active Christian revival which began on Elcho Island but has spread throughout the Central-North of Australia and, indeed, through the continent as a whole. The movement focuses on ecumenicalism as a face of political unity and operates under the banner of the phrase 'Father make us one' (Bos, 1988). Aboriginal theologians from this area have sought reconciliation between their All-Mother and the new All-Father.

Mission influence had made an impact prior to this most recent revival, although it was poorly documented. Berndt (1952b) recorded a Christian myth cycle transposed into a Dreaming form long after the relevant mission had been abandoned. The best known Christian development in Arnhem Land was the Elcho Island Adjustment Movement, in which previously secret *rangga* were placed on public display in association with a crucifix and outside the local church. Berndt has interpreted this in terms of political goals and deliberate cultural reformulation (1962), but more recently Morphy (1983) has argued for its significance as a means of educating Europeans in the ways of Aboriginal land tenure. I have analysed a comparable phenomenon among the Warlpiri, showing that, in a variation on Morphy's argument, what is involved is indeed a merging of views on land or, more precisely, the complementary co-joining of two principles of spatial organisation—the locative and the universal.

South-East

The South-East corner of Australia is the area with the longest and most intense colonial history. Considering the immense disruption to Aboriginal traditions in this region, the body of literature on Aboriginal religions is surprisingly large. The quality of the publications, however, leaves much to be desired. Most are from the nineteenth and early twentieth centuries and modern students search in vain for answers to many of their research questions.

The defining feature of this area is the sky-dwelling transcendental All-Father. There is no reason to hesitate in calling him a Supreme Being. Throughout the region he is the focus of all belief and ritual, and his home, usually said to be somewhere beyond the clouds, is the locus of all power and the paradise to which people aspire upon death. This religious understanding is so at odds with that of the rest of the continent that it was from an early date the subject of controversy (Swain, 1985: 34–9 and 79–85). Are we witnessing Christian teachings blended with pre-contact ideas? Or is it the case, as earlier scholars maintained, that the more fertile climate of the South-East had allowed these peoples' beliefs to 'evolve' to a 'higher' level? My own position (Swain, 1990) is a variant of the former view, but I see no real case for the argument that Christian ideas had become 'confused' with tradition. Rather, it seems that these Aborigines had deliberately employed and reworked the cosmology of their invaders in order to come to terms with their own place in a radically changing world.

The first thing to note in this regard is the depreciation of the Earth. Although it was still possible to find remnants of ideas about 'increase' rites and site-based spirit essences early this century, most researchers reported beliefs which indicated the Earth was of secondary importance to an unknown Heaven. Upon death the spirit no longer returned to its territory but found 'its way to the sky-country, where it lives in a land like the earth, only more inhabitable, better watered, and plentifully supplied with game' (Howitt, 1904: 440). Insofar as the more typically Aboriginal locative notions of Earth-bound sites as the eternal home of spirit essences are discernible in some studies of the South-East, it seems reasonable to suspect the Heavenly scenario was a relatively recent innovation.

Turning to the All-Father himself, our suspicions are intensified. The earliest reference to him (as *Baiami*) came from the Wellington Valley Mission, where Rev. James Günther claimed he had found the belief in a God said to be eternal, omnipotent and good (cit. Ridley, 1875: 135). James Manning's account is even more surprising. Several critics have accused Manning of embellishing his report, but as the author was himself uncomfortable with his data and thus double-checked the details, it is quite possible that he faithfully relates what he was told by Aborigines. This was that *Baiami* lives in Heaven on a throne of crystal, but because he was lonely made a son whose spirit dwelt on Earth from 'England to Sydney' (Manning, 1882: 160). Other reports, such as Howitt's, were less anachronistic, but none countered the view that an other-worldly Supreme Being was the key to religious belief in the region.

Ritual in the South-East was dominated by the 'clever men' who officiated at the deities' ceremonies. The cults, most commonly referred to by scholars as *Bora*, were initiatory, with the novice being taught of the true powers and attributes of their High God. Howitt, Mathews and others have left us with numerous accounts of the physical dimension of the rituals, including the ground sculptures and dendroglyphs (carved trees), but what they signify or mean we are mostly not told. It would seem that they were depictions in part of *Baiami's* first camp, and the god was typically portrayed in a recumbent position. But what of the other icons said to depict his benefactions? The majority were of indigenous themes, but there were also cattle, horses, pigs, trains, ships, playing cards (four aces, to be specific) and even effigies of whites themselves (for full references, see Swain, 1990).

Whatever the origin of the All-Father, in more recent years he has come to be associated by Aborigines with the Christian God. Howitt was in fact told *Brewin* (the Kurnai term) was 'Jesus Christ' (Fison and Howitt, 1967: 255), and similar opinions have been expressed by Aborigines throughout New South Wales and Victoria. In unpublished notes from the 1930s, Elkin (n.d.) referred to data collected from informants initiated around the time of Howitt's and Mathews' fieldwork. He does not actually acknowledge synthetic elements, although references to 'our saviour' with a virgin mother clearly indicate their presence. By the 1950s, when Calley (1964) performed his fieldwork with the Bandjalang, the same myth had been quite explicitly linked with Christian imagery. Variants of this account have been reported along the mid-north South-East coast and in each case the site of Christ's grave is located in the nearby landscape. This doctrine and the more general equation of the All-Father with the Christian God is still very active in New South Wales and Victoria.

As for the earlier period, it seems conclusive that the High God, while probably having some indigenous roots, only came to be an *otiose* Supreme Being in the wake of invasion. This is perhaps to argue no more than the Wuradjeri man who said: 'He was always among the people long ago ... when the white people came out to Australia, Baiami heard that they were coming. He then got "frightened", and cleared away' (Berndt, 1947: 334). The significant thing about this shift in religious orientation is that it undermined localised spatial demarcations by acknowledging a non-worldly focus of religious authority. The already universal and pan-Aboriginal structure of that tradition has made it particularly enduring in the ongoing social upheavals in rural and urban South-East Australia.

Lake Eyre

While the peoples of Lake Eyre, and the Dieri in particular, were the focus of early missionising and consequently had their religious life documented by the pioneering proselytisers, colonial pressures weighed heavily upon their traditions and thus, with a few exceptions, little investigation of any quality has been carried out there this century. In many respects Lake Eyre religious life was close to that of the Desert, although it was also influenced by the Gulf and South-Eastern regions. Ancestral Beings (*muramura*) had transformed themselves at specific sites which became the focus of patrilinear rituals performed by members of the *bindara* or patrilineal clan. This is in keeping with the typical Desert segmentary religious structure.

Two distinctive features, both possibly post-mission innovations, are worthy of note. One is the *toas*, 'guide posts' or 'direction markers' which symbolically refer to particular *muramura* and, by extension, sites with which they are associated. The antiquity of *toas* has been the subject of debate, and their origin will now probably never be fully understood (Jones and Sutton, 1986). The second noteworthy feature is the Lake manifestation of the *Molonga* cult. The cult itself came to the area from Queensland and was also recorded elsewhere in Australia. But in the Lake, according to the missionary Siebert (1910: 57–9), it was a millennial movement, focusing on a future battle between Aborigines and whites which would climax with the appearance of *Ka'nini*, the spirit of 'the Great Mother of the Water', who was to swallow all the colonial Australians. Alas for the Aboriginal people of Lake Eyre, she did not come.

Kimberley

Complex historical processes have obviously been involved in shaping the religious traditions of the areas discussed so far, but published accounts often downplay this factor. The Kimberley, in contrast, is typically depicted as a cross-road of religious innovation. In reality, it is probably no more innovative than other regions, but the presence of scholars schooled in German historical anthropological traditions in this area has resulted in publications with a concern for documenting change. Elkin (who studied under the British pan-Egyptian diffusionists) and Capell (introduced to Australian anthropology by Elkin) also consider such factors. Teasing apart the older threads of history is a complex and perhaps ultimately impossible task. Capell (1939), for instance, discerned three layers of mythic traditions. The oldest, a cult of the dead, was followed by the *Wandjina* cult, which he suggests has its origins in Timor, and was finally overlaid with narratives of the Rainbow Serpent and others. Aboriginal myth does not really help to resolve the chronology. According to Ungarinyin cosmogony, for example, the androgynous serpent *Ungud* first emerged from the oceans, created various lands, and then deposited the eggs of the *Wandjina* throughout the area. In other versions, however, the *Wandjina* are self-created. Whatever the order of emergence of these cults, we can at least say that the mouthless *Wandjina* have been the most noted element of Kimberley iconography and mythology.

The next waves of religious development in the Kimberley came from the east, via the northern Warlpiri at the apex of the Central Desert, and ultimately from Arnhem Land. These were a range of cults of the 'Fertility-Mother' genre—*Kunapipi* in Arnhem Land (Berndt,1951), *Gadjari* among the Warlpiri (Meggitt, 1966) and, travelling west (through Balgo, Hall's Creek, Sturt Creek, etc.), taking the forms of *Dingari*, *Kurrangara* and *Worgaia*. *Kurrangara* is particularly interesting. Although this is the name of one section of the Arnhem Land *Kunapipi* rituals, according to Lommel (1950) it had transformed into a cult with a pessimistic eschatology anticipating the destruction of the earth. Petri (1950) also found this situation, with the elders concerned about a poison accompanying the *Djanba* spirits associated with the cult. Older men advocated returning to the traditions of the *Wandjina* and Rainbow Serpent as the only means of preventing the disastrous world-end.

By the 1960s the Petris found things had again transformed. The *Kurrangara* and *Wandjina* traditions had to some extent merged, and there had been revivals of *Dingari*. In 1963, a full-blown messianic movement appeared. The Ancestral Being leading it was *Tjinimin* (see above), now equated with Jesus. He was said to have revealed himself to Aborigines, given them a 'new' Law called *Worgaia*, told them to be steadfast in their traditions and promised that they would then, and only then, defeat the Europeans. They would themselves receive white skin and great wealth from Noah's ark which was filled with gold and crystals and was located in Aboriginal lands. The boat would also save Aborigines from a second, European-destroying flood (Petri and Petri-Odermann, 1988).

While the cults derived from the fertility ceremonies have travelled from the Central-North westwards, a more recent innovation, *Julurru*, has been traded in the opposite direction. Having begun on the west coast (some Aborigines say from as far south as Perth) it has passed across Fitzroy Crossing, through Balgo into the Central Desert. It shares some of the *Kurrangara* ritual and, like the Jesus–*Tjinimin* cult, it has explicit Christian elements and cargoistic expectations (Glowczewski, 1984). Yet it is a movement of even wider synthetic parameters, incorporating everything from the Christian God to Islamic 'Malay' cultural elements, and from traditional Dreaming tracks to motorbikes and aeroplanes.

There is still more to the rich religious tapestry of this region. There are, for instance, stories of actual historic personalities who were nonetheless of great religious significance. Shaw (1983: 137ff) has recorded the narratives of Boxer, a 'magic' man from Queensland said to have brought *Djanba* traditions with him while Kolig (1979) and D. Rose (1984) have each documented narratives dealing with Captain Cook, showing how he has been located within Aboriginal cosmologies. Kolig (1988) and D. Rose (1988) have also done much to investigate the impact of Christian missions in this area, although to my mind their respective claims for minimal influence require qualification.

Conclusion

Having provided a sketch of Australian Aboriginal religions within an historic framework, I will conclude with some basic generalisations regarding the impact of strangers through time upon Aboriginal attitudes towards the sacred structures of space.

My contention is that many scholars who have claimed that Aboriginal religions have remained static and relatively unchanging have been led astray by the attention they paid to a lack of explicit so-called syncretisms. Aboriginal religions have primarily responded *not* by blending myths, but by reformulating ontology. Although there are references to originally non-Aboriginal religious stories, more dramatic is the accommodation of alien ways of being-in-the-world. And I must agree with their view that being is more fundamental than names. It is perhaps interesting to compare mere words like *'Baiami'* and 'Jesus Christ', but surely the true issue, irrespective of titles, is the relationship between sacred powers and the structures of the world.

Once we relegate myth to a secondary place and turn foremost to ontology, the pattern becomes clear. I began by discussing Desert traditions because, while changes have occurred there in more recent years, this has been relatively the most isolated region of Aboriginal Australia. Desert religion is, as I explained, entirely pluralistic and until the advent of Christian missions had no place for transcendent beings. This is a model of Aboriginal religion seen by many scholars to be its basic form and these principles can be discerned throughout the continent, although elsewhere other principles have been added to the essential paradigm.

In Cape York, where the changes resulting from Melanesian contacts were relatively mild, the Hero cults offered but a veneer of socio-spatial continuity over predominantly locative traditions. The All-Mother cults emerging in Arnhem Land in the wake of Indonesian contacts were far more innovative, reflecting the greater threat posed by the Indonesian presence, yet even here we are dealing with a religious understanding which is this-worldly and which, while acknowledging an Aboriginal unity and a spatial continuity, does not threaten the pre-existing order of the world.

It is only with invasion that the *otiose* Supreme Beings (including the Christian God) emerge, and often their presence becomes a threat to the ideals of Earth-based powers. It is when such radical social and spatial transcendence combine—when the structures of the world are dissolved into a momentary liminality—that we see Aboriginal millennialism emerge with promises of total worldly transformation. Such movements are not common in Australia, but they have been recorded throughout the continent. That they have been shortlived indicates that Aboriginal people only rarely fully abandon their trust in a place-based ontology. To date, with some notable exceptions, Aborigines who have become Christians or embraced other pan-Aboriginal and universal creeds have done so in a way which ensured that older ideals of ubiety also endured. This is what is encapsulated by the statement, so frequently heard in contemporary Aboriginal communities, that they are a people with 'two Laws'.

It is beyond the historian's skills to predict the future. It is, however, at least certain that Aborigines today increasingly identify themselves with *the* Land as well as their lands, and many see their concerns as transcending land itself, spreading across the globe to unite all oppressed peoples. Whether they make this link in terms of the Christian God or some revival or reinvention of Aboriginal tradition is arguably of minor importance. When reaching, of necessity, out beyond the bounds of place, Aboriginal people will perhaps feel themselves best served by that faith which will allow them, at the same time, to be true to those places eternally called their homes.

12 Religious conflict and integration among some ethnic Christian groups
Jim McKay and Frank Lewins

This paper examines how inter-relationships between ethnic and religious forces affect the identities and relations of members of immigrant populations. Research on ethnic and religious interactions among immigrants can be divided into three main categories. First, there are situations in which ethnic and religious identities and structures have mutually reinforcing tendencies. For instance, Yinger (1969: 89–90) notes that, among some immigrant groups in the United States, ethnic and religious attachments constitute a single identity—one is simultaneously Irish *and* Catholic, Swedish *and* Lutheran, Greek *and* Orthodox. Phrases such as the 'sacralisation' or 'sanctification' of ethnicity and/or the 'ethnicisation' of religion have been used to describe this symbiotic link between ethnic and religious affiliations (Mol, 1979). Second, there are contexts in which religious unity is destabilised by ethnic diversity. For instance, Irish hegemony in the Catholic Church in Australia, Canada and the United States has often been a source of tension and conflict with subordinate Southern and Eastern European Catholics (Lewins, 1978). Finally, there are cases in which religious differences fracture the stability of an ethnic population. One example is the division which often occurs between Orthodox and Catholic Armenians. In this paper we examine some antinomies and reciprocations between ethnicity and religion among several ethnic Christian groups in Australia. We use the term 'ethnic groups' to refer to collectivities of people who meaningfully interact with one another because they share a particular symbol (e.g. language or dialect, national ancestry, physical appearance) which represents their cultural and/or social distinctiveness. 'Ethnicity' or 'ethnic identity' refers to the cognitive and affective attachments which people display towards such symbols.[1] Before proceeding, it is necessary to explain the theoretical framework which will be used to present our case studies.

Theoretical framework

Our analysis of ethnic and religious connections relies on Schermerhorn's (1970; 1978) theoretical framework for studying inter-ethnic relations (see Figure 12.1).

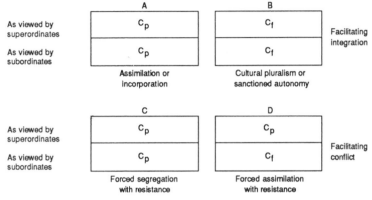

C_p = Ideology preferring centripetal goals for subordinates
C_f = Ideology preferring centrifugal goals for subordinates

Source: Schermerhorn, 1978: 22

Figure 12.1 Reciprocal goal definitions of centripetal and centrifugal trends of subordinates, as viewed by themselves and superordinates

According to Schermerhorn, inter-ethnic relations are characterised by synchronic patterns of conflict *and* integration. Integration is generally defined as a '*process* whereby units or elements of a society are brought into active and coordinated compliance with the ongoing activities and objectives of the dominant group in that society' (Schermerhorn, 1970: 14). The specific configurations of conflict and integration are the outcomes of power struggles between dominant and subordinate groups and are largely conditioned by the kinds of goals the former stipulate for the latter. In some cases dominant groups specify *centrifugal* goals, which sustain various degrees of social and/or cultural compartmentalisation between themselves and subordinates. These can range from acceptance of multiculturalism through to enforced apartheid. At other times, dominant groups have *centripetal* aims, which overtly or covertly force subordinates to assimilate into dominant institutions. Since ascendant groups are never omnipotent and subordinate groups are never impotent, Schermerhorn stresses that permutations of conflict and integration also are partially shaped by the extent to which subordinate groups 'comply' with or resist the prescriptions of dominant groups. Relations tend towards integration when the intentions of *both* dominant *and* subordinate groups are *either* centripetal *or* centrifugal. For instance, when dominant groups pursue centripetal policies of assimilation and subordinate groups 'consent' to be incorporated, then relations are inclined to be integrative. Relations also manifest a relatively integrative orientation when dominant groups institutionalise centrifugal programs such as cultural pluralism, which satisfies those subordinate groups wanting to maintain some degree of distinctiveness. Conflictive relations predominate when subordinates desire to be relatively autonomous but are compelled to assimilate, or when their demands for access to dominant institutions are overtly or covertly denied. We now use this theoretical scheme to examine some interrelationships between ethnic and religious forces among Lebanese Catholic and Orthodox, Ukrainian Catholic and Orthodox, Polish Catholics, Croatian Catholics and Italian Catholics.

Ethnic and religious inter-relationships among ethnic Christian populations

Lebanese Catholics and Orthodox

The Lebanese Christians who came to Australia before World War II, together with their descendants,[2] exemplify how the potential for ethnic coherence can be weakened by religious cleavages. Before migrating, the primary loyalties of most Lebanese were to their extended family and their village church, both of which were closely enmeshed. Moreover, most villagers were faithful to one of the following Eastern churches: Maronite Catholic, Melkite Catholic or Antiochian Orthodox; intermarriage among members of these three groups was relatively uncommon. Since nationalistic feelings were minimal among these villagers, the 'cultural baggage' of first-generation immigrants did little to foster a sense of community encompassing Maronites, Melkites and Orthodox after they arrived in Australia. Offspring of these Lebanese migrants were often strongly discouraged both by relatives and by priests from marrying Lebanese migrant offspring belonging to a different denomination.

The prospect of forging a cohesive ethnic community was further diminished by the assimilative demands which Australian Catholic and Protestant Churches made on first-generation immigrants and their offspring. Attachments to the Eastern churches quickly attenuated as second-generation Lebanese were baptised in Australian Catholic and Protestant Churches and attended Catholic and Protestant schools. Consequently, few second- and third-generation Lebanese attend the Maronite, Melkite or Antiochian churches or understand any Arabic. Most second- and third-generation Lebanese of Maronite and Melkite ancestry define themselves as 'Catholic' rather than according to their specific Eastern rite. Nearly all see themselves as *Catholic*–Lebanese rather than

Lebanese-Catholics. For example, there are about a dozen Catholic priests in New South Wales of Maronite or Melkite descent, all of whom have been ordained in the Latin rite and have little or no contact with the Eastern churches. Although a small number of third-generation Maronites and Melkites have married Lebanese of Orthodox descent, the great majority have stayed within their denomination by marrying Anglo-Australian Catholics rather than Lebanese Orthodox. Whereas Lebanese with Maronite and Melkite heritages see themselves as parts of a larger Catholic community, those from an Antiochian background have little or no feelings of sodality with Armenian, Greek, Russian, Serbian or Ukrainian Orthodox. Most second- and third-generation Lebanese with Antiochian backgrounds define themselves as 'Christian' instead of 'Orthodox' or 'Antiochian'. A few third-generation Antiochians have married Maronites and Melkites, but most inter-denominational marriages have occurred with Anglo-Australian Catholics, Anglo-Australian Protestants and people with assorted religious and ethnic lineages. Traditionally, Lebanese have followed an unwritten agreement that the bride should follow the faith of the groom. Some Orthodox allege that Lebanese Catholics frequently have violated this norm by expecting an Orthodox groom to convert to his bride's Catholicism. Given this history of antagonism between the two denominations, it is not surprising that only a relatively small number of marriages have occurred between Catholic and Orthodox Lebanese.

The religious relations between Australians and Lebanese typify cell A of Schermerhorn's typology of centripetal/centrifugal trends. Lebanese 'acquiescence' to forces of Anglicisation and Latinisation has resulted in second- and third-generation descendants having only residual and ephemeral feelings of Lebanese identity. They have *individual* identifications with family traditions, but no *collective* linguistic, religious or nationalistic ties to Lebanon or to a Lebanese community in Australia. In this way Lebanese are markedly different from Armenians, Croatians, Greeks and Ukrainians in Australia. The Lebanese also indicate how the potential for ethnic unity can be abraded by religious divergences. If Maronites, Melkites and Orthodox had been able to overcome their sectarian and denominational differences and married each other, then they may have been able to maintain a semblance of ethnic cohesion. However, their mutual animosity and their 'compliance' with Australian Catholicism and Protestantism militated against this possibility. Consequently, about half of all third-generation Lebanese have non-Lebanese spouses and there is virtually no likelihood that this exogamic trend will be reversed.

Ukrainian Catholics and Orthodox

Ukrainian Christians share some important qualities with Lebanese Christians. Specifically:

1 their numbers comprise both Catholics and Orthodox;[3]
2 their Catholic component follows an Eastern (i.e. Byzantine) rite; and
3 the Australian Catholic Church has played an important role in
   shaping the ethnic and religious lives of Ukrainian Catholics.

However, in terms of the nexus between ethnicity and religion, the differences are more significant than the similarities. Ukrainian Christians in Australia are, at the same time, Ukrainian nationalists, who see themselves primarily as *Ukrainian* Catholics or *Ukrainian* Orthodox. In contrast to Lebanese Christians, whose religious differences have inhibited the development of any corporate *Lebanese* consciousness, Ukrainians' strong sense of *Ukrainian* identity generally has transcended Catholic–Orthodox differences.

The main factor which explains this national focus of the Ukrainian identity is the nature of Ukraine's history. Whereas patterns of ethnic identification among Lebanese Christians revolve around individual attachments to family customs, Ukrainians' ethnic consciousness is rooted in their collective experience of a homeland lost, as they often put it, as a result of 'the oppression of Russian communists', and their being political refugees or children of refugees who fled the advancing Russian army at the close of World War II. Given that most Ukrainians in Australia came as refugees in the early years following the war, thematic in their perception of Ukrainian identity is the strong historical sense of national suffering and the tragedy of Ukraine's absorption into the Soviet Union. This viewpoint is evident in the Ukrainian press—for example, in their displays of photographs of political heroes who fought for Ukrainian independence. It is also prominent in the curriculum used in Ukrainian schools (Kringas and Lewins, 1981: 45–51), in the pre-Russian occupation memorabilia in Ukrainians' homes, and in the strong anti-communist/anti-Russian stance generally adopted by Ukrainians. An anecdotal illustration of this encompassing *Ukrainian* identity is Ukrainian Catholics' frequent claim that they would prefer their daughters to marry Ukrainian Orthodox rather than Australian Catholics.

Although today there is widespread awareness and acceptance in the Australian Catholic Church of the Ukrainian rite's legal independence from the jurisdiction of the local church, Ukrainians' early post-migration experience was similar to that of other migrants. The Australian Catholic Church, like other Australian institutions, expected migrants to fit into the existing parish structure and refused to set up special migrant structures to meet their needs. The ignorance in the Australian Catholic Church of the distinctive rites of Eastern Catholics has caused jurisdictional conflicts with Ukrainians over parish territories and who has the right to officiate at marriages of Ukrainian Catholics.

Closely related to the mutually reinforcing link between a beleaguered feeling of nationalism and religion, especially among Catholics, is the attempt to institutionalise a Ukrainian way of life in Australia. For example, in Catholic circles, priests have been actively involved in organising ethnic or Saturday schools, consistently acting as financial advisers, business advocates and initiators of efforts to establish special institutions for Ukrainians, such as an old people's home in Sydney. It is this approximation of 'institutional completeness' (Breton, 1964) which has led many Ukrainians to 'opt out' of what they see as the strictures of a Ukrainian-controlled way of life. As one prominent Ukrainian in Sydney noted: 'unless families are prepared to be wholly in by participating in things such as church, scouts, and social activities, then it's best to be wholly out and not be Ukrainian at all'.

In the case of Ukrainian Catholics, the early conflict based on the centripetal expectations of Australian Catholics alongside the centrifugal desires of Ukrainians fits Schermerhorn's cell D. More recently, this relationship approximates cell B, because in Schermerhorn's model of conflict and integration, the Australian Church has accepted Ukrainians' Eastern rite status and, hence, their religious autonomy. This is a contrast with Lebanese Maronites and Melkites, who largely 'conformed' to the assimilative policies of the Australian Catholic Church. Despite the recent change towards accommodation, the early conflict between Australian and Ukrainian Catholics illustrates the impact ethnic heterogeneity can have on eroding cohesion within the Australian Catholic Church, a situation more explicitly illustrated among Poles, Croats and Italians.

Polish and Croatian Catholics

Polish and Croatian Catholics are not only empirically similar in that both are a part of the Latin rite, but they also have similar relations within the Australian Catholic Church. For these reasons they will be dealt with together.

Among Polish Catholics there is a jointly reinforcing relationship between religion and ethnicity. For instance, Majka (1972) claims that Polish identity and Catholic identity go hand in hand. A similar emphasis is evident in Kaluski's (1988: 91) comment that 'Since the tenth century, Polish culture has been dominated by Roman Catholicism. Poland became and is Catholic to its roots.' Accordingly, it is difficult to give primacy to either element in Polish Catholic identity. Although Polish organisations in Australia generally have no official links with the church, members often claim that it is taken for granted that the bulk of their number is taking part in religious life. This link between religion and ethnicity is illuminated by the claims of some Polish priests that, for Poles, religion is a vehicle with which to attack communism and, in this sense, Poles share an important quality with Ukrainians. In relation to communism, conflict among Poles manifests a strong link between Polish religion and politics. It is significant that conflict both among Polish groups, and between Polish groups and Polish priests has been precipitated by 'confrontation between hard line anti-communists and moderates' (Martin, 1972: 56), and also by importing political differences which existed in Poland prior to World War II.

Like Poles, Croats in Australia exhibit a strong blend of Catholicism, nationalism and anti-communism. However, they differ from Poles in that national identity takes precedence over religious orientations—most see themselves as Croats first and Catholics second, or as *Croatian* Catholics. Like Ukrainians and Poles, this meld of religion and nationalism is mutually reinforcing and cannot be understood independent of factors pertaining to Croatia in contemporary Yugoslavia. The dominant orientation among Croatian Catholics in relation to their homeland is their refusal to recognise Yugoslavia, which is synonymous with domination by Serbian communists (Schopflin, 1973). This strong political conviction is evident among Croatian chaplains and other Catholic Croats. In homes and church offices, maps and flags of Croatia are openly displayed alongside religious symbols, making it difficult to distinguish between the religious and political nature of the setting. Among Croatian Catholics, claims of fighting for the freedom of Croatia have frequently been heard over the past couple of decades and numerous references in the media corroborate this claim.

To distinguish the priority of religious and political beliefs, the anecdotal litmus test (as in the case of Lebanese and Ukrainians) is who should marry whom, especially one's daughter. Croats seem as equally definite as Ukrainians that it is better if 'like marries like'; that is, Croat marries Croat, even if it involves marriage between Croatian Catholics and Muslims. As one chaplain put it: 'It is better if Croat marries Croat, after all we are all brothers [sic] ... '

Poles' and Croats' locations within the Australian Catholic Church have accentuated their respective national identities and simultaneously undermined the uniformity of Australian Catholicism. Being of the Latin rite, Poles and Croats have been expected to be absorbed into the existing parish structure as *Australian* Catholics. However, the refusal of Australian bishops and priests to admit national differences in the structure of the Australian Church has resulted in these groups organising as *Polish* Catholics and *Croatian* Catholics in order to meet their religious needs. Such ethnic mobilisation in the form of migrant chaplains providing Mass in the native language and, especially in the case of the Croats, the establishment of Croatian Catholic Centres, has produced many jurisdictional disputes and a milieu of conflict. Polish and Croatian priests have felt as if they were 'second class citizens' and 'outcasts' for having to be beholden to Australian parish priests for the use of buildings in which they could say Mass.

Historically, it is worth noting briefly that, among both Poles and Croats, the successive waves of migration correspond to changing circumstances in Poland and Yugoslavia. Specifically, this is borne out by the correspondence between the decline of religious participation among some Poles and Croats and their deviation from strong anti-communism. Previously, alleged Croatian terrorist activities in Australia have been identified by Croats as responsible for a decline in Croats' participation in Croatian Catholic life.

These nationalistic articulations of religious identity in an Australian Catholic Church which traditionally has either ignored or incorporated national differences conforms to Schermerhorn's cell D. Thus there has been a tendency towards conflict because of the incongruent nature of Australian Catholics' assimilative expectations (centripetal orientations) and Poles'[4] and Croats'[5] desires to maintain their specific national religious practices (centrifugal orientations).

Italian Catholics

Italian Catholics do not normally have a strong, national sense of being *Italian*. Instead, their strongest tie is to their *paese*; that is, their village of origin and surrounding area (Lewins, 1978: 95–108). Like Lebanese, but unlike Ukrainians, Poles and Croats, they generally do not easily organise on the basis of national loyalty. 'Normally' and 'generally' are used to indicate the overall pattern of Italians' behaviour and to provide a contrast with the specific situation which has arisen in the territorial parishes of the Australian Catholic Church. The vast majority of Italians worship in their local Catholic parish, with a smaller number catered for by religious orders, such as the Scalabrinians and Capuchins, which care principally for Italians.

Despite almost a century of Italian migration (Pyke, 1948; Borrie, 1954), there has been since the 1970s a crystallisation of Italian ethnic identity in the parish context. This *Italian* consciousness stems largely from the political nature of relations within the parish and is expressed most clearly in parishes which contain significant numbers of Italians and (other) Australians. In this context, Italians from a variety of regional backgrounds organise as *Italians* in a religious environment which has a history of resentment to the maintenance of Italians' cultural traits. The emergence of an Italian identity centres around Italians' perception that Australians have a disregard for Italians and the worth of their religious traditions. It has been a frequent complaint among Italians that they are subject to ethnocentric and incorporative practices in Australian parishes. They note that Australian priests still use the term 'assimilation', even though it has been superseded by 'integration' and, more recently, 'multiculturalism'. In some parishes, Italians have felt sufficiently aggrieved to claim publicly that unless more concessions were made to allow for regional styles of worship, many Italians would not have anything further to do with the Church. It is this insensitivity by

Australians to the diversified nature of Italians' religious customs which has long been recognised as at least one factor in lowering the participation of Italians in Australian Catholic life (Borrie, 1954). For some time scholars have linked Italians' feelings of rejection by the Australian Catholic Church with their attraction to Jehovah's Witnesses (Phillips, 1970). Italians comment on the 'neglect' of Italian Catholics by the Australian Church and the often-disastrous consequences of Jehovah's Witnesses filling the religious vacuum produced by this insensitivity.

The genesis and development of this *Italian* consciousness has not occurred in a vacuum. The convergence of regional backgrounds in parishes derives primarily from the individual Italian's recognition, that although regional backgrounds are relatively unimportant in the parish, a combined Italian voice is a viable method of obtaining some measure of political power. As Italians perceive it, there has been a need to have political power in light of Australians' disrespect and prejudice towards them for worshipping as Italians. The propensity of Australians to put migrants with regional differences into one category—Italians—has had the effect of reinforcing an Italian consciousness, because of the functional correspondence between Australians' perception that Italians constitute a homogeneous category and Italians' realisation of the value of a unified Italian voice.

In Schermerhorn's terms, the centripetal wish of Italian Catholics to participate as *Italians* in Australian parish life clashes with Australians' centrifugal desire to exclude them as *Italians*, as well as Australians' centipetal aim to incorporate them as *Australian* Catholics. Such permutations are associated with conflict (cell C of Schermerhorn's typology) and highlight the manner in which, again, ethnic dissonance corrodes the religious cohesion of the parish context of Australian Catholicism.[6]

Summary and conclusions

In this paper we have analysed some religious experiences of a variety of ethnic Christian populations in Australia. Our case studies, making use of Schermerhorn's theoretical insights, were selected in order to demonstrate three points. First, we have tried to show that ethnic identities, group unity and inter-ethnic relations are processual in form and contextually related.[7] Our second aim has been to illustrate the divergent connections between religion and ethnicity, especially in terms of the capacity of each to reinforce or undermine the solidarity of the other. These varying relationships illustrate the different histories of both ethnic and religious groupings and the need to examine each on its own terms. As Nahirny and Fishman (1965: 316) remind us, immigrants possess 'many different ethnic pasts rather than one national past'. Just as there is no universal theory governing the formation of ethnic identities and structures, there also is no axiom which posits a determinate association between religious and ethnic forces. Our final concern has been to argue that religious institutions are sites of power struggles between dominant and subordinate groups. These three factors have been emphasised in order to demonstrate that understanding the ethnic diversity of religious institutions is essential for comprehending patterns of conflict and integration in polyethnic societies like Australia.

Notes

1   See McKay and Lewins (1978) for a comprehensive analysis of ethnic identities and structures.
2   For a comprehensive analysis of these Lebanese Christians, see McKay (1989).
3   There are also other denominational groupings among Ukrainians, such as Baptists, but these are small; see Lawriwsky (1988).
4   For more details on the religious heterogeneity of Poles in Australia, see Kaluski (1988).
5   For a further discussion of Croats as a part of the wider category of Yugoslavs, see Tisay (1989).
6   For further discussions of Italians see Bertelli and Pascoe (1988), Lewins (1978) and Pittarello (1980).
7   See McKay (1982) and McKay and Lewins (1978) for detailed discussions of the dynamic and contextual nature of ethnic identities and structures.

13 Islam, immigrants and the state: religion and cultural politics in Australia[1]
Michael Humphrey

In the West contemporary Islam has become equated with fundamentalist and assertive Islam encapsulated in a cluster of international cultural symbols and images. The chador, veil, mosques, bearded sheikhs and angry Muslim crowds have come to represent irrationality, archaism, repression, intolerance and violence. Muslim culture is regarded as alien and unmanageable, while the politics of radical Islamic movements and states are seen as uncontrollable through the normal rules of international diplomacy. One consequence of the international politicisation of Islamic culture is that manifestations of individual belief and practice or Muslim community solidarity are often treated with suspicion. Muslim immigrant communities in Western societies experience the consequences of the politicised cultural symbols most directly. Muslims tend to be regarded as unyielding to the demands of the modern world either as migrants or as states.

Yet the 'Muslim problem' in the West is part of a larger political question about the impact of the massive recruitment of labour from underdeveloped regions and its incorporation into Western societies. Racist political movements and changes in immigration policy in Western states strictly regulating entry, work and residence rights are the context in which the strong prejudice and antagonism towards Muslim immigrants have emerged. But because immigration is often as important for the donor as the host states—as labour for the former, and as remittances and a safety valve against pressures of unemployment for the latter—the politics of immigration policy have assumed national and international dimensions. Behind the issues of immigration policy and the treatment of immigrants are broader questions of the relationship between the developed and underdeveloped world and the articulation of this political relationship in transnational culture, in this case Islam.

This chapter explores the relationship between religious practice and the cultural marginality of Islam in the West, focusing on the religious organisation and practice of Muslim immigrant communities in Australia. It interprets immigrant religious culture as a dimension of the process of incorporation of migrants in class cultures. The theoretical approach used derives from Bourdieu's (1984) analysis of the social world as both a symbolic system and a system of power relations. It argues that the process of incorporation of immigrants selectively structures the reconstitution of religious culture in migration.

Immigration for most Muslim migrants transforms their status from a majority to a minority culture. However, in the process of relocation and incorporation, the religious category is usually subordinated to class and ethnic divisions in the organisation of immigrant religious life. In this context, religion does not usually act as a socially or organisationally cohesive or overarching category. In fact, the character of religious organisation, the kind of Islamic orientation found in mosques and the links between organisations reflect the different social and class positions of Muslim immigrants. Because these religious institutions are locally grown, they articulate the social experience of discrete groups. Even with the development of national Islamic institutions, local mosque communities resist the pressure to dissolve their specific ethnic and class basis. The historical plurality of Islamic authority—that is, the absence of a Church—only serves to strengthen the autonomy and independence of mosque communities.

Class and Muslim cultural identity in Australia

A cultural history of Islam in the West must be set in the social and cultural context into which immigrants are incorporated. Because of the character of Australian immigration, this has mainly involved the adjustment of migrants to the social and work rhythms of the immigrant working class.

The 1986 Census revealed that there were around 110 000 Muslims in Australia. While they have come from all parts of the globe, including the Middle East, Southern Europe, Africa, South Asia, Southeast Asia, East Asia and the Pacific, more than 80 per cent are from Turkey and Lebanon. The distribution of Muslims in Australia is heavily concentrated (87 per cent) in the two most populous states, New South Wales and Victoria, with the former having around 53 per cent of the total Muslim population. The concentration of Muslim communities in particular working-class suburbs of Sydney and Melbourne also parallels Mediterranean immigrant working-class settlement patterns. Chain migration has had a strong influence in clustering immigrants, emphasising ties of family, community and ethnic group. The names and addresses of Islamic voluntary associations and mosques reveal the ethnic, sectarian and linguistic demarcations of Muslim cultural and religious identity and community settlement. Thus the addresses of the Amal Charitable Association, the Lebanese Muslim Association and the Sydney Turkish Islamic Cultural and Mosque Association identify the residential concentrations of Shi'a from South Lebanon, Sunnis from North Lebanon and Turks from Eastern Turkey respectively.

Occupational status and unemployment levels are also indicators of the class position of Muslim immigrants. Like most members of the Mediterranean immigrant working class, Muslims from the majority of Lebanese and Turkish communities are concentrated in manufacturing, construction and retail trade. While the proportion varies, on average Lebanese and Turks are twice as likely as the Australian-born population to be in manufacturing jobs. Amongst the most recent arrivals, the proportion employed in unskilled work is even higher. One study found that between 1972 and 1983 and average of 35.2 per cent of Lebanese (Christian and Muslim) were engaged in manufacturing jobs, and among recent Lebanese arrivals the figure was as high as 47.2 per cent. A detailed study on employment and unemployment amongst Sydney Lebanese in 1984 found that 75 per cent of Lebanese Sunni Muslim males who had been employed in Australia were concentrated in unskilled work, compared with 53 per cent of Shi'a, 52 per cent of Antiochian Orthodox and 45 per cent of Maronite Catholic males who had been employed in Australia (Humphrey, 1984b). Unemployment amongst Turkish- and Lebanese-born Australians has been consistently high, running between 30 per cent to 35 per cent since the early 1980s, when the national average has ranged from 6 per cent to 8 per cent (Young, Petty and Faulkner, 1980; Mackie, 1983; Humphrey, 1984b).

Wolf (1982: 363) argues that 'The migrant's position is determined not so much by the migrant or his culture as by the structure of the situation in which he finds himself.' For most Muslim immigrants to Australia, their incorporation into the immigrant working class of the two major industrial cities of Sydney and Melbourne dominates their individual and social experience. In this context, the social and cultural capital derived from other societies and social positions has limited value except in the formation of new local cultures. Ties of family, community, mosque and patronage are eclipsed by the primary characteristics of education, qualifications, skills, English language and savings in securing good jobs and social mobility in Australian society. Even Muslim immigrants from middle-class backgrounds often find that poor English-language skills and the non-portability of qualifications severely restrict the possibility of realising a similar class position and lifestyle. The selective character of the official recognition of others' culture—for example, professional training and qualifications—reflects historical and institutional ties between Australia and other countries (Mitchell, Tait and Castles, 1990).

Hence, for the immigrant working class, basic choices of consumption, housing, suburb of residence, quality of education and the character of youth culture are largely determined by factors beyond their control and outside the domain of family or community organisation.

The social and cultural capital 'of another place' forms the core of a new local culture based on social ties and religious affiliation.[2] The process of cultural regeneration is, however, necessarily selective. The act of immigration itself begins selective reinforcement of social and cultural practices. Immigration law determines the kinship ties (consanguinal and affinal) which are deemed most important under 'family reunion' provisions. In this way, the state's selection procedures strongly shape the future character of immigrant family and community ties, often more so than traditional marriage preferences, Islamic law or patterns of kinship obligations. State-sanctioned family ties are in turn reinforced by the experience of settlement where familiar ties assume value as resources for providing the basic needs of housing, services and employment channelled through community networks which are themselves generated by the process of selection and settlement. Ethnic communities have long been regarded as the initial providers of assistance in settlement.

If the experience of initial location of immigrants selectively reinforces social ties, then the experience of incorporation in the ethnic working class shapes the potential development of the social and cultural capital and thus the social trajectory of migrants. This can be quite specific in terms of the kind of employment one enters and the social activities and leisure time it allows. As Bourdieu (1984) points out in his analysis of working-class culture, the time available to acquire new social and cultural capital or make use of the old is strongly influenced by the conditions and requirements of work. Hours of work (e.g. rotating shift work, long hours imposed by self-employment in a shop), place of work (e.g. factory, office, taxi), working in more than one job, social isolation by task and/or noise, opportunities for interaction with others socially from your own or other ethnic backgrounds at work, the chance to interact in English and whether you work with others from a wider community or with your own community or family—all these factors influence the relevance of one's social and cultural capital and the potential to transform it. Cultural identity forms in the context of life possibilities, strongly influenced by daily experience of isolation or interaction with wider class cultures.

The ethnography of Muslim immigrants in Australia reveals a strong concern with family morality and the sexual division of labour focused on the regulation of women's behaviour. The importance of gender relations in Muslim immigrant culture reflects on one hand the centrality of gender relations in traditional Islamic social practice with its ideals about dress, segregation and domestic confinement, and on the other the increased significance of the family in sustaining social and cultural continuity in immigrant life. Lives previously enmeshed in a Muslim social and cultural environment find in migration that the major responsibility for the regeneration and maintenance of Muslim culture falls on the family, itself frequently reduced to the members of a household.

The heightened significance of the family for cultural and group survival makes the regulation of these arenas particularly sensitive. Islamic law, customary practices and social etiquette are invoked to regulate marriage, divorce and inheritance, the segregation of women and rules of modesty in such areas as dress. The sensitivity of these issues in Muslim immigrant communities in the West has become apparent in controversies over wearing of the headscarf in French state schools, the tests for virginity of prospective Muslim and Hindu brides arriving in Britain and the continuing force of Islamic law preventing Muslim women remarrying even after they have secured a civil divorce through the courts in Australia.

In migration the cultural sensitivity of male–female relations becomes particularly acute as social ties contract around a nuclear household. Removed from an environment in which degrees of social distance could be differentiated and regulated by kinship, marriage, family standing and membership of a religious community, gender is recast as a confrontation between the inside/outside, the familiar/foreign and the safe/dangerous in an alien social environment. In this context, a gender ideology which celebrates modesty, privacy, dependence and obedience seeks to enclose women within a socially narrowed arena. They are made the object of male 'protection' and the vehicle through which the moral preservation of the family is secured or lost. Comments by Lebanese Muslim women that they had greater personal freedom to choose a marriage partner in Lebanon than they do in Australia are in part a reflection of the intensified focus of male authority among Muslim immigrants.

However, the social position of Muslim women is extremely ambiguous. At the same time as Muslim males seek to restrict their women's independence, the very process of incorporation and class location imposes economic and social demands which must be accommodated. This ambiguity can be seen in the way strategies are developed to preserve gender identities in areas where women are drawn into broader social and cultural arenas. One area is wage work. The need to earn an income through wage work, especially since working-class migrants usually arrive with few economic resources, places immediate demands on family members of working age to enter the labour market irrespective of gender. The dilemma becomes how to maximise wage contributions to the household while at the same time preserving gender roles and identity within the context of the family.

One solution is to try to continue the practice of domestic confinement of women and to limit their participation in the workforce. As few as 11 per cent of Lebanese Muslim women, but as many as 45 per cent of Turkish Muslim women, participate in wage work. The total Australian female labour force participation rates are around 43 per cent. Large families and an extended period of childbearing continue as the main factors perpetuating the domestic confinement of women in the role of mothers and housekeepers.[3] While it is often argued by welfare workers that it is inadequate childcare facilities that prevent mothers from entering the paid workforce, this ignores the cultural reinforcement of gender roles that having large families represents.[4]

The entry of Muslim women into the workforce usually creates considerable concern amongst men about the work environment and kind of work their women undertake. A local cultural map develops, tacitly classifying jobs by their degrees of closeness to cultural ideals of domestic confinement (i.e. close supervision) and mothering. Some work environments are represented as familiar and culturally permissible (e.g. working with family members in a family business, working with members from the same community or ethnic group, working only with women). Also acceptable are jobs associated with traditional gender roles of caring and nurturing (e.g. cook, welfare worker, childcare, making clothes, teacher). The most acceptable jobs are those regulated in familiar environments and involving work associated with the home. For example, women may be employed in a family business such as a restaurant where they can cook removed from public view; or they may provide home-based care for the children of other working mothers.

Employment of women in family businesses also serves to reinforce male authority through economic control over the distribution of household income. Usually takings in family businesses are not dispersed in the form of wages but allocated according to the competing needs of family members (e.g. buying a house, providing bridewealth, paying for travel, a car or consumer goods). Employment of women in family businesses can also provide the opportunity for males to assert authority in public life. Flexibility of working hours and the availability of family labour (wife and children) allows the household head to become involved in community politics and thereby locate himself within a competitive and honour-defined male arena.

Women's participation in wage work, especially factory work, is regarded as particularly threatening because of the unsegregated character of the workplace and the economic independence wages can create. A common Muslim male view that factories are sites of moral corruption and sexual promiscuity historically parallels attitudes towards the entry of English working-class women into factory employment in the mill towns in the nineteenth century (Thompson, 1968: 452). In Sydney, a scandal involving Lebanese Muslim and Christian women employed to clean railway carriages on night shift and coerced by their supervisors in the State Rail Authority to grant them sexual favours only heightened fears about the dangers of women's work outside the home.[5]

Where women are employed in factory wage work, men often adopt controlling strategies which seek to restrict the independence usually associated with work outside the home. They may seek to regulate the unsupervised time women spend outside the household by personally driving them to and from work by car, by permitting employment only in workplaces where another family member is already employed or by ensuring they work in a segregated female workforce from their own ethnic and/or religious background.

Observance of dress rules, especially wearing the headscarf, often becomes a condition for permission to work outside the home. The headscarf serves as an external symbol of modesty and responsibility, but in fact its wearing can be ambiguous. On the one hand it can be seen as a condition imposed by males marking their authority over women, but on the other it signifies the 'coming out' of Muslim working-class women who for the first time are entering the industrial workforce. The dominant Australian culture generally sees the headscarf as a symbol of male domination and an intrusion of religious practice into secular arenas of life. The negative response has actually seen the women themselves, rather than their husbands, brothers or fathers, become the victims of discrimination in the workplace because they 'look different' and are accused by employers of disrupting the workplace.

The interdependence of Muslim gender identities and the fragility of traditional gender boundaries are dramatically expressed in the impact of industrial injuries on male roles in the household. The working-class status of most Muslim male immigrants places many of them in jobs where self-worth is intimately tied up with physical strength. If the physical 'macho' self-image is undermined through injury, there frequently occurs a psychological crisis which is expressed in a gender role reversal. Household heads who were physically strong, independent and proud providers may fall into the role of being dependent and weak. When this occurs, women can find themselves fulfilling the role of mother rather than wife and partner to their injured husbands. Injury which might not be physically incapacitating can become chronic and incurable because of the need for a continuous sick performance in order to justify claims for worker's compensation and to give cultural legitimation to one's inability to fulfil the competitive male image.

The education of women is another area where men intervene by seeking to regulate dress rules and supervise social interaction. Just as migration offers women possibilities for industrial employment, it also offers many Muslim women opportunities for education previously unavailable for reasons of gender bias and cost. Headscarves are common amongst Muslim female students in Australia, sometimes from the early age of 5 years. The government policy of multiculturalism encourages tolerance of dress rules as an expression of cultural difference. Conflicts over dress do arise, however, when Muslim parents restrict their daughters from participating in the full range of school activities, especially sporting activities. Muslim fathers frequently prevent their daughters from doing sports such as swimming or athletics, which require clothing that is brief and physically non-constraining. The usual outcome of these conflicts is that Muslim girls either participate with such cumbersome clothing that they are effectively excluded—they cannot learn to swim—or they attend sports days as mere spectators.

Early marriage still serves as an important means of control over the activity of migrant Muslim women. The continued high levels of endogamy, the selection of a spouse in the country of origin, the high instance of first-cousin marriage amongst Lebanese Muslims, and legal conflicts over the age at marriage are all an indication of pressures to retain male responsibility for women. In fact, because of the perceived moral permissiveness of Australian society, concerns over chastity and supervision can actually be heightened. Such concerns can occur even amongst those males who might prefer to allow their daughters or sisters to take full opportunity of education. In one case where a Lebanese Muslim ethnic intermediary was confronted with demands for his younger sister to marry at the age of 14 years he submitted because he feared the consequences of dishonour for his own position in the community he served (Humphrey, 1984c).

The idea that Muslim women should always be under the protection/supervision of men has presented acute problems when, because of conflict or violence, women leave the marital household. As the traditional response of going to one's father's house is often not available, women may seek help and shelter outside their community. One source of help is Australian women's refuges, which are regarded by Muslim men as being subversive of Muslim family life by encouraging women to assert their legal rights to live a life independent of their husband or to charge husbands with assault in cases of domestic violence. If women seek help in these refuges they can find themselves isolated from their children and even rejected by their own families. Muslim women's groups have responded by establishing 'Islamic' refuges to provide a culturally acceptable, neutral and uncompromised space to allow for the settlement of marital conflicts. Islamic refuges are an attempt to prevent the 'pollution' of women brought about by going outside permitted social boundaries and authority; they serve to reinforce Islamic morality by emphasising a woman's duties towards husband and family.

Communities and mosques

Beyond the family, men seek to create an institutional environment which supports their efforts to retain authority in the household. The same ideals of segregation and confinement which help to demarcate gender roles in the family are continued in the public arena. The domains of authority are delineated by formal institutional participation as well as by the retention of an honour culture which maintains an assertive male image of social responsibility and personal power.

Voluntary associations and mosques are two institutional arenas which men dominate. Even though many voluntary associations are nominally village-based organisations, for most purposes they act as male clubs (Humphrey, 1984b). The involvement of women in these associations is usually limited to special occasions such as family social functions and picnics. Where women do become actively involved in voluntary associations, they undertake welfare and charitable activities, areas associated with caring and generosity rather than public power.

The formation of this kind of male-oriented community culture is common amongst many Mediterranean immigrants in Australia. It is built on social ties derived from kinship and friendship, often within the context of members of an original village. Factional divisions, status competition and conflicts from the home community can persist and influence competition over prizes of rank in voluntary associations (e.g. president of an association). The cultural capital of former personal ties (kinship, friendship and community networks) achieves new relevance for the immigrant working class by allowing links to develop between males of the same ethnic group through inter-associational activities or in the context of larger encompassing cultural organisations. Parochial ties become the focus for cultural incorporation within the immigrant working class.

While voluntary associations can link males of the same ethnic group, religious institutions are most commonly the broadest social arena for a particular ethnic community. The link between male culture and religious organisation in immigrant communities is an area which has seen little investigation. Male authority is extended beyond the sphere of the household through the formation of community and religious institutions. In Lebanese Muslim communities, the close association between community and religious organisation as a domain of male authority is evident in the careers of the early imams and the role of village factionalism in decision-making on mosque committees. In the absence of established Islamic institutions, personal devoutness and charitable works provided a path to community leadership in the case of the first imam among the Lebanese Sunni Muslims. Inter-village factional rivalry in the mosque committee played an important role in dismissing incumbent imams and recruiting new ones (Humphrey, 1987).

The close relationship between the development of Islamic religious institutions and voluntary community ones is entirely compatible with the egalitarian status of 'believers' and their religious capacities as members of the Muslim community ('*umma*). Locally grown and without the need for external clerical authority, such communities readily recreated a synthesis of the secular and religious in the context of social ties circumscribed by migration. Reinforcing the ideological and historical basis for local

Muslim organisation are the state politics of multiculturalism, which seek to legitimise broadly based ethnic identities as strategies of incorporation. It is because religion is often the broadest social identity above the village that religious organisations and leadership play such prominent roles in the politics of multiculturalism.

An important dimension of the establishment of formal religious institutions is the role they play in the general reaffirmation of male social space and authority. This is most apparent in the organisation and practice of public ritual (especially communal prayer, fasting and the celebration of female modesty through dress) and the identification of the imam as an Islamic legal authority in the regulation of family life. This is particularly the case amongst Lebanese Muslim immigrants because of the legal and religious status of imams conferred by the Lebanese state in a plural legal system which gave religious courts exclusive jurisdiction over family and inheritance matters.

Participation in mosque activities of prayer, Qur'anic education and Arabic language classes continues to be male dominated. Women participate, but to a much lesser degree and in formally segregated space within the mosque or separate premises removed from the mosque. On large public ritual occasions such as Id al Fitr at the end of Ramadan, when mosques overflow with families, the male-dominated nature of the institution is symbolically affirmed in the proportion of males and females inside and outside the mosque. As a result of the unequal allocation of space in the mosque, the majority of women are to be found outside in the street, clustered together.

The authority of the imam as a source of Islamic law acts as a conservative force to buttress male authority in a legal environment which radically challenges traditional ideas of morality, legal rights and prerogatives of gender. The continued identification of the imam with religious legal capacity, even though Australian law has restricted his capacity to the performance of marriage ceremonies under the *Marriage Act,* means that people seek his services as a marriage counsellor and the only person capable of effecting a religious divorce. Conflicts over the minimum age of marriage, custody rights and property settlement reflect an interest in having traditional male rights prevail over those which obtain under Australian civil law (Humphrey, 1984c). As a result of these conflicts of civil and religious law, Lebanese religious leaders, Muslim and Christian, proposed a special mixed council of religious representatives to counsel Lebanese couples before they approached the Family Court of Australia.

As well as helping to reassert the public realm as the male domain and to confirm the authority of males in family life through the support of Islamic law and the imam's prestige, the mosque also provides a focus for male competition and standing within the broader ethnic working-class arena. As the pre-eminent community institution, the mosque becomes the domain for the assertion of separate identity and status within a pluralist political environment in which ethnicity has legitimacy. It is a centre from which demands are made on Australian political, legal and bureaucratic structures about the needs and rights of the 'community' *vis-a-vis* other groups. Within the Lebanese Muslim and Christian communities, this has led to intense competition between the different sects (Humphrey, 1990).

Demands from the mosque address those issues which are seen as essential to the maintenance of the religious and moral integrity of Muslims in migration. These include demands on public health services for culturally sensitive practices respecting gender rules (e.g. making women doctors available for Muslim women patients in public hospitals), legal recognition of the right of imams to conduct marriage and burial according to Muslim rites, acknowledgement of the right of Muslims to pray at work and permission from local government to close streets around major mosques to traffic on feast days. These demands represent more than the mere re-establishment of Muslim cultural practice in migration. They are an integral part of the constitution of male cultural domain based on parochial ties in the political arena of ethnic pluralism.

The issue of religious leadership at the mosque has dramatically highlighted the overlap in the development of community and religious organisation in immigrant communities in Australia. The absence of an Islamic clerical bureaucracy has, in most cases, seen mosque leadership remain in the hands of the men of the community rather than a separate religious body external to the social ties which have shaped immigrant mosque communities. The process of development of mosques reflects distinctive ethnic, linguistic and regional backgrounds of Muslim communities in Australia. Religion has not yet been separated from working-class position and ethnic origin for most Muslims. Consequently, local community politics derived from former family, factional and even party competition in parent communities remain an integral part of mosque politics (Humphrey, 1987). In this political environment, the assertion of Muslim identity and the demands for recognition of Muslim religious and legal practices are essentially competitive and drawn into the politics of community standing and defence of cultural autonomy.

However, the movement of the organisational focus from primarily community associations to mosque is transformative. The very nature of cultural capital and political resources changes as demands initially generated from parochial ties of kinship, friendship and community networks are placed within very different political and institutional environments. Organised under legal structures which stipulate formal organisational and management procedures (e.g. formal annual elections of the executive), and within a political arena in which assertion of separate identity has legitimacy in an Australian political party patronage system seeking links into the grassroots of ethnic communities, the mosque becomes a focal point of interest and mobilisation of Muslim migrants.

Defence of Muslim culture at the mosque most commonly arises out of working-class culture, but its political significance goes beyond the arena of ethnic politics. Focused on cultural autonomy and authenticity, it finds common ground with diverse Islamic movements internationally. The local mosque, connected through its imam, links experience in the developed world with the position of most Muslim states and societies in the underdeveloped world. It is at this point that the state intervenes to shape the character of Islamic organisation, seeking to limit the religious domain to ethnic competition.

Local and national Islamic organisations

While local mosques have for the most part grown out of ethnic working-class immigrant communities, umbrella Islamic organisations have been generated from different sources. They have evolved from the responsibility assumed by the Muslim professional middle class to develop a national Islamic organisation. In Australia the Muslim immigrant middle classes have come mainly from South Asia, Southeast Asia and the Pacific and are part of small Muslim communities with little scope to secure the patronage in the ethnic political arena available to the larger Lebanese and Turkish Muslim communities.

The largest and oldest national Islamic organisation is the Australian Federation of Islamic Councils (AFIC), which evolved from the Australian Federation of Islamic Societies established in 1964. The change in name reflected the formation of a federal structure based on seven state or regional councils of member Islamic societies.[6] Not all 'Islamic societies' included on the state councils are mosque-centred organisations. Educational, national and youth organisations are also members. Moves to create a national organisation were prompted by the need to have Muslim clerics recognised as authorised marriage celebrants in Australia and to establish procedures to certify hallal meat for the large Australian meat export trade to the Middle East.[7]

Although the AFIC is a national organisation, it has never had legal or religious authority to organise or decide issues within any local mosque community. It does not provide religious training for imams nor has it any legal capacity to interpret Islamic law on matters that arise amongst Muslims in a secular state. Its role has been largely confined to the promotion of Islamic culture and support of educational and religious activities. Through funds received from the Government of Saudi Arabia (Muslim World League), AFIC contributes to the salaries of imams of member Islamic societies, but any attempts to assume responsibility for the selection and appointment of imams to mosques have been strongly resisted by local communities. The recommendation of imams to serve as marriage celebrants for Muslims and the development of educational and welfare activities have all been the domain of local communities.

The strong autonomous sentiment of local Islamic societies is reflected in their titles. AFIC's efforts to make uniform the constitutions of its constituent local Islamic societies was strongly resisted when it came to the matter of requiring member societies to drop the ethnic, national or Islamic sect affiliation from their titles.[8] The attachment to ethnic, national and sect affiliation is particularly marked in the two main states of immigrant settlement, New South Wales and Victoria.[9] In other states, member Islamic societies are differentiated by Australian regional or place names only.

AFIC has assumed the role of advocate and representative of Australian Muslim interests with government departments and in areas affecting Muslim businesses dealing with the Middle East. Its role has essentially been as an advocate for Muslim rights in Australian society, taking up such issues as the difficulty in finding mosque sites in the suburbs, the right to a Muslim burial and media discrimination against Muslims. Recently state councils of AFIC have been involved in putting submissions to government-sponsored inquiries into religious discrimination and racist violence.

This broadly representative character of AFIC in fact reflects the plurality of authority within Australian Muslim communities. This derives on one hand from the historical autonomy of mosque communities in Islam, but on the other from the autonomy small immigrant communities have in recreating their culture and organisation outside the domain of parent institutions and social environments. These traditional and situational sources of autonomy have resulted in continuing tensions over efforts to establish a national representative organisation. This tension between autonomy and incorporation is not confined to Muslim immigrants. Conflicts have occurred on several occasions between locally grown minority churches seeking to preserve their autonomy, and representatives of the parent church overseas trying to incorporate or control them. Such conflicts have arisen in the Maronite Catholic, the Greek Orthodox and the Assyrian Churches in Australia. However, in the Islamic case, such incorporation is not possible because there is no external hierarchical or bureaucratic structure which can legitimately impose itself.

The appointment of imams by local mosque communities clearly expresses the impact of plural religious authority. In contrast to the immigrant minority churches, which establish a clear hierarchy of authority and procedure for the appointment of clerics, the mosque communities remain independent and located in their specific ethnic, cultural and political contexts. Local mosque committees and not AFIC recruit and dismiss imams according to the wishes of the mosque executive. Thus an imam's security of tenure of office lies with the mosque community and not with a superior religious body. The exceptions are the Turkish imams who are salaried appointees of the Turkish state.

The plurality of religious authority is also revealed in the process of consultation on religious matters. Imams in Australia may consult one another, but more frequently they consult their own personal overseas network. The tradition of learning under the guidance of a respected scholar (*ulama*) places each imam in his own circle, from which he can seek advice and guidance. While there are learned individuals in AFIC, they do not have the status of religious networks emanating from al-Azhar in Cairo and Qom in Iran. This issue of religious authority has presented problems to Australian government departments seeking some overarching authority to resolve problems. At one stage of a dispute over the deportation of a radical imam there were suggestions that the Mufti of Cairo should be consulted to find a suitable alternative.

The imam derives his authority not purely from his religious standing, but also from ethnic community leadership. According to the specific ethnic and class background of the mosque community, the imam may or may not be in direct competition for support and influence with competing organisations. In the case of the Lebanese Sunni Muslims, the growth in pre-eminence of the mosque association saw regional associations like the Tripoli al-Mina Association eclipsed. Moreover, because of heightened sectarian divisions between Lebanese, the status of Sunni Muslim religious leader carried with it the baggage of the Lebanese conflict (Humphrey, 1987). Yet in the ethnically mixed middle-class mosque communities, the assertion of parochial differences by an imam would be seen as contrary to the spirit of Islam.

The desire to organise Australian Muslims under one national body is more than simply an enterprise of the Muslim middle classes. Islamic states and the Australian government also share the goal of encouraging the formation of truly national organisations.[10] In the case of the former, the concern focuses on the religious welfare and needs of Muslim minorities in the West, and in the latter the concern is to create representative cultural and ethnic organisations not only for simplified management but also to regulate any expressions of Islamic radicalism, especially the multiplicity of links between local mosque communities and Islamic foreign governments. What has emerged is a convergence of interests between the Australian state and particular outside Islamic states to have an orderly and regulated immigrant Islamic community expressing compatible cultural values.

In Australia, the most active Islamic state tending to the religious and educational needs of Muslim immigrant communities has been Saudi Arabia through the agency of the Muslim World League. It has been closely involved over the years in the formation of AFIC and has made recommendations about organisational matters. It has also donated funds to AFIC for the salaries of imams and for mosque building. While Saudi Arabia has been pre-eminent in this field, there has always existed an element of competition with other Islamic states, including Kuwait,

Egypt, Libya, Iraq, Lebanon, Turkey and Iran. These states have established links with a variety of local Islamic societies and mosque communities to meet religious needs and provide funds for mosque building.

There was a particularly tense period in 1987 when AFIC fell out of favour with representatives of the Saudi Arabian government. This saw the proliferation of parallel national Islamic organisations sponsored by the Saudi Arabian government in order to challenge AFIC's national standing.[11] In the end the move failed, but it highlighted tensions between Australian Muslim organisations and revealed the rivalries of outside states *vis-a-vis* Muslims in Australia.

One of the main sources of conflict between AFIC and the Saudi government was in relation to an Egyptian imam who had close involvement with a pro-Iranian Islamic movement in Lebanon and had brought his Islamic radicalism and anti-Saudi opinions to Australia. The imam had been recruited from Tripoli in 1982 by Lebanese Sunni organisations for the Imam Ali mosque in Sydney, whose congregation was overwhelmingly Lebanese Sunni Muslim. The close relationship between Islamic radicalism and working-class origins in Lebanon was reconstituted in Sydney in the context of ethnic working-class politics. The imam emerged as a Sunni charismatic leader who actively set out to expand mosque activities in the areas of welfare, education, marriage counselling and women's issues under a *shura* committee at the mosque. The often conservative and fundamentalist pronouncements of the imam about the values of Australian society and Middle East politics mobilised broad opposition to him.[12] Nevertheless he has managed to avoid deportation to date, primarily because of the character of his leadership, based in an ethnic constituency, not because of the influence of national Islamic organisations.

As a consequence of the plurality of Islamic religious authority at both the international and the Australian national level, the enterprise of establishing national Islamic organisations has been problematic. However, the expression of Islamic diversity in Australia is not simply the product of sectarian division in Islam; it must be understood also in the context of the institutions of the ethnic working class. The religious and the secular overlap in the state's interest to create forums and a discourse for the incorporation of the unintegrated immigrant working class. Islamic religious plurality grows from the competitive nature of ethnic immigrant parochialism without the possibility of a single recognised authority being imposed at the national level.

Incorporation of the Australian Muslim immigrant working class, in this generation or the next, will be seen in the routinisation of Islamic religious organisation and practice, the centralisation of Islamic religious administration, the establishment of a compatible Islamic religious leadership and the ascendancy of the view that religion is primarily a personal rather than communal activity.

Conclusion

The cultural history of Islam in the West has been shaped by Muslim immigrant experiences of their respective host societies. In Australia most Muslims have formed part of the large-scale migration of the working class from underdeveloped regions, especially the Mediterranean. Their social experience of the process of incorporation has seen them generate cultural institutions derived from the parochial ties which in many cases facilitated their migration. The reconstitution of Islamic organisations and practices has been greatly influenced by the social reality of the process of incorporation. Little of the cultural and social capital of previous lives based on intimacy of ties and the personalisation of power can be transferred except in the context of a competitive, pluralist, ethnic political arena.

The reconstitution of cultural practices rests on narrowed institutions, especially the family, which initially carries the burden of maintaining a discrete cultural identity based on language, etiquette and morality. Gender differentiation, an important historical dimension of the social organisation of Islamic societies, bears the burden of this process of differentiation, becoming a strong symbolic issue in the defence of culture and autonomy. However, it also symbolises the demarcation between the inside and the outside, the foreign and the familiar, which males assume the authority to define. Here the symbols of conservative Islamic practice become strongly political and assertive, focused on the rights of cultural autonomy. Headscarves, mosque building, prayer in the workplace, Islamic burial rights, religious instruction and demands for culturally sensitive government services become political issues in the context of ethnic pluralism and rights.

Male authority is also expressed in the community arena. In mosques and Islamic societies the historical plurality of Islamic religious authority expresses itself. Mosque communities appoint their own imams, who are expected to reflect the mosque community's own political and ideological dispositions. Local cultural autonomy is edified by currents of international religious culture. However, it is important not to forget the impact of racism and rejection by host societies. Hostile public opinion shaped by racism and by the representation of Islamic international politics as irrational, violent and fanatical only serves to delineate difference more sharply.

The development of Islamic culture in Australia is a product of the interaction between the developed and underdeveloped world. It has grown out of the experience of migrants who as yet do not know whether they are to be Australians or only Muslims in exile in the developed world.

Notes

1 This chapter is a condensation of a paper which originally appeared in the *Journal of Islam and Christian–Muslim Relations*. It is used here with the kind permission of the Editor of that journal.
2 Joseph (1982) discusses the importance of the Lebanese family in the context of social and political upheaval in Beirut and its vital role in providing security and solidarity.
3 Caroline de Costa (1988) notes in a study on Lebanese pregnancy outcomes in Sydney that there were disproportionate numbers of Lebanese mothers giving birth in the 15–20 years and more than 36 years categories. While this included all Lebanese, Christian and Muslim, my own research in Sydney would suggest that her findings apply no less strongly to the Muslim Lebanese than to the Christians.
4 See, for example, the report by the Lebanese Community Council of New South Wales, *Community Profile of the Lebanese Community in the St George Area*, 1989. Acknowledging that Lebanese women have one of the lowest workforce participation rates, they argue for 'affordable childcare for women in employment' and employment training program which have been designed in 'a culturally appropriate and sensitive way' (p. 32). The former suggests it is the children who inhibit mothers' workforce participation, while the latter suggests it is the work and its environment which do so.
5 See *State Rail Authority v. Australian Railways Union* 'Bans on Lifting Seats' before Commissioner Walker, Arbitration and Conciliation Commission, Sydney, 1982.
6 For membership on a state council, an Islamic society must have a minimum of 100 members and be registered under the *Charitable Collection Act*. There cannot be more than one Islamic society in any city, town shire or region unless the adult financial membership exceeds more than 500. See *Constitution of the Australian Federation of Islamic Councils* 1980.
7 Because Shi'a organisations are not member societies of AFIC, separate channels had to be established with Iranian clergy to facilitate the meat export trade to Iran. See Peter Diegutis 'Trade in balance, says Iranian delegate' *Sydney Morning Herald*, 1 May 1979.
8 Despite the advice of a visiting Saudi Arabian advisor on Muslim minorities and a note in the 'The Islamic Council of New South Wales President's Annual Report 1981–1982', indicating it had advised member societies to delete all names that suggest any ethnic, national or Islamic sect affliation, many member societies retain such affiliations in their titles; e.g. Lebanese Muslim Association; Muslim Alawy Society, The Albanian Muslim Society, Turkish Society of Victoria.
9 Twelve out of the 26 Islamic organisations in New South Wales and fourteen out of the 24 Islamic organisations in Victoria listed in the Department of Immigration, Local Government and Ethnic Affairs'

Directory of Ethnic Community Organisations in Australia 1989 (Canberra: Australian Government Publishing Service) have sect, ethnic or national affiliations in their titles.

10 The French government has also taken initiatives to bring French Muslims under a national organisation. Recently the French Interior Minister announced the establishment of a Consultative Council of France's Muslims 'to give opinions and make recommendations which could help me administer as well as possible the practical problems arising from Islamic worship in France'. His aim in creating this national Islamic body was to create a French frame of reference for the Muslim community rather than allow the differentiation of Muslims into nationally based ethnicities with their own links to external Islamic governments. See Henri Tincq 'French government takes a hand in organising Islam' *Guardian Weekly*, 25 March 1990.

11 One newspaper report at the time stated that Saudi Arabian government had spent $66 000 in grants to Muslim organisations who opposed the imam. See Barry Lowe 'Saudis spend up big to depose Muslim leader' *Weekend Australian*, 5–6 December 1987.

12 The most recent crisis over the iman's leadership involved complaints by the Jewish Board of Deputies over the iman's racist language about Jews in the Middle East in an address to Muslim university students at a university in Sydney. A secret video-recording of a speech was forwarded to the Jewish Board of Deputies in order to further undermine his leadership position and presumably hasten his deportation. The recording was made by a Muslim opponent.

Bibliography

Allport, G. (1950) *The Individual and His Religion* New York: Macmillan.

Anderson, M. (1983) ' "Helpmeet for Man": Women in Mid-Nineteenth Century Western Australia' in P. Crawford (ed.) *Exploring Women's Past* Sydney: Allen & Unwin.

Anderson, R. M. (1979) *Vision of the Disinherited: The Making of American Pentecostalism* New York: Oxford University Press.

—— (1987) 'Pentecostal and Charismatic Christianity' in M. Eliade (ed.) *Encyclopedia of Religion* vol. 11, New York: Macmillan.

Anthony, D., Ecker, B. and Wilber, K. (1987) (eds) *Spiritual Choices, the Problem of Recognizing Authentic Paths to Inner Transformation* New York: Paragon House.

Ata, A. W. (ed.) (1988) *Religion and Ethnic Identity: An Australian Study* [vol. 1] Richmond, Vic.: Spectrum Publications.

—— (1989) *Religion and Ethnic Identity: An Australian Study* vol. 2, Richmond, Vic.: Spectrum Publications.

The Australian Hymn Book (1977) Sydney: Collins.

An Australian Prayer Book (1978) Sydney: Standing Committee of the General Synod of the Church of England in Australia.

Bainbridge, W. S. and Stark, R. (1980) 'Scientology: To Be Perfectly Clear' *Sociological Analysis* 41: 128–36.

Barth, F. (1969) 'Introduction' F. Barth (ed.) *Ethnic Groups and Boundaries* London: Allen & Unwin.

Bartley, W. W. III (1978) *Werner Erhard, The Transformation of a Man, The Founding of est* New York: Clarkson N. Potter Inc.

Behnke, D. A. (1982) *Religious Issues in Nineteenth Century Feminism* New York: Whitson Publishing Co.

Bell, R. R. (1981) *Worlds of Friendship* Beverley Hills, California: Sage.

Bellah, R., Madsen, R., Sullivan, W., Swidler, A. and Tipton, S. (1985) *Habits of the Heart: Individualism and Commitment in American Life* Berkeley: University of California Press.

Benson, P. and Spilka, B. (1973) 'God-image as Function of Self-esteem and Locus of Control' *Journal for the Scientific Study of Religion* 12: 296–310.

Bentley, C., Blombery, 'T. L. and Hughes, P. J. (1986) *Australian Beliefs and Practices Project* Sydney: Christian Research Association.

Berger, P. L. (1967) 'Religious Institutions' in N. Smelser (ed.) *Sociology* New York: Wiley.

—— (1973) *The Social Reality of Religion* Harmondsworth: Penguin.

Berger, P. L. and Kellner, H. (1970) 'Marriage and the Construction of Reality' in H. Dreitzel (ed.) *Recent Sociology 2* New York: Macmillan.

Berger, P. L. and Luckmann, T. (1971) *The Social Construction of Reality* Harmondsworth: Penguin.

Berndt, R. M. (1947) 'Wuradjeri Magic and "Clever Men" ' *Oceania* 17(4): 327–65; 18(1): 60–86.

—— (1948) 'Badu, Islands of the Spirits' *Oceania* 91(2): 93–103.

—— (1951) *Kunapipi: A Study of An Australian Aboriginal Religious Cult* Melbourne: Cheshire.

—— (1952a) *Djanggawul: An Aboriginal Religious Cult of North-Eastern Arnhem Land.* London: Routledge and Kegan Paul.

—— (1952b) 'Surviving Influence of Mission Contact on the Daly River, Northern Territory of Australia' *Neue Zeitschrift für Missionswissenschaft* 8(2/3): 1–20.

—— (1962) *An Adjustment Movement In Arnhem Land: Northern Territory of Australia.* Paris: Mouton.

—— (1974) *Australian Aboriginal Religion.* Four Fascicles. Iconography of Religions, section V. Leiden: E. J. Brill.

Berndt, R. M. and Berndt, C. H. (1951) *Sexual Behaviour in Western Arnhem Land* New York: Viking.

—— (1954) *Arnhem Land: Its History and Its People.* Melbourne: F. W. Cheshire.

Bertelli, L. and Pascoe, R. (1988) 'Immigrant Italians and the Australian Catholic Church: Folk Festivals and the Evil Eye' in A. W. Ata (ed.) *Religion and Ethnic Identity: An Australian Study* [vol. 1] Richmond, Vic.: Spectrum Publications.

Birke, L., Faulkner, W., Bert, S., Jansen-Smith, D. and Overfield, K. (eds) (1980) *Alice through the Microscope* London: Virago.

Birke, L. and Silvertown, J. (eds) (1984) *More than the Parts: Biology and Politics* London: Pluto Press.

Black, A. W. (1976) *Organizational Genesis and Development* St Lucia: University of Queensland Press.

—— (1983a) 'Church Union in Canada and Australia: A Comparative Analysis' *Australian–Canadian Studies* 1 (1983): 44–56.

—— (1983b) 'The Sociology of Ecumenism: Initial Observations on the Formation of the Uniting Church in Australia' in A. W. Black and P. E. Glasner (eds) *Practice and Belief: Studies in the Sociology of Australian Religion* Sydney: Allen & Unwin.

—— (1985) 'The Impact of Theological Orientation and of Breadth of Perspective on Church Members' Attitudes and Behaviors' *Journal for the Scientific Study of Religion* 24: 87–100.

—— (1986) 'Some Aspects of Religion and Law: The Case of Church Union in Australia' *Religion* 16: 225–47.

—— (1988a) 'The Context for Rural Ministry' in *Bearers of Hope: Report of the Rural Ministry Conference of Australian and New Zealand Churches* Sydney: Uniting Church in Australia.

—— (1988b) 'A Marriage Model of Church Mergers' *Sociological Analysis* 49: 281–92.

—— (1988c) 'Unity, Renewal and Participation in United and Uniting Churches' in T. F. Best (ed.) *Living Today Towards Visible Unity* Geneva: World Council of Churches.

—— (1990a) 'Organizational Imagery and Interdenominational Mergers' *British Journal of Sociology* 41: 105–27.

—— (1990b) 'Pentecostal Churches in Australia' in P. Bentley, 'T. Blombery and P. J. Hughes (eds) *A Yearbook for Australian Churches 1991* Hawthorn Vic.: Christian Research Association.

Black, A. W. (forthcoming) *The Quest for Church Union*, Wesport, Conn.: Greenwood Press.

Black, A. W. and Glasner, P. E. (eds) (1983) *Practice and Belief: Studies in the Sociology of Australian Religion* Sydney: Allen & Unwin.

Bleier, R. (ed.) (1986) *Feminist Approaches to Science* New York: Pergamon Press.

Bloch-Hoell, N. (1964) *The Pentecostal Movement: Its Origin, Development, and Distinctive Character* Oslo: Universitetsforlaget.

Blombery, 'T. (1988) *Religious Broadcasting in Australia* Wangaratta, Vic.: Christian Research Association.

—— (1989a) *God Through Human Eyes: Report from the Combined Churches Survey for Faith and Mission* Hawthorn, Vic.: Christian Research Association.

—— (1989b) *Tomorrow's Church Today: Report from the Combined Churches Survey for Faith and Mission* Hawthorn, Vic.: Christian Research Association.

Blombery, 'T. and Hughes, P. J. (1987) *Combined Churches Survey for Faith and Mission: Preliminary Report* Wangaratta, Vic.: Christian Research Association.

Bodycomb, J. F. (1984) *Quo Vadis, Ecclesia?*, D. Theol. thesis, Melbourne College of Divinity.

—— (1985) 'Women, Religion and Australian Society' *Religious Education Journal of Australia* 1(1): 15–21.

—— (1986) *A Matter of Death and Life: The Future of Australia's Churches* Melbourne: Joint Board of Christian Education.

Boisen, A. T. (1939) 'Economic Distress and Religious Experience: A Study of the Holy Rollers' *Psychiatry* 2: 185–94.

Bollen, J. D., Cahill, A. E., Mansfield, B. and O'Farrell, P. (1980) 'Australian Religious History, 1960–80' *Journal of Religious History* 11: 8–44.

Borrie, W. (1954) *Italians and Germans in Australia* Melbourne: Cheshire.

Bos, R. (1988) 'The Dreaming and Social Change in Arnhem Land' in T. Swain and D. B. Rose (eds) *Aboriginal Australians and Christian Missions: Ethnographic and Historical Studies* Adelaide: Australian Association for the Study of Religions.

Bouma, G. D. (1983) 'Australian Religiosity: Some Trends Since 1966' in A. W. Black and P. E. Glasner (eds) *Practice and Belief: Studies in the Sociology of Australian Religion* Sydney: Allen & Unwin.

—— (1988a) 'Assessing Trends in the Position, Strength and Role of Religion in Australian Society' in R. S. M. Withycombe (ed.) *Australian and New Zealand Religious History 1788–1988* Canberra: Australian and New Zealand Association of Theological Schools and Society for Theological Studies.

—— (1988b) 'The Sociology of Religion in Australia' *Australian Religion Studies Review* 1(2): 44–9.

Bouma, G. D (1991) *Religion: A Sociological Analysis of Religion in Australia* Melbourne: Longman.

Bouma, G. D. and Dixon, B. R. (1986) *The Religious Factor in Australian Life* Melbourne: MARC Australia.

Bourdieu, P. (1984) *Distinction: A Social Critique of the Judgement of Taste* London: Routledge and Kegan Paul.

Breton, R. (1964) 'Institutional Completeness of Ethnic Communities and Personal Relations of Immigrants' *American Journal of Sociology* 70: 193–205.

Britt, M. (1988) *In Search of New Wineskins: An Exploration of Models of Christian Community* Melbourne: Collins Dove.

Bromley, D. G. (1985) 'Financing the Millennium: the Economic Structure of the Unificationist Movement' *Journal for the Scientific Study of Religion* 24: 253–75.

Bromley, D. G. and Shupe, A. D. (1979) *Moonies in America* Beverly Hills: Sage.

Buckley, V. (1983) *Cutting Green Hay* Ringwood: Penguin Books.

Byrne, B. (1988) *Paul and the Christian Woman* Sydney: St Paul Publications.

Calley, M. J. C. (1964) 'Pentecostalism Among the Bandjalang' in M. Reay (ed.) *Aborigines Now: New Perspectives in the Study of Aboriginal Communities* Sydney: Angus and Robertson

—— (1965) *God's People: West Indian Pentecostal Sects in England* London: Oxford University Press.

Cambridge, A. (1903) *Thirty Years in Australia* London: Methuen.

Campbell, D. F. (1985) 'The Canadian and Australian Church Unions: A Comparison' *International Journal of Comparative Sociology* 26: 181–97.

Capell, A. (1939) 'Mythology in the Northern Kimberley, North-West Australia' *Oceania* 9(4): 382–404.

Chant, B. (1984) *Heart of Fire: The Story of Australian Pentecostalism* 2nd edn, Unley Park, South Australia: House of Tabor.

Christian, W. A. Jnr (1972) *Person and God in a Spanish Valley* New York: Seminar Press.

Church of England (1925) *The Church and the New Age: Official Report of the Ninth Australian Church Congress held at Melbourne, May 3–13* Melbourne: Diocesan Registry.

Collins, P. (1986) *Mixed Blessings: John Paul II and the Church of the Eighties* Ringwood: Penguin.

Cowie, B. H. L. (1906) *One of Australia's Daughters: An Autobiography of Mrs Harrison Lee* London: Osborn.

Cox, H. (1968) *The Secular City* rev. edn, Harmondsworth: Penguin.

—— *The Silencing of Leonardo Boff: The Vatican and the Future of World Christianity* Oak Park, Ill.: Meyer-Stone.

Currie, R., Gilbert, A. and Horsley, L. (1977) *Churches and Churchgoers: Patterns of Church Growth in the British Isles since 1700* Oxford: Clarendon Press.

Da Free John (1983) *The Dawn Horse Testament: The Secret Revelation Book of Heart Master Da Love Ananda* San Raphael, Calif.: Dawn Horse Press.

Davison, G. (1978) *The Rise and Fall of Marvellous Melbourne* Melbourne: Melbourne University Press.

de Costa, C. (1988) 'Preganancy Outcomes in Lebanese-born Women in Western Sydney' *Medical Journal of Australia* 149: 457–60.

de Vaus, D. (1980) 'Education and Religious Change Among Senior Adolescents: I. Questioning Some Common Research Assumptions' *Journal of Christian Education* Papers 69: 13–24.

—— (1981a) 'Education and Religious Change Among Senior Adolescents: II. Findings of an Enquiry' *Journal of Christian Education* Papers 70: 33–45.

—— (1981b) 'The Impact of Catholic Schools on the Religious Orientation of Boys and Girls' *Journal of Christian Education* Papers 71: 44–51.

—— (1982a) 'The Impact of Geographical Mobility on Adolescent Religious Orientation: An Australian Study' *Review of Religious Research* 23: 391–405.

—— (1982b) 'Does Tertiary Education Produce Religious Change?' *Australian Journal of Education* 26: 101–4.

—— (1983) 'The Relative Importance of Parents and Peers for Adolescent Religious Orientation: An Australian Study' *Adolescence* 18(69): 147–58.

—— (1984) 'Workforce Participation and Sex Differences in Church Attendance' *Review of Religious Research* 25: 247–56.

—— (1985) 'The Impact of Tertiary Education on Religious Orientation' *Journal of Christian Education* Papers 84: 9–20.

de Vaus, D. and McAllister, I. (1987) 'Gender Differences in Religion: A Test of The Structural Location Theory' *American Sociological Review* 52: 472–81.

Demerath, N. J. III (1965) *Social Class in American Protestantism* Chicago: Rand McNally.

Dempsey, K. (1983a) *Conflict and Decline: Ministers and Laymen in an Australian Country Town* North Ryde, NSW: Methuen Australia.

—— (1983b) 'Country Town Religion' in A. W. Black and P. E. Glasner (eds) *Practice and Belief: Studies in the Sociology of Australian Religion* Sydney: Allen & Unwin.

—— (1985a) 'The Fate of Ministers' Wives' *La Trobe University Sociology Papers* 15.

—— (1985b) 'Have the Churches a Future?' *La Trobe University Sociology Papers* 16.

—— (1986) 'Identity and the Rural Minister' in V. C. Hayes (ed.) *Identity Issues and World Religions* Bedford Park, South Australia: Australian Association for the Study of Religions.

—— (1987) 'Gender and Economic Inequality in an Australian Rural Community' *Australian and New Zealand Journal of Sociology* 23: 357–74.

—— (1988) 'Exploitation in the Domestic Division of Labour Through Major Stages of the Life Course: An Australian Case Study' *Australian and New Zealand Journal of Sociology* 24: 420–36.

—— (1989a) 'Is Religion Still Relevant in the Private Sphere?' *Sociological Analysis* 50: 247–63.

—— (1989b) 'Women's Leisure, Men's Leisure: A Study in Subordination and Exploitation' *Australian and New Zealand Journal of Sociology* 25: 27–45.

—— (1990a) 'The Aged: Integrated or Segregated?' *Australian Journal on Ageing* 9(2): 37–43.

—— (1990b) *Smalltown: A Study of Inequality, Cohesion and Belonging* Melbourne: Oxford University Press.

Dening, G. (1978) *Xavier: A Centenary Portrait* Melbourne: The Old Xaverians Association.

Diesendorf, E. (1988) 'Why Women Leave the Church' *Women–Church: An Australian Journal of Feminist Studies in Religion* Autumn: 25–30.

Dixson, M. (1984) *The Real Matilda* rev. edn, Ringwood: Penguin.

Douglas, M. T. (1970) *Natural Symbols* London: Barrie and Rockliff.

—— (1975) *Implicit Meanings* London: Routledge and Kegan Paul.

—— (1982) *In the Active Voice* London: Routledge and Kegan Paul.

Dowell, S. and Hurcombe, L. (1981) *Dispossessed Daughters of Eve* London: SPCK.

Dumont, L. (1986) *Essays on Individualism* Chicago: University of Chicago Press.

Duncan, B. F. (1987) From Ghetto to Crusade: A Study of the Social and Political Thought of Catholic Opinion-Makers in Sydney During the 1930s, Ph.D. thesis, University of Sydney.

Easthope, G. (1985) 'Marginal Healers' in R. K. Jones (ed.) *Sickness and Sectarianism* Aldershot: Gower.

Eco, U. (1979) *A Theory of Semiotics* Bloomington: Indiana University Press.

Elkin, A. P. (n.d.) 'Kattang Inititation' manuscript, *Elkin Papers*, Fisher Library, p. 130, Box 11, folder 1/3/10.

Elshtain, J. B. (1981) *Public Man Private Woman: Women in Social and Political Thought* Oxford: Martin Robertson.

Ely, R. (1981) 'Secularisation and the Sacred in Australian History' *Historical Studies* 19(77): 553–66.

Epstein, B. (1981) *The Politics of Domesticity: Women, Evangelism and Temperance in Nineteenth Century America* Middletown, Conn.: Wesleyan University Press.

Fenn, R. K. (1982) *Liturgies and Trials: The Secularization of Religious Language* Oxford: Blackwell.

Field, B. (ed.) (1989) *Fit for This Office: Women and Ordination* Melbourne: Collins-Dove.

Fiorenza, E. S. (1984) *Bread not Stone* Boston: Beacon Press.

Fison, L. and Howitt, A. W. (1967 [1880]) *Kamilaroi and Kurnai: Group-Marriage and Relationship, and Marriage by Elopement* The Netherlands: Anthropological Publications.

Flaherty, C. and Roberts, M. (1989) 'The Reproduction of Anzac Symbolism' *Journal of Australian Studies* 24: 52-69.

Foss, D. A. and Larkin, R. (1986) *Beyond Revolution: A New Theory of Social Movements* Massachusetts: Bergin and Garvey.

Foucault, M. (1972) *The Archaeology of Knowledge* New York: Harper Colophon.

—— (1979) *Discipline and Punish: The Birth of the Prison* New York: Vintage/Random House.

Franklin, M. A. (ed.) (1986) *The Force of the Feminine: Women, Men and the Church* Sydney: Allen & Unwin.

Franklin, M. A. and Sturmey-Jones, R. (eds) (1987) *Opening the Cage: Stories of Church and Gender* Sydney: Allen & Unwin.

Freeland, G. (1985) 'Death and Australian Civil Religion' in M. Crouch and B. Hüppauf (eds) *Essays on Mortality* Kensington: Faculty of Arts, University of New South Wales.

Freud, S. (1962) T*he Future of an Illusion* New York: Doubleday.

Frost, L. (1984) *No Place for a Nervous Lady: Voices from the Australian Bush* Ringwood: McPhee Gribble/Penguin.

Garland, P. (1981) Continuity and Conflict: Symbolic Mediation in a Religious Context: a Case Study of the Confraternity of Christian Doctrine (Melbourne) 1961–1975, M.A. thesis, La Trobe University.

Gerlach, L. P. and Hine, V. H. (1968) 'Five Factors Crucial to the Growth and Spread of a Modern Religious Movement' *Journal for the Scientific Study of Religion* 7: 23–40.

—— (1970) *People, Power, Change: Movements of Social Transformation* Indianapolis: Bobbs–Merrill.

Gerrard, N. L. (1970) 'Churches of the Stationary Poor in Southern Appalachia' in J. D. Photiadis and H. K. Schwarzweller (eds) *Change in Rural Appalachia: Implications for Action Programs* Philadelphia: University of Pennsylvania Press.

Gerth, H. H. and Mills, C. W. (eds) (1948) *From Max Weber: Essays in Sociology* London: Routledge and Kegan Paul.

Gilbert, A. D. (1980) *The Making of Post-Christian Britain* London: Longman.

—— (1988a) 'Religion and the Bicentenary' *Journal of Religious History* 15: 12–19.

—— (1988b) 'Religion and Politics' in A. Curthoys, A. W. Martin and T. Rowse (eds) *Australians From 1939* Sydney: Fairfax, Syme and Weldon .

Gilchrist, M. (1986) *Rome or the Bush: the Choice for Australian Catholics* Melbourne: John XXIII Fellowship.

—— (1987) *New Church or True Church: Australian Catholicism Today and Tomorrow* Melbourne: John XXIII Fellowship.

Giles, K. (1985) *Created Woman* Sydney: Acorn Press.

Glasner, P. (1983) 'The Study of Australian Folk Religion: Some Theoretical and Practical Problems' in A. W. Black and P. E. Glasner (eds) *Practice and Belief: Studies in the Sociology of Australian Religion* Sydney: Allen & Unwin.

Glock, C. Y. (1964) 'The Role of Deprivation in the Origin and Evolution of Religious Groups' in R. Lee and M. E. Marty (eds) *Religion and Social Conflict* New York: Oxford University Press.

Glowczewski, B. (1984) 'Manifestations Symboliques d'une Transition Économique: Le "Juluru", Culte Intertribal du "Cargo" ' *L'Homme* 23(3): 7–35.

Graetz, B. and McAllister, I. (1988) *Dimensions of Australian Society* Melbourne: Macmillan.

Greeley, A. (1985) *American Catholics since the Council* Chicago: Thomas More Press.

Griffith, J. D. (1989) 'When Men Are Women Too' *Doctrine and Life* 39: 4–8.

Grimshaw, P. (1979) 'Women and the Family in Australian History—a Reply to *The Real Matilda' Historical Studies* 18(72): 412–21.

Grimshaw, P., McConville, C. and McEwen, E. (eds) (1985) *Families in Colonial Australia* Sydney: Allen & Unwin.

Grocott, A. M. (1980) *Convicts, Clergymen and Churches* Sydney: Sydney University Press.

Guthrie, S. (1980) 'A Cognitive Theory of Religion' *Current Anthropology* 21 (2): 181–203 and 21 (4): 535–8.

Halley, C. (1980) *Migrants and the Australian Catholic Church, Multi-cultural Australia Papers No. 6* Richmond, Vic.: Clearing House in Migration Issues and National Catholic Research Institute.

Halliday, M. A. K. (1975) *Learning How to Mean—Explorations in the Development of Language* London: Edward Arnold.

Hamilton, A. (1982) 'Descended from Father, Belonging to Country: Rights to Land in the Australian Western Desert' in E. Leacock and R. Lee (eds) *Politics and History in Band Society* Cambridge: Cambridge University Press.

Harris, D., Hynd, D. and Millikan, D. (eds) (1982) *The Shape of Belief: Christianity in Australia Today* Homebush West, NSW: Lancer.

Heelas, P. (1982) 'Californian Self Religions and Socializing the Subjective' in E. Barker (ed.) *New Religious Movements: A Perspective for Understanding Society* Toronto: Edwin Mellen.

Heelas, P. and Kohn, R. (1986) 'Psychotherapy and the Techniques of Transformation' in G. Claxton (ed.) *Beyond Therapy: The Impact of Eastern Religions on Psychological Theory and Practice* London: Wisdom Publications.

Heeney, B. (1972–73) 'On Being a Mid-Victorian Clergyman' *Journal of Religious History* 7: 208–24.

—— (1982) 'The Beginning of Church Feminism: Women and the Councils of the Church of England, 1897–1919' *Journal of Ecclesiastical History* 33: 89–109.

Heirich, M. (1977) 'Change of Heart: A Test of Some Widely Held Theories About Religious Conversion' *American Journal of Sociology* 83: 653–80.

Herrmann, C. (1981) in E. Marks and I. de Courtivron (eds) *New French Feminisms* Brighton: Harvester Press.

Hill, M. (1973) *A Sociology of Religion* London: Heinemann.

Hirst, J. (1988) 'Egalitarianism' in S. L. Goldberg and F. B. Smith (eds) *Australian Cultural History* Melbourne: Cambridge University Press.

Hodge, R. and Kress, G. (1988) *Social Semiotics* Oxford: Polity Press.

Hogan, M. (1984) 'Whatever Happened to Australian Sectarianism?' *Journal of Religious History* 13: 83–91.

—— (1987) *The Sectarian Strand: Religion in Australian History* Ringwood: Penguin.

Hoge, D. R. and Roozen, D. A. (eds) (1979) *Understanding Church Growth and Decline: 1950–1978* New York: Pilgrim Press.

Hollenweger, W. (1986) 'After Twenty Years' Research on Pentecostalism' *International Review of Missions* 75(297): 3–12.

Holt, J. B. (1940) 'Holiness Religion: Cultural Shock and Social Reorganization' *American Sociological Review* 5: 740–47.

Hornsby-Smith, M. (1987) *Roman Catholics in England: Studies in Social Structure since the Second World War* Cambridge: Cambridge University Press.

Hornsby-Smith, M. and Lee, R. (1979) *Roman Catholic Opinion* Guildford: Department of Sociology, University of Surrey.

Horton, R. (1960) 'A Definition of Religion, and its Uses' *Journal of the Royal Anthropological Institute of Great Britian and Ireland* 90: 201–26.

Howitt, A. W. (1904) *The Native Tribes of South-East Australia* London: Macmillan.

Hubbard, L. R. (1950) *Dianetics, the Modern Science of Mental Health* Los Angeles: The American Saint Hill Organization (Scientology).

—— (1951) *Science of Survival* Los Angeles: The American Saint Hill Organization (Scientology).

Hughes, P. J. (1988a) *The Church's Mission: Report from the Combined Churches Survey for Faith and Mission* Melbourne: Christian Research Association.

—— (1988b) *Faith and Work: Report from the Combined Churches Survey for Faith and Mission* Melbourne: Christian Research Association.

—— (1989) *The Australian Clergy: Report from the Combined Churches Survey for Faith and Mission* Hawthorn, Vic.: Christian Research Association.

Hughes, P. and Blombery, 'T. (1990) *Patterns of Faith in Australian Churches: Report from the Combined Churches Survey for Faith and Mission* Hawthorn, Vic.: Christian Research Association.

Hume, D. (1957 [1757]) *The Natural History of Religion* Stanford: Stanford University Press.

Hume, L. (1988) 'Christianity Full Circle: Aboriginal Christianity on Yarrabah Reserve' in T. Swain and D. B. Rose (eds) *Aboriginal Australians and Christian Missions: Ethnographic and Historical Studies* Adelaide: Australian Association for the Study of Religions.

Humphrey, M. (1982) 'Disputes and Law: A Study of Lebanese Immigrant Communities in Sydney' Ph.D. thesis, Macquarie University.

—— (1984a) 'Community Disputes, Violence and Dispute Processing in a Lebanese Muslim Immigrant Community' *Journal of Legal Pluralism* 23: 53–88.

—— (1984b) *Family, Work and Unemployment: A Study of Lebanese Settlement in Sydney* Canberra: Australian Government Publishing Service.

—— (1984c) 'Religion, Law and Family Disputes in a Lebanese Muslim Community in Sydney' in G. Bottomley and M. de Lepervanche (eds) *Ethnicity, Class and Gender in Australia* Sydney: Allen & Unwin.

—— (1986) 'The Lebanese War and Lebanese Immigrant Cultures: A Comparative Study of Lebanese in Australia and Uruguay' *Ethnic and Racial Studies* 9: 445–60.

—— (1987) 'Community, Mosque and Ethnic Politics' *Australian and New Zealand Journal of Sociology* 23: 233–45.

—— (1989) 'Is This a Mosque Free Zone? Islam and the State in Australia' *Migration Monitor* 12: 12–17.

—— (1990) 'Sectarianism and the Politics of Immigrant Identity: the Lebanese in Sydney' in Nadim Shehadi (ed.) *Lebanese Emigration* London: I. B. Tauris (forthcoming).

Hyslop, A. (1976–77) 'Temperance, Christianity and Feminism: The Women's Christian Temperance Union of Victoria 1887–97' *Historical Studies* 17: 27–49.

Inglis, K.S. (1987) 'Memorials of the Great War' *Australian Cultural History* 6: 5–17.

Ireland, R. (1988) *The Challenge of Secularisation* Melbourne: Collins Dove.

Jackson, H. (1988) 'White Man Got No Dreaming: Religious Feeling in Australian History' *Journal of Religious History* 15: 1–11.

Jones, P. and Sutton, P. (1986) *Art and Land: Aboriginal Sculptures of the Lake Eyre Region*. Adelaide: South Australia Museum/Wakefield Press.

Joseph, S. (1982) 'Family as Security and Bondage: A Political Strategy of the Lebanese Urban Working Class' in H. Safa (ed.) *Towards a Political Economy of Urbanistaion in Third World Countries* Delhi: Oxford University Press.

Judd, S. E. and Cable, K. J. (1987) *Sydney Anglicans* Sydney: Anglican Information Office.

Jupp, J. (ed.) (1988) *The Australian People* North Ryde, NSW: Angus and Robertson.

Kaldor, P. (1987) *Who Goes Where? Who Doesn't Care?* Homebush West, NSW: Lancer.

Kaldor, P. and Homel, R. (1988a) 'The 1986 Joint Church Census, Report No. 1: Looking in the Mirror—A Profile of Attenders' Sydney: Joint Church Census Interchurch Steering Committee.

—— (1988b) 'The 1986 Joint Church Census, Report No. 2: Fresh through the Door—Newcomers to Church Life' Sydney: Joint Church Census Interchurch Steering Committee.

—— (1988c) 'The 1986 Joint Church Census, Report No. 3: Keepers of the Word' Sydney: Joint Church Census Interchurch Steering Committee.

—— (1988d) 'The 1986 Joint Church Census, Report No. 4: Two Generations—Age Differences in Church Attendance' Sydney: Joint Church Census Interchurch Steering Committee.

—— (1989) 'The 1986 Joint Church Census, Report No. 5: Religious Musical Chairs' Sydney: Joint Church Census Interchurch Steering Committee.

Kaluski, M. (1988) 'Polish Religious Life in Australia' in A. W. Ata (ed.) *Religion and Ethnic Identity: An Australian Study* [vol. 1] Richmond, Vic.: Spectrum Publications.

Kapferer, B. (1988) *Legends of People, Myths of State* Washington, DC: Smithsonian Institution.

Kayal, P. M. and Kayal, J. M. (1975) *The Syrian–Lebanese in America* New York: Twayne.

Keller, E. J. (1985) *Reflections on Gender and Science* New Haven: Yale University Press.

Kelley, D. M. (1972) *Why Conservative Churches Are Growing* New York: Harper and Row.

Kiev, A. (1964) 'Psychotherapeutic Aspects of Pentecostal Sects among West Indian Immigrants to England' *British Journal of Sociology* 15: 129–38.

Kitley, P. (1979) 'Anzac Day Ritual' *Journal of Australian Studies* 4: 58–69.

Knight, J. (1985a) 'Fundamentalism and Education: A Case-Study in Social Ambiguity' *Discourse* 5(2): 19–38.

—— (1985b) 'Creation-Science, Evolution-Science, and Education: Anything Goes?' *Australian Journal of Education* 29: 115–32.

—— (1986) 'Creation-Science' in Queensland: Some Fundamental Assumptions' *Social Alternatives* 5(3): 26–31.

Knight, J., Smith, R. and Maxwell, J. (1986) 'The Right Side: "Creation-Science" in Queensland, Australia' *New Zealand Sociology* 1(2): 88–103.

Knox, R. A. (1950) *Enthusiasm* Oxford: Clarendon Press.

Kolegar, F. (1964) 'The Concept of "Rationalization" and Cultural Pessimism in Max Weber's Sociology' *Sociological Quarterly* 5: 355–73.

Kolig, E. (1979) 'Captain Cook in the Western Kimberley' in R.M. and C.H. Berndt (eds) *Aborigines of the West: Their Past and Their Present* Nedlands: W.A.: University of Western Australia Press.

—— (1988) 'Mission Not Accomplished' in T. Swain and D. B. Rose (eds) *Aboriginal Australians and Christian Missions: Ethnographic and Historical Studies* Adelaide: Australian Association for the Study of Religions.

Kringas, P. and Lewins, F. (1981) *Why Ethnic Schools? Selected Case Studies* Canberra: Australian National University Press.

Lasch, C. (1979) *The Culture of Narcissism: American Life in an Age of Diminishing Expectations* New York: Warner.

Lawriwsky, M. (1988) 'The Role of Ukrainian Churches in the Ukrainian Community in Australia' in A. W. Ata (ed.) *Religion and Ethnic Identity: An Australian Study* [vol. 1] Richmond, Vic.: Spectrum Publications.

Lawton, W. B. (1983) The Better Time To Be: The Kingdom of God and Social Reform. Anglicans and the Diocese of Sydney, 1885–1914 Ph.D. thesis, University of New South Wales.

Leavey, C. and Hetherton, M. (1988) *Catholic Beliefs and Practices* Melbourne: Collins Dove.

Lees, H. C. (u.d.) *The Divine Master in Home Life,* London: Religious Tract Society.

Lewins, F. W. (1978) *The Myth of the Universal Church* Canberra: Faculty of Arts, Australian National University.

—— (1983) 'Wholes and Parts: Some Aspects of the Relationship between the Australian Catholic Church and Migrants' in A. W. Black and P. E. Glasner (eds) *Practice and Belief: Studies in the Sociology of Australian Religion* Sydney: Allen & Unwin.

Lewis, I. (1971) *Ecstatic Religion: An Anthropological Study of Spirit Possession and Shamanism* Harmondsworth: Penguin.

—— (1977) 'Introduction' in I. Lewis (ed.) *Symbols and Sentiments: Cross-cultural Studies in Symbolism* London: Academic Press.

Linder, R. D. (1988) 'Civil Religion in America and Australia' *Lucas: An Evangelical History Review* 3: 6–23.

Lommel, A. (1950) 'Modern Culture Influences on the Aborigines' *Oceania* 21(1): 14–24.

Luckmann, T. (1967) *The Invisible Religion* New York: Macmillan.

MacGinley, M. R. (1988) 'The Church's Mission' in M. R. MacGinley and T. Kelly *The Church's Mission in Australia* Melbourne: Collins Dove.

Mackie, F. (1983) *Structure, Culture and Religion in the Welfare of Muslim Families* Canberra: Australian Government Publishing Service.

Maddock, K. (1974) *The Australian Aborigines: A Portrait of Their Society* 2nd edn, Ringwood: Penguin.

—— (1988) 'Myth, History and a Sense of Oneself' in J. R. Beckett (ed.) *Past and Present: the Construction of Aboriginality* Canberra: Aboriginal Studies Press.

Majka, J. (1972) 'Poland' in H. Mol (ed.) *Western Religion* The Hague: Mouton.

Manning, J. (1882) 'Notes on the Aborigines of New Holland' *Journal and Proceedings of the Royal Society of New South Wales* 16: 155–73.

Martin, B. (1981) *The Sociology of Contemporary Social Change* London: Basil Blackwell.

Martin, D. (1978) *A General Theory of Secularization* Oxford: Basil Blackwell.

—— (1990) *Tongues of Fire: The Explosion of Protestantism in Latin America* Oxford: Blackwell.

Martin, J. (1972) *Community and Identity: Refugee Groups in Adelaide* Canberra: Australian National University Press.

Mason, M. and Fitzpatrick, G. (1982) *Religion in Australian Life: A Bibliography of Social Research* Adelaide: Australian Association for the Study of Religions and National Catholic Research Council.

McAllister, I. (1988) 'Religious Change and Secularization: The Transmission of Religious Values in Australia' *Sociological Analysis* 49: 249–63.

McCallum, J. (1986) 'The Dynamics of Secularisation in Australia: 1966–1985' SAANZ '86 Conference, Armidale.

—— (1987) 'Secularisation in Australia between 1966 and 1985: A Research Note' *Australian and New Zealand Journal of Sociology* 23: 407–22.

—— (1988) 'Belief versus Church: Beyond the Secularization Debate' in J. Kelly and C. Bean (eds) *Australian Attitudes: Social and Political Attitudes from the National Social Science Survey* Sydney: Allen & Unwin.

McCann, D. P. and Strain, C. R. (1985) *Polity and Praxis: A Program for American Practical Theology* Minneapolis: Winston Press.

McConnel, U. H. (1936) 'Totemic Hero-Cults in Cape York Peninsula, North Queensland' *Oceania* Part I 6(4): 452-77;. Part II 7(1): 69–105.

McGuire, M. B. (1982) *Pentecostal Catholics: Power, Charisma, and Order in a Religious Movement* Philadelphia: Temple University Press.

McKay, J. (1982) 'An Exploratory Synthesis of Primordial and Mobilizationist Approaches to Ethnic Phenomena' *Ethnic and Racial Studies* 5: 395–420.

—— (1985) 'Religious Diversity and Ethnic Cohesion: A Three-Generation Analysis of Syrian-Lebanese Christians in Sydney' *International Migration Review* 19: 318–34.

—— (1989) *Phoenician Farewell: Three Generations of Lebanese Christians in Australia* Surrey Hills, Vic.: Ashwood House.

McKay, J. and Lewins, F. (1978) 'Ethnicity and the Ethnic Group: A Conceptual Analysis and Reformulation' *Ethnic and Racial Studies* 1: 412–27.

McKinney, W. and Roof, W. C. (1986) 'Liberal Protestantism: A Sociodemographic Perspective' in W. McKinney and W. C. Roof, *Liberal Protestantism: Realities and Possibilities* New York: Pilgrim Press.

McSweeney, B. (1980) *Roman Catholicism: The Search for Relevance* Oxford: Basil Blackwell.

Meaney, N. K. (1964-65) 'The Church of England in the Paradise of Dissent—A Problem of Assimilation' *Journal of Religious History* 3: 137–57.

Meggitt, M. J. (1962) *Desert People: A Study of the Walbiri Aborigines of Central Australia* Sydney: Angus & Robertson.

—— (1966) *Gadjari Among the Walbiri Aborigines of Central Australia* Oceania Monographs No. 14. Sydney: The University of Sydney.

Mercer, J. (ed.) (1975) *The Other Half: Women in Australian Society* Ringwood: Penguin.

Michaelsen, R. S. and Roof, W. C. (1986) 'Introduction' in W. McKinney and W. C. Roof *Liberal Protestantism: Realities and Possibilities* New York: Pilgrim Press.

Miller, C. and Swift, K. (1976) *Words and Women* New York: Anchor Press.

Mitchell, C., Tait, D. and Castles, S. (1990) *The Recognition of Overseas Professional Qualifications* Canberra: Australian Government Publishing Service.

Moi, T. (1985) *Sexual Textual Politics: Feminist Literary Theory* London: Methuen.

Mol, H. (J. J.) (1971) *Religion in Australia: A Sociological Investigation* Melbourne: Nelson.

—— (1976) *Identity and the Sacred: A Sketch for a New Social–Scientific Theory of Religion* Oxford: Blackwell.

—— (1979) 'Theory and Data on the Religious Behavior of Migrants' *Social Compass* 26: 31–9.

—— (1985) *The Faith of Australians* Sydney: Allen & Unwin.

Morphy, H. (1983) ' "Now You Understand": An Analysis of the Way Yolngu Have Used Sacred Knowledge to Retain Their Autonomy' in N. Peterson and M. Langton (eds) *Aborigines, Land and Land Rights* Canberra: Australian Institute of Aborginal Studies.

Nahirny, J. and Fishman, J. (1965) 'American Immigrant Groups: Ethnic Identification and the Problem of Generations' *Sociological Review* 13: 321–32.

Needleman, J. (1972) *The New Religions* 2nd edn, New York: Pocket Books.

Nelson, H. M., Clark, N. H. Jnr and Au, P. (1985) 'Gender Differences in Images of God' *Journal for the Scientific Study of Religion* 24: 396–402.

Nicholls, P. (1987) The Social Expectations of Anglican Clergymen in England and Australia, 1850–1910, D. Phil. thesis, Oxford University.

Nichols, A. (ed.) (1990) *The Bible and Women's Ministry* Canberra: Acorn Press.

Niebuhr, H. R. (1929) *The Social Sources of Denominationalism* New York: Holt, Rinehart and Winston.

O'Farrell, P. (1976) 'Writing the General History of Australian Religion' *Journal of Religious History* 9: 65–73.

—— (1977) *The Catholic Church and Community in Australia: A History* Melbourne: Nelson.

—— (1981) 'The Cultural Ambivalence of Australian Religion' *Australian Cultural History* 1: 3–8.

Oddie, W. (1984) *What Will Happen to God? Feminism and the Reconstruction of Christian Belief* London: SPCK.

Ostling, R. N. (1989) 'Those Mainline Blues' *Time* 22 May: 52–4.

Pattison, E. M. (1974) 'Ideological Support for the Marginal Middle Class: Faith Healing and Glossolia' in I. I. Zaretsky and M. P. Leone (eds) *Contemporary Religious Movements in America* Princeton: Princeton University Press.

Pawsey, M. (1982) *The Demon of Discord* Melbourne: Melbourne University Press.

Pell, G. (1988) *Catholicism in Australia* Bundoora: Seminar on the Sociology of Culture, La Trobe University.

—— (1989) 'The Future of the Local Parish' *AD 2000* 2, 9: 10–11.

Petri, H. (1950) 'Kurangara: neue magische kulte in Nordwest-Australien' *Zeitschrift für Ethnologie* 75: 43–51.

Petri, H. and Petri-Odermann, G. (1988) 'A Nativistic and Millenarian Movement in North West Australia' in T. Swain and D. B. Rose (eds) *Aboriginal Australians and Christian Missions: Ethnographic and Historical Studies* Adelaide: Australian Association for the Study of Religions.

Phillips, D. (1970) Italians and Australians in the Ovens Valley Area; a Sociological Study of Interaction Between Migrants and the Host Population in a Rural Area of Victoria, Ph.D. thesis, Australian National University.

Pittarello, A. (1980) *'Soup Without Salt': The Australian Catholic Church and the Italian Migrant* Sydney: Centre for Migration Studies.

Pope, L. (1942) *Millhands and Preachers* New Haven: Yale University Press.

Porter, M. (1989) *Women in the Church: The Great Ordination Debate in Australia* Ringwood: Penguin.

Potvin, R. H. (1977) 'Adolescent God-images' *Review of Religious Research* 19: 43–53.

Pyke, N. (1948) 'An Outline of Italian Immigration into Australia' *Australian Quarterly* 20: 99–109.

Ratzinger, J. and Messori, V. (1986) *The Ratzinger Report: An Exclusive Interview on the State of the Church* San Francisco: Ignatius Press.

Richardson, J. T. (1982) 'Financing the New Religions: Comparative and Theoretical Considerations' *Journal for the Scientific Study of Religion* 21: 255–68.

Ridley, W. (1875) *Kámilarói and other Australian Languages* 2nd edn, Sydney: Government Printer.

Robbins, T. and Anthony, D. (1972) 'Getting Straight With Meher Baba: a Study of Drug Rehabilitation, Mysticism and Post-Adolescent Role Conflict' *Journal for the Scientific Study of Religion* 11: 122–40.

Robertson, R. (1972) *The Sociological Interpretation of Religion* Oxford: Basil Blackwell.

Robin, A. de Q. (1967) *Charles Perry, Bishop of Melbourne* Nedlands: University of Western Australia Press.

Roe, J. (1968–69) 'Challenge and Response: Religious Life in Melbourne, 1876–86' *Journal of Religious History* 5: 149–66.

—— (1985) *Beyond Belief* Kensington: University of New South Wales Press.

Rogers, L. J. (1988) 'Biology, the Popular Weapon: Sex Differences in Cognitive Function' in B. Caine, E. A. Grosz and M. de Lepervanche (eds) *Crossing Boundaries: Feminisms and the Critique of Knowledges* Sydney: Allen & Unwin.

Roof, W. C. (1976) 'Traditional Religion in Contemporary Society: A Theory of Local–Cosmopolitan Plausibility' *American Sociological Review* 41: 195–208.
—— (1978) *Community and Commitment* New York: Elsevier.
Rose, D. B. (1984) 'The Saga of Captain Cook: Morality in Aboriginal and European Law' *Australian Aboriginal Studies* 2: 24–39.
—— (1988) 'Jesus and the Dingo' in T. Swain and D. B. Rose (eds) *Aboriginal Australians and Christian Missions: Ethnographic and Historical Studies* Adelaide: Australian Association for the Study of Religions.
Rose, F. G. G. (1965) *The Wind of Change in Central Australia: The Aborigines at Angus Downs 1962* Berlin: Akademie.
Ruether, R. (1983) *Sexism and God-Talk* London: SCM Press.
Russell, L. (1974) *Human Liberation in a Feminist Perspective—a Theology* Philadelphia: Westminster Press.
Sackett, L. (1985) 'Marching into the Past: Anzac Day Celebrations in Adelaide' *Journal of Australian Studies* 17: 18–30.
Santamaria, B. A. (1939) 'The Italian Problem in Australia' *Australasian Catholic Record* 16: 291–305.
Saussure, F. D. (1966) *Course in General Linguistics* (transl. W. Baskin) New York: McGraw Hill.
Scarfe, J. (1974) Bridge of Polished Steel as Fine as Hair: The Oxford Movement in South Australia, 1836–1881 M.A. thesis, University of Adelaide.
Schermerhorn, R. (1970) *Comparative Ethnic Relations: A Framework for Theory and Research* New York: Random House.
—— (1978) *Ethnic Plurality in India* Tucson: University of Arizona Press.
Schopflin, G. (1973) 'The Ideology of Croatian Nationalism' *Survey* 19: 123–46.
Seligman, C. G. (1916) 'An Australian Bible Story' *Man* 16: 43–4.
Sharp, L. (1952) 'Steel Axes for Stone-Age Australians' *Human Organisation* 11(1): 17–22.
Shaw, B. (1983) *Banggaiyerri: The Story of Jack Sullivan* Canberra: Australian Institute of Aboriginal Studies.
Shaw, G. (1988) 'Beyond Discipline: The Historical Context of Theological Thought in Australia' *St Mark's Review* 133: 14–20.
Siebert, O. (1910) 'Sagen und Sitten der Dieri und Nachbarstämme in Zentral-Australien' *Globus* 97(3): 44–50; 97(4): 53–9.
Sless, D. (1986) *In Search of Semiotics* Sydney: Croom Helm.
Spilka, B., Addison, J. and Rosensohn, M. (1975) 'Parents, Self and God: a Test of Competing Theories of Individual-Religion Relationships' *Review of Religious Research* 16: 154–64.
Stanner, W. E. H. (1959–1963) *On Aboriginal Religion* Oceania Monographs No. 11, Sydney: University of Sydney.
Star, S. L. (1979) 'The Politics of Right and Left: Sex Differences in Hemispheric Brain Asymmetry' in R. Hubbard, M. S. Henifin and B. Fried (eds) *Women Look at Biology Looking at Women* Boston: G. K. Hall.
Stone, D. (1976) 'The Human Potential Movement' in C. Glock and R. Bellah (eds) *The New Religious Consciousness* Berkeley: University of California Press.

—— (1978) 'New Religious Consciousness and Personal Religious Experience' *Sociological Analysis* 39: 123–34.

Sturmey, R. I. (1989) Women and the Anglican Church in Australia: Theology and Social Change, Ph.D. thesis, University of Sydney.

Summers, A. (1975) *Damned Whores and God's Police* Ringwood: Pelican.

Suttor, T. L. (1965) *Hierarchy and Democracy in Australia, 1788–1870* Melbourne: Melbourne University Press.

Swain, T. (1985) *Interpreting Aboriginal Religion: An Historical Account* Adelaide: Australian Association for the Study of Religions.

—— (1988) 'The Ghost of Space: Reflections on Warlpiri Christian Iconography and Ritual' in T. Swain and D. B. Rose (eds) *Aboriginal Australians and Christian Missions: Ethnographic and Historical Studies* Adelaide: Australian Association for the Study of Religions.

—— (1990) 'A New Sky Hero From A Conquered Land' *History of Religions* 29(3): 195–232

—— (1991) 'The Earth Mother from Northern Waters' *History of Religions* 30 (3): in press.

—— (n.d.) Songs of a Wayfarer, manuscript.

Swain, T. and Rose, D. B. (eds) *Aboriginal Australians and Christian Missions: Ethnographic and Historical Studies* Adelaide: Australian Association for the Study of Religions.

Swanson, G. E. (1960) *The Birth of the Gods* Ann Arbor: University of Michigan Press.

Taylor, J. (1988) 'Goods and Gods: A Follow-Up Study to "Steel Axes for Stone-Age Australians" ' in T. Swain and D. B. Rose (eds) *Aboriginal Australians and Christian Missions: Ethnographic and Historical Studies* Adelaide: Australian Association for the Study of Religions.

Thiering, B. (1982) *God's Experiment—Australian Religion* Perth: Murdoch University.

Thompson, D. (1988) 'Bora, Church and Modernization at Lockhart River, Queensland' in T. Swain and D. B. Rose (eds) *Aboriginal Australians and Christian Missions: Ethnographic and Historical Studies* Adelaide: Australian Association for the Study of Religions.

Thompson, E. P. (1968) *The Making of the English Working Class* Harmondsworth: Penguin.

Thomson, D. F. (1933) 'The Hero Cult Initiation and Totemism on Cape York' *Journal of the Royal Anthropological Institute of Great Britain and Ireland* 63: 453–537.

—— (1934) 'Notes on a Hero Cult from the Gulf of Carpentaria, North Queensland' *Journal of the Royal Anthropological Institute of Great Britain and Ireland* 64: 217–35.

Tisay, L. (1989) 'Ethnic Identity and Religion Among Yugoslavs in Australia' in A. W. Ata (ed.) *Religion and Ethnic Identity: An Australian Study*, vol. 2, Richmond, Vic.: Spectrum Publications.

Tonkinson, R. (1970) 'Aboriginal Dream-Spirit Beliefs in a Contact Situation: Jigalong, Western Australia' in R. M. Berndt (ed.) *Australian Aboriginal Studies: Modern Studies in the Social Anthropology of the Australian Aborigines* Nedlands: University of Western Australia Press.

—— (1974) *The Jigalong Mob: Aboriginal Victors of the Desert Crusade* Menlo Park, California: Cummings.

—— (1978) *The Mardudjara Aborigines: Living the Dream in Australia's Desert* New York: Holt, Rinehart and Winston.

Towler, R. (1984) *The Need for Certainty: A Sociological Study of Conventional Religion* London: Routledge and Kegan Paul.

Troeltsch, E. (1931) *The Social Teachings of the Christian Churches* New York: Macmillan.

Tu Wei-ming (1979) *Humanity and Self-cultivation* Berkekey: Asian Humanities Press.

Turner, B. S. (1987) 'Religion, State and Civil Society: Nation-Building in Australia' in T. Robbins and R. Robertson (eds) *Church–State Relations: Tensions and Transitions* New Brunswick: Transaction Books.

Vergote, A., Tamayo, A., Pasquali, L., Bonami, M., Pattyn, M. and Custers, A. (1969) 'Concepts of God and Parental Images' *Journal for the Scientific Study of Religion* 8: 79–87.

Wallace, R. A. (1985) 'Religion, Privatization and Maladaptation: A Comment on Niklas Luhmann' *Sociological Analysis* 46: 27–32.

Wallis, R. (1975) 'Relative Deprivation and Social Movements' *British Journal of Sociology* 26: 360–63.

—— (1976) *The Road to Total Freedom* London: Heinemann Educational.

—— (1986a) 'The Dynamics of Change in the Human Potential Movement' in R. Wallis and S. Bruce *Sociological Theory, Religion and Collective Action* Belfast: The Queen's University Press.

—— (1986b) 'Social Construction of Charisma' in R. Wallis and S. Bruce *Sociological Theory, Religion and Collective Action* Belfast: The Queen's University Press.

Warner, W. L. (1958 [1937]) *A Black Civilization: A Social Study of an Australian Tribe* New York: Harper.

—— (1959) *The Living and the Dead: A Study of the Symbolic Life of Americans* New Haven: Yale University Press.

Weber, M. (1947) *The Theory of Social and Economic Organization* New York: Oxford University Press.

—— (1963) *The Sociology of Religion* Boston: Beacon Press.

Weedon, C. (1987) *Feminist Practice and Poststructuralist Theory* London: Basil Blackwell.

West, W. J. (1987) *Opus Dei: Exploding a Myth* Crows Nest, NSW: Little Hills Press.

Westley, F. (1978) ' "The Cult of Man": Durkheim's Predictions and New Religious Movements' *Sociological Analysis* 39: 135–45.

Wetherell, D. (1987) *Women Priests in Australia? The Anglican Crisis* Melbourne: Spectrum.

White, R. (1981) *Inventing Australia* Sydney: Allen & Unwin.

Williams, E. (1980) *A Way of Life: The Pastoral Families of the Central Hill Country of South Australia* Adelaide: University of Adelaide Press.

Willis, S. (1980) 'Homes are Divine Workshops' in E. Windschuttle (ed.) *Women, Class and History: Feminist Perspectives on Australia, 1788–1978* Melbourne: Fontana.

—— (ed.) (1977) *Women, Faith, and Fetes* Melbourne: Dove and Australian Council of Churches.

Wilson, Bruce (1982) 'The Church in a Secular Society' in D. Harris, D. Hynd and D. Millikan (eds) *The Shape of Belief: Christianity in Australia Today* Homebush West, NSW: Lancer.
—— (1983) *Can God Survive in Australia?* Sutherland: Albatross.
Wilson, Bryan (1969) *Religion in Secular Society* Harmondsworth: Penguin.
—— (1982) *Religion in Sociological Perspective* Oxford: Oxford University Press.
Wimber, J. and Springer, K. (1986) *Power Healing* London: Hodder and Stoughton.
Wolf, E. (1982) *Europe and the People Without History* Berkeley: University of California Press.
Wood, W. W. (1965) *Culture and Personality Aspects of the Pentecostal Holiness Religion* The Hague: Mouton.
Wuthnow, R. (1976) 'Recent Patterns of Secularization: A Problem of Generations?' *American Sociological Review* 41: 850–67.
Wuthnow, R., Hunter, J. D., Bergesen, A. and Kurzweil, E. (1984) *Cultural Analysis* Boston: Routledge and Kegan Paul.
Yinger, J. (1969) *Sociology Looks at Religion* Toronto: Macmillan.
Young, C., Petty, M. and Faulkner, A. (1980) *Education and Employment of Turkish and Lebanese Youth* Canberra: Australian Government Publishing Service.
Zaunbrecher, M. (1980) 'Henry Lawson's Religion' *Journal of Religious History* 11: 308–19.

Index